Aug 10, 2016

Helen & Tony

I sure hope you enjoy
learning more about
diamonds

Karen

ADVANCE PRAISE FOR
PERFECTLY CLEAR

"A beautiful book that sparkles with stories and practical know-how on virtually every important aspect of diamonds, especially their value. Diamonds have been truly a great investment for centuries, especially in today's uncertain world, where they hold and increase their value as well as being portable and wearable Taking the reader behind the arcane industry of diamonds, Diamond expert Karen Simmons provides valuable knowledge and insights for the novice and even globetrotting collector and investor alike. Simmons has written a real gem of a book and a must read."
—ERNEST D. CHU, AUTHOR OF *SOUL CURRENCY*, FORMER WALL ST. JOURNAL FINANCIAL COLUMNIST

"From the layman to the diamond expert, Karen Simmons has written a comprehensive book that will have something of interest for everyone. Investing in diamonds is a complex art, and it is critical to have all the criteria and talking points at your fingertips. That is exactly what Karen has produced with this thorough examination of all the issues from rough mining to investment portfolio."
—ERNEST BLOM, PRESIDENT OF THE WORLD FEDERATION OF DIAMOND BOURSES

"Karen Simmons is a life-long gemologist and diamond enthusiast. I should know. I taught her colored gemstones almost four decades ago before becoming the President of the Gemological Institute of America. Karen was a star pupil, and again stars with a fun and informative read in *Perfectly Clear: Buying Diamonds for Pleasure and Profit*. Enjoy it, but be prepared! You'll get hooked on diamonds. Then again, what a way to go!"
—BILL BOYAJIAN, PAST PRESIDENT, GEMOLOGICAL INSTITUTE OF AMERICA (GIA)

"Karen Simmons' seven shining reasons why everyone needs to include some S-P-A-R-K-L-E™ to their portfolio is brilliant! Her crystal clear view of the diamond industry provides an in-depth look at this alternative asset class with all the necessary background information available within. All the unbelievable facts presented that prove how natural fancy color diamonds have appreciated so much over the years, makes this book a delight to any investment strategist looking for the right investment vehicle with ultimate gain."

—LEIBISH POLNAUER, PRESIDENT AND FOUNDER OF LEIBISH & CO., TEL AVIV, ISRAEL

"Superb! What an amazing book! After completely reading *Perfectly Clear* over the weekend, I was engrossed by the content and how well Simmons has described our small, hush-hush like industry. It's a book that's fun to read, and speaks to you like a diamond does. Simmons has flawlessly illustrated an intricate and mesmerizing portrayal of the diamond business and its culture. I look forward to being a part of this amazing adventure sharing the world with diamonds!"

—HARSH MAHESHWARI, G.G. DIRECTOR, KUNMING TRADING COMPANY, KOWLOON HONG KONG

"In her book *Perfectly Clear: Buying Diamonds for Pleasure and Profit*, Karen Simmons creates a story of romance for the world of diamonds. This two-part manual serves diamond jewelry buyers for both enjoyment and investment. Simmons has eloquently described the important distinction between the two categories of diamond purchases. When one adds in the intrinsic value of enjoyment while wearing the diamond to the resale value it brings over time, diamonds become a good investment. Hugely inspired by Warren Buffet, Karen is poised to give the seekers of quality jewelry a 'Borsheim Experience,' a term coined by Mr. Buffet that means a nice product at a reasonable price, and act as a curator of fine diamonds for investment clients."

—RAJIV AGRAWAL, GG, MBA, L.K. IMPORTS, PRINCIPAL & QJM CORP., LOS ANGELES, CA

Perfectly Clear

BUYING DIAMONDS
FOR PLEASURE AND PROFIT

KAREN SIMMONS

Perfectly Clear: Buying Diamonds for Pleasure and Profit
Copyright © 2016 by Karen Simmons
Published by Exceptional Resources, Incorporated
1425 Broadway, #444, Seattle, Washington 98122

Contributing Writer: Chris J. Schumacher

Production Management: Write to Sell Your Book, LLC
Copyeditor: Annie Nichol
Cover Design: Kathi Dunn and Hobie Hobart
Interior Design: Steven Plummer
Author photo: Rocco Macri

Printed in the United States of America for Worldwide Distribution
ISBN: 978-0-9831308-8-8

First Edition

CONTENTS

FOREWORD

I T IS A pleasure to be asked to write this Foreword for such a comprehensive book on the diamond industry – and at such an important time for the global business. In my role as President of the World Federation of Diamond Bourses (WFDB), it is my duty to hold widespread consultations and meetings with all members of the diamond pipeline. This enables me to keep my pulse on the state of the trade globally and to have an ongoing understanding of topics of interest to my members.

The WFDB represents all the official diamond bourses in the world, with 30 affiliated diamond exchange members in 24 countries covering the whole diamond world and on every continent. The WFDB plays a critical role in the global diamond industry, with our members trading 95% of the world's rough and polished via the affiliated bourses.

The aim of the WFDB is to protect the interests of our affiliated bourses and their individual members, and to enable the friendly settlement or arbitration of differences and disputes between the individual members of the affiliated bourses and between the affiliated bourses. We insist that diamond exchange members promise to uphold our traditions, principles of mutual trust, consideration and friendship. Abiding by these principles ensures that they serve as a basis in business relations between members of the affiliated bourses worldwide.

The WFDB also aims to promote global diamond trading and to encourage the establishment of bourses, with the view of eventual affiliation of all centres in which diamonds are actively traded. Needless to say, we have stringent requirements, and the WFDB insists these are met and diamond exchanges operate according to the highest international standards.

We also play a critical role in the issue of conflict diamonds and were founding members of the World Diamond Council which represents the WFDB on the Kimberley Process which was established in the year 2000 and which has almost completely eradicated trading in such stones. In addition, we work with international bodies such as the Financial Action Task Force to ensure that the diamond industry is completely transparent in its financial dealings.

Members of the diamond business are optimistic by nature – we cannot be otherwise due to the beauty of the products we deal with day by day and for what they represent: love, commitment and long-lasting relationships.

I am encouraged by the continuous stream of young people joining the diamond trade in all the major centres around the world which gives the business great confidence for the future. And a book such as this one will help give them the history of the industry and a long-term perspective.

In conclusion, I would like to recommend this book for its global look at the diamond trade. It is important because Karen is not only an experienced gemmologist and expert on diamonds, but she has also carried out a great deal of research to provide the very latest insights into the trade.

From describing how fancy colour diamonds are created and the investment opportunities they, along with jewellery, represent and who is investing in them; from how and where diamonds are found and mined and appraised to how they end up on the Red Carpet at globally covered events; from the range of fancy shaped diamonds to global economic trends and how they affect diamond sales and much more all spiced up with fascinating anecdotes and nuggets of information. This is truly a book with something for everyone, whether you are new to diamonds or an industry veteran.

Karen is to be congratulated for writing a book that gets to the heart of the issues that are vital to an understanding of the diamond business. There are relatively few books that have managed to tackle such a wide range of topics, which makes this book all the more important.

ERNIE BLOM
PRESIDENT OF THE WORLD FEDERATION OF DIAMOND BOURSES

DEDICATION

I dedicate this book to the hardworking individuals in the diamond business all the way from the miners sweating to bring them from the earth to the wholesalers who risk their lives to bring them to the jewelers around the globe, to the gemologists who evaluate them and value them, the cutters who create their masterpieces with much risk and to the jewelers that have built their livelihood bringing diamonds to their clients, embracing them with love, joy and enthusiasm. Also to the diamond world leaders who have stepped up to the table by establishing organizations that will someday soon eradicate the trading of conflict diamonds. Diamonds, the hardest substance on earth is truly Mother Nature's most magnificent gift!

Karen Simmons

ACKNOWLEDGEMENTS

IRST AND FOREMOST I thank my loving husband Jim Sicoli, of 31 years, and my six children, Kimberly, Matthew, Christina, Jonathan, Stephen and Alex for tolerating all my wild and crazy escapades, literally and metaphorically, while sacrificing our time together while I traveled the globe and took exceptional risks to bring this book into reality. Also, my extended family, Susan Simmons, Tiffany Sicoli, Amanda Shyiak, Miranda Englesby, Marcin Krol, Anna Ehli, Josephine Pino and their children, sisters, brothers and relatives.

Other very important folks to acknowledge are Chris Schumacher, Lawrence Draut, Karen Doucherty, Piero Karam who loves blue diamonds, Jeunesse Francis, Anna Rossi, Thuyen Doan, Fabiola Bince, Brianna Bince, Larry Clark, Jim's staff, support team and business partners and the testimonial providers who have willingly and lovingly extended their time, energy and resources to the diamond cause as well. I couldn't possibly list all the names of people that have helped me, so rather than leave anyone out, I am recognizing you all and thanking you for your efforts. You know who you are!

The real reason I wrote this book is to help the jewelry industry, which I am deeply in love with. I want the jewelers of the world to have this book to share with their many clients so they realize that diamonds are not just about the money, they are about beauty, splendor, assets, durability and the most precious symbol of love! I especially want the younger generation to once again, *fall in love with diamonds* as the symbol of love and for the value they retain. Additionally, the process by which diamonds are retrieved has been dramatically overhauled. The industry has moved toward an ethical system of both mining diamonds and bringing them to market without conflict. The diamond industry leaders are working hard to make the world a better place. The wonderment of diamonds in general have "facet-nated" me since I was a young girl wanting to be covered from head to toe with them. As Mae West says, *"I never worry about diets. The only carrots that interest me are the number you get in a diamond."*

My hope is that this book will open more eyes and help everyone enjoy them, especially the younger generation for what they truly are and move beyond the past press since the issues that were taking place have shifted to a more positive approach towards diamond retrieval and marketing. Diamonds will always be magical, brilliant, sparkles of color that can bring joy to any wearer that chooses to see them in the right light.

CHAPTER 1

FANATICAL FANCIES

ROM FANCY REDS to deep blues to radiating greens to fancy intense orangey-pink to cognac, colored diamonds have taken the diamond industry by storm.

Colored diamonds have earned the right to stand on their own, anytime, anyplace. Formerly reserved as complements to colorless (white) diamonds, colored diamonds are a force to be reckoned with.

Walk the show room floor with us, if you will, and discover the treasure that all colored diamonds can offer you over the next several pages.

An Eye On Color

Color is nature's variety, offering us the means of enjoying visual treats from our world.

"The quality of an object or substance with respect to light reflected by the object, usually determined visually by measurement of hue, saturation, and brightness of the reflected light; saturation or chroma; hue," is Dictionary.com's definition of color.

Our world is awash in an array of almost endless hues. Without light the human eye is unable to detect, much less appreciate color since light waves being absorbed and reflected from diamonds is what ultimately gives them color.

Diamonds need light to sparkle as well as to show off their distinctive "hue" and spectacular saturation of color. Properly proportioned (cut) diamonds are extremely proficient at reflecting light. Similar to other colored objects, diamonds not only reflect light waves but absorb others (light spectrum) resulting in the "color" we actually see, our visual perception.

Reflected light from an object determines what we perceive as color. On the contrary, all light waves absorbed by an object are never picked up by the eye.

A "colorless" (white) diamond that has a pure arrangement of carbon atoms reflects all light waves making it clear in appearance. None of the light is absorbed in this case. Black would come about if all light waves were absorbed.

It is a fluke of nature that colored diamonds exist. Certain imperfections related to a developing diamond's crystal structure determine its color. Location, geography, and other elements interacting with the crystal all play a part in coloring a diamond.

When a diamond's color reaches a certain level of saturation, they are called "fancy" colored diamonds. It used to be that flawless clear diamonds fetched the highest prices. That has changed with the popularity and beauty that fancy colored diamonds bring to the market.

Colored diamonds represent many shades of the rainbow. GIA (Gemological Institute of America) simplifies the spectrum of color down to 27 different hues for naturally colored diamonds. Colorless diamonds are graded on a D-to-Z scale. GIA estimates that 1 in 10,000 diamonds of color are outside of this scale.

What Color Do You Fancy?

When only carbon atoms bond, a pure clear diamond is born. Here is how some popular diamond colors are believed to come to life:

Red

Distortion and absorption of green light by the diamond's crystal lattice structure in concert with electron charges during diamond growth is key to the red hue. Reds are very rare and expensive.

Yellow

Nitrogen is definitely tied to the creation of the common yellow diamond. Since a carbon–nitrogen bond is a covalent bond between carbon and nitrogen and is one of the most abundant bonds in organic chemistry and biochemistry, carbon atoms allows nitrogen to slide in place of carbon during the formation process. Overall, the nitrogen absorbs blue light waves allowing yellow to be reflected and perceived by the human eye. Enhancement of less than vivid yellow diamonds with blue coloring is sometimes used to pass off light yellow stones as colorless diamonds.

Green

Many green diamonds have a light green surface color caused by natural radiation. Effective in trapping electrons, this radiation comes from nearby radioactive rocks. Natural green diamonds are very rare with reports indicating that only about ten come to market per year. Nickel, in trace amounts, mixed with carbon atoms also contributes to the green hue. During the polishing process some of the natural green color is lost since the rock radiation during formation of the diamond is topical in nature.

Blue

Some blue hues are hypothetically influenced by the presence of nickel and higher concentrations of hydrogen. More common is boron, which is common to carbon in size. Boron bonds with carbon and absorbs red, yellow and green, which allows beautiful blue to be reflected by the diamond. With low nitrogen levels, the blue hue really stands out.

Orange

Suspicions are that nitrogen is the modifier that leads to an orange hue.

Purple

Most purples are pale and make up about 1% of production from Siberia's Mir kimberlitic field. Strong coloration is much rarer. In addition to lattice deformation, purple diamonds have shown evidence of hydrogen in their makeup.

Pink

Similar to natural purple diamonds, pink stones are thought to endure "plastic deformation" during their travels to the Earth's surface. Unlike a green diamond's natural radiation experience, a pink diamond's movement to the surface ("mechanical" action) is what determines the electron structure.

Gray

Boron bears its presence in blue diamonds and is a trace element in natural gray diamonds. It is also possible that gray diamonds are black diamonds that did not reach full saturation.

Brown

Promotional efforts always influence our perception of diamonds. "Champagne" and "Cognac" are terms coined to describe light brown tints and darker brown diamonds. Nitrogen, along with structural "defects" in the diamond's lattice structure is attributed to the brown hue.

Black

Unique in its opaqueness, the natural black color comes about from iron and graphite inclusions, not trace elements responsible for other diamond colors. The transparency of all other colored diamonds is absent with black diamonds which explains the lack of fire and brilliance. A consequence of being a heavily included diamond is a tendency to fracture more easily than other gem-quality stones. This unfortunate trait makes cutting and polishing difficult which relegates many black diamonds to industrial use.

Further, natural black diamonds may have sections of gray, white and clear, rendering them inconsistent in "black" hue. High pressure and temperature treatments usually solve this oddity.[1,2]

> *"The sky was a sparkling succession of black diamonds on black velvet made crystal clear by the blackout."*
> *- Sara Sheridan, Brighton Belle*
>
> Brighton Belle

An inanimate dog worth $372,000?

In honor of the 60th anniversary of Charles Schulz's Snoopy cartoon-strip, a 9,917 stone Snoopy was created by Hong Kong jeweler Tse Sui Luen. The *Guinness Book of World Records* dubbed the 5 ½-inch scintillating Snoopy, "Most Valuable Snoopy."

Of the almost 10,000 stones used, 415 red ruby gems make up Snoopy's collar while 783 black diamonds make up his ears, nose, eyes, and eyebrows.

Imagine what a complimenting Charlie Brown design would look like. All those intense yellow diamonds needed to make up his famous shirt would be an amazing sight.[3]

Famous Fancies

Some of the most famous diamonds in the world are colored. A 407 carat flawless diamond is the star of a world record necklace.

In 2013, the *Guinness Book of World Records* declared the "most valuable necklace" to be the Mouawad L'Incomparable Diamond Necklace.

Valued at $55 million, this piece totals 637 carats. The star of the show is the deep yellow modified shield step-cut diamond that dangles below the 90 other diamonds of varying shapes that make up the strand of the necklace.

Origin roots of the Incomparable Diamond date back to 1980 in the Congo where it was almost lost. Similar to the Hope Diamond, the Incomparable was on display at the Smithsonian Institute in Washington D.C.[4]

A brilliant Brazilian red rough was masterfully turned into an internally flawless Fancy 5.11 carat stunner. Called the "Red Shield" due to a modified triangular shape, it was one of the largest Fancy reds GIA has graded.

An intense orange 5.54 carat diamond is known as "The Pumpkin." During the cutting process the brownish-orange stone gave way to intense orange. Back in 1997 it was graded as "the largest Fancy Vivid Orange diamond in the world." This South African-mined Fancy later sold at Sotheby's for $2,956,000, or $705,587 per carat.

Another South African beauty became one of the rarest blue diamonds in history. The trapezoid-shaped, 30.06 carat vivid blue has fiery character. William Goldberg (jeweler) named it "Blue Lili" after his wife.

Now held by a private collector, the "Pink Muse" is a William Goldberg creation weighing in at 8.9 carats. Its vivid pink color and oval shape help make the Muse a world-class diamond.

In recognition of his keen eye for diamonds, a portion of East 48th street is named "William Goldberg Way" in the New York Diamond District.[5]

Many years ago colored diamonds began to stir up the auction block at Christie's. At that time three of the top four sellers were pink diamonds.

One vivid pink set two records as far back as 2009. Christie's Hong Kong brought in almost $11 million for the five carat diamond. That record, for most expensive jewelry paired with the second record of per carat price, was $2.1 million.[6]

William Goldberg grabbed a 10.19 carat fancy orangey-pink for a cool $2.3 million. This was the highest per carat price paid at the time and doubles the estimated take according to Christie's.

The third pink diamond was a hexagonal fancy. Although "only" 3.01 carats, it brought in about $220,000/carat due to the intensity of the pink color.[7]

In 1958, with $1 million dollars of transit insurance, jeweler Harry Winston donated the largest deep blue diamond in the world to the Smithsonian Institution. Viewable at the Natural History Museum in Washington D.C., the Hope Diamond is a sight to behold. At over 45 carats, the Hope has 16 clear cushion and pear-shaped diamonds as a surround.[8]

The "Pink Dream" was short-lived for a bidder who defaulted on the $83 million required to secure the stone.

At almost 60 carats, "The Pink Star" retained its name. The pre-sale estimate was $61 million with the stone valued at $72 million. As a flawless diamond it appears the Pink Star caused emotions to run high at the 2013 auction run by Sotheby's in Geneva. Isaac Wolf, a diamond cutter, must have had big dreams for the diamond he prematurely attempted to rename.

Sotheby's Magnificent Jewels sale saw a 100.02 carat diamond go for just over $22 million. The one-of-a-kind emerald stone was far away from setting any sale records. Being a colorless diamond, one has to imagine what this stunning stone would have fetched had it been a vivid colored stone. Nonetheless, this large "Perfect" diamond grabbed headlines and helped Sotheby's New York set the local sales-room record for total jewelry auctioned at $65 million.

"Perfect" is a Type IIa, internally flawless, "D" color emerald-shaped diamond. The $22 million bid at the spring 2015 sale made this diamond the highest selling colorless stone auctioned in New York.

At the same Magnificent Jewels sale, a fancy purplish-pink diamond sold for $2.4 million. Kashmir sapphire side stones accented this spectacular 6.24 carat pear-shaped diamond.[9]

"Silvermist," a gray diamond, surprised industry insiders by pulling in $1.9 million. This "dirty" diamond is still considered an off-color despite the popularity of colored diamonds. At 10.67 carats, only time will tell if "gray" becomes the new fancy diamond.

For historical perspective, the "Graff Pink" auction sale earned $46 million in Geneva by Sotheby's. That 2010 sale made this diamond the most expensive sold at auction. It had been kept off the market for 60 years in a private collection, which increased demand. Mr. Graff recut the 24.68 carat stone after the purchase.

The "Wittelsback Blue" became "Wittelsbach-Graff" in 2008 when Graff Diamonds nabbed it at auction for $23.4 million. This high profile stone has done well since setting that sales record. Within three years it was reported that Graff sold the 31 carat deep blue to the emir of Qatar for $80 million. Being internally flawless and blue in hue is hard to beat. Only red diamonds are rarer than natural blue diamonds.

A fiery frenzy over colored stones was well under way in 2010 when "The Perfect Pink" auctioned for $23.2 million in a bidding war between four prospective buyers. Selling for $9 million over the low end expectation at the auction is quite an impressive spread. Weighing in at 14.23 carats and being a rare vivid pink made the "Jewels: The Hong Kong Sale" an auction to remember.[10]

Late 2013 saw a per-carat sale record at Christie's International.

At just under 15 carats, a fancy vivid orange sold for $36 million, well above the pre-sale estimate of between $17-$20 million. Amazingly enough, this stone was far from perfect with a VS1 clarity grade and pear shape. The longtime owner likely took advantage of the rising popularity of colored diamonds and proved that the old saying, "The best color is no color" about diamonds has clearly been debunked.

Now, take a fancy walk on the wild side...

Another world record involved 1,106 total carats that reportedly cost $23.7 million. The 8,601 flawless diamonds encrust a human skull. The centerpiece? A 52.4 carat pink diamond, right in the middle of the skull's forehead.

Guinness book dubs this skull, created by Damien Hirst, "Most Valuable Materials in a Work of Art" for the record. Damien named it "For the Love of God."[11]

Natural fancy colored diamonds are rare creations.

Being among the most scarce substances on Earth, as well as possessing inherent beauty, colored diamonds not only retain value but deliver stellar returns year in and year out. Also, as one-of-a-kind pieces of nature, value is usually determined at auction, fixed price lists are obsolete upon printing.

To this day, the fine jewelry auction market is carried by rare fancy-colored diamonds.

Could Nitrogen Be Your "Type"?

Atomic integrity, or lack thereof, has much to say about diamond color.

Diamond formation requires extremely high temperatures and pressure. This time of heat and condensing is the crystallization phase of a diamond's life. Up to 1 million pounds per square inch with up to 3,600 degrees Fahrenheit is acting on the diamond's crystal structure. Turmoil of this sort is the perfect opportunity for other atoms to be integrated into the diamond, giving it some sort of color.

Infrared spectrophotometers measure nitrogen presence as low as a few parts per million. Although such minute levels are undetected by the human eye, a more pronounced level of nitrogen becomes important in the classification and color of diamonds.

The purest diamonds, those with virtually no impurities, are quite rare. Diamond colors such as pink and red are also valued due to short supply. Diamonds of such purity and rare color have few or no nitrogen atoms and are considered "Type IIa" diamonds, the "purest of the pure." Upon rising towards the Earth's crust during formation, some diamonds' carbon lattice structure is disturbed, rendering a diamond that absorbs light to some degree, instead of reflecting light for maximum sparkle. About 1-2% of diamonds is Type IIa allowing pink, red, purple and even yellow and brown colorings.

"Type IIb" are gray, nearly colorless and blue in hue. These diamonds contain boron and no nitrogen. Only about 0.1% of diamonds are in this class.

"Super D's" is a slang term used by diamond traders referring to very pure colorless diamonds. They are members of the Type II family and some retail jewelers are quite insistent on this fact being on any certification.

Deep yellow "Canary" diamonds also make up less than 0.1% of diamonds and are considered "Type Ib" given their darker color. The presence of nitrogen atoms, which absorb blue light, and their concentration and spread throughout the diamond are a factor in color. Orange, brown and greenish diamonds are members of Type Ib.

Pale yellow diamonds contain clustered nitrogen atoms in the carbon lattice and are classified as "Type Ia" diamonds. Type I diamonds are also colorless and together with yellow make up about 98% of all diamonds.

A "perfect" natural diamond is theoretically possible. With the forces involved during natural diamond formation, perfection is most improbable. Impurities can be limited but most diamonds have at least a scintilla of structural and chemical oddities.

Nature's gift of nitrogen/carbon atom substitution and mixing give us the wonderful beginnings of colored diamonds.[12]

Fancy Grading

It was traditionally thought that a colorless (white) diamond was most treasured due to its "purity." Scientifically this is accurate. Like inclusions and blemishes, colored diamonds were technically deemed a "defect." Flawless, colorless diamonds are pure crystal carbon creations, rare indeed. In fact, a GIA Color Grading Scale ranks "light yellow" diamonds at the low end of the scale (S-Z of the entire D-Z range). This letter grading scheme is meant for colorless diamonds only. As such, a yellow tint was deemed undesirable.

In layman's terms, a diamond graded with "Fair" or "Poor" color was at the less desirable end of the grading scale (S-Z; light yellow). "Excellent" tops the chart with "Poor" bringing up the bottom of a range of five descriptors.

A "Poor" grade is effectively restricted to the W-Z range with "V" on the boarder of "Fair." Although an element of subjectivity is impossible to completely eliminate GIA color grading is performed under strictly controlled lighting conditions to aid in consistent grading conditions.

The visible spectrum of light can be finely divided into literally hundreds of colors. Color wheels show off an odd variety of hues to the uninitiated.

"Standalone" colors for diamonds on the wheel are orange, yellow, green, violet, purple, and blue. Pink is a common color mixed with others by official designation such as red pink, purplish pink and purple pink. A few other combinations are pinkish orange, orangey yellow, yellowish green and violet blue.

GIA uses the terms "hue," "tone," and "saturation" to distinctly describe color, lightness and darkness, and intensity of colored diamonds. Remember that the color grading system that jewelers offer for consumer viewing is the "4 C's" which is used to grade the absence of color, not the presence of it. A "D to Z" range is used for colorless diamonds, even though some "colorless" diamonds can have an obvious tint of yellow and have even been nicknamed "Cape Diamonds" if graded to be on the far right ("Z" side) of the scale due to higher yellow tint.

The presence of color in diamonds lends itself to a unique "Fancy" grading scale with levels named as such: Fancy Light, Fancy, Fancy Intense, Fancy Deep, Fancy Vivid or Fancy Dark. These modifiers are added to the diamond's hue. For example, Fancy Red or Fancy Deep Blue. Many times you'll see the diamond's shape added, Fancy Red Pear or Fancy Deep Princess, in online ads or other printed materials.[13]

A diamond's characteristic color is precisely determined in a consistent manner via a standard set of color comparators under controlled viewing and lighting conditions. Color graders give independent opinions. When sufficient opinions meet in agreement a color grade is assigned.

A GIA grading report for colored diamonds included "color origin," which is critical to distinguish between natural and treated stones or irradiation (artificial) after unearthing the diamond. Reports also indicate if the diamond was loose or mounted which can make a difference in finding any imperfections and possible flaws.[14]

No matter all the technical details or the special names attached to diamonds that are industry-specific, keep focused on the basic premise that colored diamond value turns grading principles on their head.

First, it may surprise you that the very popular round-shaped stone is almost always used for colorless (white) diamonds, not colored diamonds. Cushion-shaped and Radiant-shaped stones have taken the top position of popularity when it comes to colored diamonds.

Although it is true that a stone with limited inclusions boasting a proportioned (ideal) cut will add value, it is the specific color, intensity of that color, and the dispersion of color throughout the stone that are prime value drivers.

Colors such as red, blue, and yellow continually set auction records. On top of that quality, red diamonds are extremely rare which further increases value. Type II blue diamonds have also gained great value due to their limited nature. "Clean" stones have limited inclusions, which is obviously a preferred stone trait.

However, a deep and intense colored stone can effectively "hide" or "mask" any defects that are present. To a certain degree, colored stones graders favor intense color over clarity and the market agrees.

Any deep, rich color that is also evenly dispersed within the stone is the "Holy Grail" of colored diamond value. A high clarity grading would just be frosting on the cake as they say.

Of course, a poorly cut stone will oppress value quite a bit regardless of the stone's color. Just remember that all else being equal, a colored stone takes less of a value hit than its colorless cousin due to a less-than-ideal cut.

For more great details about diamond quality and investment options, refer to the chapter in this book that delves further into diamond investing.

Full Color Investing

Wondering if colored diamond investing is feasible?

Like any long-term investment, due diligence is highly advised. Back in the 1989, the "Oracle of Omaha" jumped into jewelry in a big way by buying a jewelry store. Having made out quite well with that initial venture, Warren Buffet continued investing in the diamond business for years to come.

This book contains a chapter about investing in diamonds. With that in mind, the following is meant to reveal a bit more about colored diamond investing in particular.

Following the time-honored investing principle of getting in for the long haul, Yaniv Marcus of Leibish & Co. proves how colored diamonds can provide you with a means to beat "goliath" investors and large company returns. His company's site offers data on diamond investing that may surprise you.

Not many could have predicted how and when fancy blue diamonds would be amongst the cream-of-the-crop of diamond investment returns. Prior to 1996, fancy intense blues weren't even on the radar. By the time 2006 rolled around, blues literally took off like a rocket and ever since have been amazing auctioneers around the world with their staying power.

Fancy intense pinks are also riding the wave of popularity and fantastic investment returns. On the Leibish website, graphs show that between 1995 and 2013 one and two carat pinks outperformed the Dow Jones, Nasdaq, S&P, gold, Coke and Berkshire Hathaway.

For reasonable comparison purposes Yaniv used independent third-party information over varying timeframes. Data from Sotheby's and Christie's (both respected fine jewelry auction houses) were compared to financial benchmarks as well as Coke (a Berkshire favorite stock holding) and Berkshire Hathaway itself.[15]

Any way you slice it investment grade colored diamonds come out on top. More and more investors are beginning to realize the significant advantages of diamond investing. Some of the many benefits are no maintenance costs, long-term growth, world-wide convertibility, portability, no lengthy closing or contingencies, virtually recession resistant, performance and privacy.

The United States Gold Bureau presents yet another confirmation on the viability of colored diamond performance superiority.

Sources prove that investment grade fancy colored diamonds appreciated about 350% over the twelve year period from 2000, 2012. A basic investment rule of thumb, the "Rule of 72," tells us that at an annual return of 10% an asset should double in value in about 7.2 years.

The 350% example represented a five-carat fancy intense yellow diamond that produced a 29% yearly return and effectively doubled in value in 3.4 years.

In a head-to-head competition between a fancy pink and colorless diamond we witness complete domination. In a mere ten years the fancy pink returned about 350% while the colorless diamond plodded along at a meager fraction of the pink's return.[16]

It's up to you to investigate further to determine whether you're ready to join the big leagues of serious diamond investing.

Colorful Geography

Colored diamonds come from all around the world. Some of these sources offer limited quantities of colored diamonds while others are a major supply.

It is not unusual for some Siberian diamonds to be both pink and brown before cutting. As a two-for-one natural bonus, cutters then divide the stone yielding separate pink and brown diamonds. Grayish-yellow, purple, colorless, pink and brown are common Siberian diamond hues.

Southeast Asia is the home of the Borneo river diamonds. Rare pink, blue, pink and green stones can be found with brown and yellow being more common, especially a "washed-out" yellow. Intense yellow diamonds have come from Borneo after cutting through a radiated crystalline skin.

Once again, brown and intense to fancy yellows pop up in various geographic locations. Plentiful large (up to several hundred carats) diamond production occurs in Angola. Yellows of varying saturation make up a portion of the total diamond mining the majority of which is colorless. Sometimes a pink stone is in the mix.[17]

The kings of pink diamonds are sourced from Australia's Argyle mine. Back in 1985, pink diamonds weren't really on the markets radar, even with intense hue. Prior to the mid-80s, their pale/pastel look did nothing to stimulate demand. Today, exceptional pink hues and red diamonds are very popular and most of the world's supply originate from Argyle.

Only about 1 in 1,000 Argyle diamonds have a strong hue which cannot be completely explained by specialists. Nonetheless, there is no doubt that demand for pink Argyle diamonds will boost value as production winds down at this mine known for its productivity.

Brown, brownish-pink, champagne, colorless, purple and pink champagne are famous hues coming out of Australia.

Olive-like hues are common in the country with "countless mines," Brazil.

When exposed to the sun this olive hue appears more green due to very high fluorescence. On the other end of the spectrum, Brazil is home to many rare red diamonds. Brown, yellow, green and blue round out what Brazilian artisans have to offer the diamond world.

Turquoise and aquamarine hues make British Guyana a modest diamond producer on an extremely brilliant quality level. Colorless stones are also part of the mix but not as well known. Similar to Brazil, you can thank artisans for bringing attention to these diamonds.

Natural black diamonds are plentiful in Central Africa. Quantity is lower from this area, yet stone purity is considered good and there is a plethora of colors to choose from. Typical hues are pink, yellow, blue, green, colorless, olive with black being abundant.

Setting aside Sierra Leone's history as a "conflict diamond" hotspot, this region's current claim to fame is "deep, warm and lively" yellow diamonds. Large colorless crystals are common, but many fabulous vivid yellows make the Zimi mine infamous. Less popular olive stones also originate from the Zimi mine and are of pure quality similar to sister yellow diamonds. Some of these local yellows show off a touch of orange, further contributing to their uniqueness.

Wrapping around the Northeastern boarder of Sierra Leone is Guinea. Yellow diamonds are commonly found there, as well as pinks. High-quality stones are both colored and colorless. Guinea colored stones are much smaller than much of the colorless production. Yellows range from light to intense.

Traveling South from the Sierra Leone-Guinea region along the Western coast of Africa we find one of the largest diamond producing countries, the Democratic Republic of Congo.

Up to 80% of DR Congo's production was industrial use, which has fallen under synthetic diamond dominance as of late, resulting in fewer colored diamonds given the reduced extraction schedule. As with other producers this is likely good news in the coming years for colored diamonds whose supply will continue to be restrained. The DR Congo mines output intense yellow, orange and cognac diamonds with character.

Another price impact is due to DR Congo's special "barrel" diamonds. Yellow-orange "cubic" rough stones are sometimes hollow, which leads to about an 85% loss of carats during cutting. Despite this large loss, these stones gain pricing favor due to their scarcity.

DR Congo mines put out olive, orange, cognac, yellow, colorless, brown, and gray stones.

The DR Congo also has very peculiar diamonds, called "barrels." These are beautiful yellow-orange diamonds which, in the rough, are cubic, but sometimes hollow. Cutting them therefore causes an 85% loss in the weight of the stone (the rough/cut ratio is usually 40%), which has an important impact on their price.

Yellow diamonds from the Ivory Coast lean toward a greenish hue. Yellows are prominent in this region which is regionally close to Sierra Leone and DR Congo. The Coast's production also includes colorless and brown diamonds.

Light blues and strong blue fluorescent colorless diamonds come from "value" famous South African mines. This area caters to all colors with the common appearance of being pale and "washed-out."

Diamonds of all colors can be found in South African production but their main common characteristic is that they tend to appear pale and washed-out.

South African mines are well-known for blue diamonds. All other colors lean toward lighter saturation, rarely intense.

Across the continent from DR Congo is the occasional pale pink diamond producer Tanzania. Colorless stones dominate output with pale pinks getting extraordinary attention due to popularity trends.

Interestingly enough Venezuela and some mining regions of Africa have similar diamond geological formations. High fluorescence, few impurities and a unique greenish-yellow hue are hallmarks of diamonds common to these two regions.

Intense yellows, brown, colorless, and greenish-yellow diamonds are common fare from Venezuela.

Colorless diamonds make up the great majority of Chinese production. Rarely, pink stones of average quality are unearthed.

In the Arctic reaches of the Northwest Territories, colorless diamonds monopolize mine output with the exception of a few lightly yellow colored stones.

Old terminology for color diamond grading included "Top Cape" and "Cape" to describe yellow diamonds. The International Diamond Council (IDC) has used the terms "Tinted White" and "Tinted Color" for a similar hue. Yellow and yellowish diamonds from South Africa, Guinea, Angola, and Borneo have been referred to as "Cape" depending upon the source.

Colored Diamonds vs. Colored Gems

7.5, 8, 9, 10.

What do these numbers represent?

Judge scoring cards at a boxing match...Olympic competition scores...Ring finger sizes?

First, let's consider that minerals of the Earth have their own physical and chemical properties. Diamonds are made of carbon and rank as one of the hardest minerals while other materials, such as gypsum and talc, are among the softest. Alumina and beryllium are the foundational structures of rubies, sapphires, and emeralds respectively.

German mineralogist Friedrich Mohs created a "hardness" scale several hundred years ago that is still used today. It ranks minerals on their ability to scratch (score) each other, or not. Based on a one-to-ten scale, a diamond ranks as "10" (hardest) which is 46 times harder than ruby giving them the ability to scratch any mineral ranked lower than "10" (softer) on the scale. According to the Mohs scale a "7.5" represents the hardness of emeralds, "9" covers rubies and sapphires, and of course a "10" is the coveted diamond top position.

In evaluating diamonds versus gems the role of scarcity also applies. Gems can be found measured in pounds while it is rare indeed to find a diamond pushing four grams. Depending on the mine, about 250 tons of ore typically yield a one carat (02. Grams) diamond. On top of that, colored diamonds aren't found in every diamond mine and when present only account for a small percentage of carats mined.[18]

Terms such as "stone," "gem," and "gemstone" are frequently thrown around without much thought. GIA grades colorless and colored diamonds, not colored stones. Like diamonds, colored stones require a complex analysis with countless variables. Colored stones have no standardized grading system embraced by the trade like diamonds have. Some gems are subjected to heating processes that alter their appearance (color) up to three grades. Diamond grading is very strict.[19]

Many gemstones can be considered precious yet, when measured by hardness and scarcity, colored diamonds are in a class all their own.

Color Your Own Rainbow, With Diamonds

Diamonds come in a variety of shapes and sizes, offering you almost endless options to match color with your preference and personality.

Colored diamonds have caught the attention of movie stars and fashion designers alike. Even the budget-minded have options to satisfy their desire to get in on the colored diamond train.

Even collectors are getting in on colored diamonds by seeking out natural diamonds that mimic chameleons. These bicolor diamonds encompass two colors in one stone and are amazing to see.

The acceptance and value of colored diamonds even extends to rough stones. These "fresh-from-the-mine" uncut diamonds are making marvelous marriage bands. Rough colored diamonds are completely natural as they are left in their unearthed virgin form and are uncut.

Follow the rainbow of the symbol of love that diamonds symbolize, and see where it takes you.

CHAPTER 2

DIAMONDS: A PROFITABLE PORTFOLIO

W HAT COMES TO mind when you ponder the term "great investment," stocks, real estate, IRA's, precious metals, inflation-protected bonds, classic cars, or maybe a business venture?

We've all seen the stock rush up and down like a roller coaster, heard about numerous "pump and dump" securities scams, watched the bond market linger and witnessed paltry savings interest rates. Bernie Madoff, Enron, bankrupt airlines, the skeletal remains of US steel manufacturing and the latest "Great Recession" that sunk real estate values and swallowed life savings along with it will remain fresh in our memories.

With all this market turmoil, what check-list criteria do you use when evaluating investments? How do you remain rational and objective before committing your hard earned money?

Warren Buffet Demands Diamonds

Americans have become familiar with the ubiquitous "Southwest effect" and the "Wal-Mart market" but never heard about the very successful "ratchet-up effect" related to what became known as the "Borsheim's price."

Jewelry industry insiders know full well how difficult it is to keep overhead and fixed costs low while attempting to earn a fair margin. By the time a rough diamond makes its way to a retail display counter as a sparkling gem, many stops along the value-chain (miner, cutter, polisher, etc.) have taken their profit cut.

Nonetheless, Warren Buffet's investment in the jewelry industry officially began in 1989 with the acquisition of the Borsheim's chain of jewelry stores. Everyone knows that when Buffet makes an investment almost everybody pays attention.

So what about diamonds caught Buffet's keen investment eye compelling him to jump into the retail ring and invest?

First off, he studied the behind-the-scenes operations sur-rounding the dazzle and glitter that makes up the glamorous jewelry retail industry. Although some gem-loving patrons pay the going market price Buffet understood that the majority of us are not made of money, we have budgets. He also was keen to the fact that most prospective customers were looking for quality at a fair price. Sure, purchasing a diamond is usually an emotional endeavor, but only the well to do can afford Fifth Avenue or Rodeo Drive prices that include very high overhead in the sales price.

As an example, Buffet declared that jewelry costing $1,350 else-where would only cost about $1,000 at Borsheim's. This is where the term "Borsheim's Price" comes into the equation. Basically, Buffet turned the standard retail jewelry operating formula on its head to suit his stringent requirements. Store rent was a major factor of focus that was reduced many points below that of com-petitors for starters. Borsheim's business model also allowed for huge volume and single location simplicity, further lowering oper-ating expense ratio.

"Don't sell Warren the ring, sell him the store!" was the callout to Buffet who was in Borsheim's shopping for Christmas. Being a long-time customer and a stellar investor, Buffet took the suggestion to heart and early the next year made the store the first jewelry company owned by Berkshire Hathaway.[1]

Getting a good deal based on fundamentals and quality is a hallmark of Buffet's investment savvy. He approaches investments that he can understand and demonstrates fiscal responsibility. As a private gemstone investor, take heed of the fact that Buffet also recognized that diamonds are low maintenance and last a long time. On the pure business side of the equation, businesses that Buffet investigates must have staying power given his reputation as a "buy and hold" investor with a long record of great acclaim. Sure, you might find that on occasion Berkshire Hathaway has held conservative yet "speculative" positions in their history, but overall, like a diamond, the company's money is placed on the long-term position.

Of course running out and structuring a leveraged buyout of the nearest jewelry store is not advisable for many businesses, much less the average layman.

However, you clearly need to approach investing in a strategic manner, similar to Buffet's example, if you are to be successful weaving gemstones in your portfolio. No doubt investing in a retail jewelry store is much more complex than seeking out a loose diamond, or two, for investment purposes. Witnessing how one of the world's most famous conservative investors took on gems at the retail level presents big lessons relevant to wealth creation on an individual level.

Borsheim's created scalability by creating a direct selling pipeline courtesy of their "shop-at-home" program. Similar to investing in gems as an individual, a wide selection and infrequent purchases is the reality of retail jewelry sales.[2]

It turns out that Borsheim's was just the beginning of Buffet's venture into the diamond industry. After being around for 80 years, Helzberg Diamonds was acquired by Buffet in 1995 and had 200 stores by 1999, up from 101 in 1990. There were 230 stores by 2010 when Helzberg also qualified for American Gem Society membership.

In 1996, a year after the Buffet acquisition, Helzberg.com hosted their ecommerce site.[3]

That was almost 20 years ago and it was a pioneering move that allowed unmatched accessibility to diamonds.

"From Wall Street to Main Street, financial investors follow his every move, assured in knowing that where Warren goes, success is sure to follow," says Robert Miles, professional speaker and the author. Dedicated investing requires monitoring your holdings and that is precisely what Buffet did. As you can see within about six years of the Borsheim's purchase, Berkshire Hathaway, under Buffet's keen guidance, doubled down on the diamond industry in grand fashion with the Helzberg acquisition. Where its shining, spectacular sparkle is a likely source. Buffet became aware of a diamond-in-the-rough and capitalized on it, immediately. Serious investors rise to the top by assessing value and risk. When the numbers work there is no reason to delay, carpe diem!

Warren Buffet's tenured and stable reputation is one of investing in quality and knowing exactly what is being bought. The jewelry industry, diamonds in particular, have stood the test of time. It's an "old economy business," as the Buffet camp commonly states, that has survived market changes for over 100 years.

For a private portfolio investor, the advantages of diamonds are clear. To reap the rewards of increasing returns, one must be disciplined and methodical when pursuing a diamond investment strategy.

Unlike traditional acquisitions such as take-overs and mergers where an extensive "house cleaning" is standard operating procedure, when Berkshire Hathaway buys a business, it retains talented management staff, talent being a key factor and due diligence prior to sealing the deal a major component to ensuring success. Such was the case with the jewelry store acquisitions.

That Buffet quote is sage advice to ponder. That quote tells us you can't know everything about a deal. For those with capital to invest but less depth of knowledge, a wise move is to seek out competent counsel (diamond dealers) from those "in-the-know."

Success attracts success. Critics have been silenced. Buffet's eye for quality investments was so sharp that his initial foray into the diamond industry (Borsheim's) competes against his second (Helzberg) with great spirit in Omaha. The Helzberg brand has about 250 stores across the country yet local Borsheim's remains a solid performer despite its sister company competition. Now there's proof of a solid investment.

> *"If you don't know jewelry, know the jeweler."*
> Warren Buffet

But wait, there's more!

In 2000 Buffet added a third gem to "Berkshire Hathaway's crown" by buying Ben Bridge Jeweler. Founded by Samuel Silverman in 1912, Ben Bridge was originally a Rolex watch dealer. Despite casting synergy to the side all three Berkshire Hathaway "gems" shine due to their independent operation. There is no "jewelry division" at Berkshire Hathaway combining the three jewelry store operations. Each operation (Borsheim's, Helzberg, and Ben Bridge) stand on their own merit.

When describing his diamond purchase back in 1993, Bill Gates said, "Warren had them open up the store on a Sunday especially for us."[4]

Open up your own "door" to diamond investing. Make it happen today.

Move Over Wall Street!

According to the Leibish & Company website, "Fancy color diamonds are the most concentrated and portable form of wealth on the planet."

Now that is a bold claim. As thousands of investors worldwide have discovered for themselves, it's true. Jeweler Leibish & Co. is an internationally recognized dealer specializing in fancy and colored jewelry that not only makes this claim but proves it.

Also claimed on the Leibish & Company website, outperforming "all other major assets including stocks, bonds, gold, silver, and platinum" is the claim to fame of colored diamonds. "They have proven themselves over time to be the strongest asset classes around" and investors are flocking to get their piece of the pie.

Fancy colored's performance trajectory is so stunning that they rocketed above all other asset classes even during the 2008 financial crisis. Investors have found that being timid or overly conservative during and after the "Great Recession" led to meager returns if not outright losses. Lack of tangibility and other constraints of traditional assets have put them at a disadvantage in this new world of economic decay.

"After many comprehensive hours of research, we managed to collect ROI statistics and the historical price performance for bullion, precious metals, major currencies, US inflation, general stocks and bonds, colorless diamonds, and of course natural fancy colored diamonds," according to Leibish & Co.

In an attempt to compare apples to apples, a search of the "most popular financial websites" was conducted over many asset investment classes. Historical price performance and trends were investigated.

When speaking of Fancy Intense Pink diamonds, a 443% gain was consistently achieved over a twelve year period. That is a stellar 37% gain per year for a three-carat stone! Only select stocks can even come close to that run-up. Even the most desirable classic cars can't sustain year-over-year appreciation in the same ball park. Further, you'd have to be crazy to think any real estate capital gains were even close when the market was at its peak prior to the crash.

350% appreciation over twelve years (2000 - 2012) accrued to a Fancy Intense Yellow diamond over five carats.

There is no comparison to these rare gems. "Although other assets have improved, and some significantly over the period of time, none can compare to the performance of colored diamonds."[5]

Feel free to do your own research. As the world welcomes diamond investment, pricing platforms help ease the way via Rapaport and IDEX online. Assistance can be had by experienced diamond traders or you can even join a diamond investment fund. Either way, discriminating investors have been realizing that tangible assets like diamonds are a sensible option to disappointing returns from "paper" assets.

If nothing else, investment grade diamonds secure confidence in your portfolio knowing an exquisite yet timeless alternative is backing you up.[6]

Today greater potential returns are much more likely to materialize with investment grade gemstones than any other asset class. Similar to certain other assets, one must accept the fact that long-term holding periods allow these returns to become reality. The risk inherent with reduced liquidity is much more acceptable when there is no self-imposed rush to sell. Be patient and plan your exit strategy for maximum profit potential.[7]

Treasure Trends

A spotlight on alternative investments has revealed telling facts about the habits of those with high wealth and how, as well as with what, that net worth is built to form a sizable nest egg.

Barclays Wealth and Investment division teamed up with Ledbury Research in an effort to better understand the motives that influence wealth creation on the highest level. Heading to the source, more than 2000 high-net-worth individuals were surveyed from 17 countries.

Thomas Kalaris, Barclay Chief Executive, catches crowd curiosity in the opening pages of the report by declaring " ... *the notion that art, or indeed, any commodity, is worth whatever someone is willing to pay for it is worthy of further scrutiny.*"

Trends and surprising facts in the fifteenth volume of *Wealth Insights,* Barclays report on net wealth and alternate investments (otherwise known as "treasures") reveals secrets of the rich you can profit from. All of the individuals in the report had at least $1.5 million in investable assets, 200 of them over the $15 million threshold.

Simply put, those around the world with high net worth have adjusted their investing strategy to include tangible assets including jewelry, precious metals, artworks, wine, classic autos, etc. Assets such as these can be considered collectables. This tactic is part of an overall strategy to diversify portfolios in an effort to mitigate the failures of traditional assets as witnessed over the last several years.

Wealth Insights stated, "*Owning possessions that are financially valuable, emotionally pleasing and culturally significant is a timeless tradition and one that shows no sign of abating.*"

A "Treasure Map" seems to back up that premise in the form of a large two page color spread within the report. This map lays out the world's continents and illustrates, in graphical from, how the ultra-wealthy have chosen to invest in "treasures." 17 major locales around the world representing concentrations of high wealth were highlighted. Percentages of total wealth held as "treasure" are as follows:

US	09%
Ireland	10%
S. Africa	11%
Monaco	14%
Hong Kong	14%
Brazil	15%
Singapore	16%
China	17%
Saudi Arabia	17%

Classic cars, despite being quite popular in the US, were held as a larger part of a treasure portfolio only in Saudi Arabia and India. Precious metals made the top of the treasures list in only four of the 17 locales.

"In times when paper wealth is seen to be more risky, investors are drawn to real, tangible assets," the report stated.

No one will argue that classic cars are not only tangible but seem to have a steely spirit of their own. A wise treasure investor realizes that no matter how well cared for they may be, treasure assets like classic cars require high overall maintenance (even when accrued miles are kept low), scratch easily, can rust or rot if not stored properly, and a small dent can significantly affect value if not repaired. Said repairs can reach into the thousands of dollars depending on size and quantity. Similar to art, wines, and other treasure investments, insurance and transactions costs required to buy and sell add up quickly. Also, in the case of classic cars, upkeep, maintenance and storage costs quickly cut into any profits.

Jewelry was a coveted treasure in *all* 17 high-net-worth locales worldwide.

The Ledbury Research team discovered that India's precious jewelry as a preferred investment treasure was held by 98% of the respondents. 93% of China's responding investors held jewelry. The ratio was at about 50% in Monaco and Switzerland while the US rate was 77% with Brazil at 80%.

These numbers are revealing in many aspects. In particular, India's very high rate of jewelry held as investment treasure was closely tied to portability and simplicity of safe storage. Despite diamonds being a popular concentration of wealth, they allow investors, as well as everyday citizens, to avoid seizure (from opposing private parties as well as the reigning government) that is more difficult to deter if holding other investment treasures such as cars, art and heavy gold bars. This fact is becoming more relevant given the recent "Great Recession" and other financial crises around the world.[8]

Most Popular Treasure

Jewelry was tops in yet another category: standing the test of time.

When high net worth respondents were surveyed about what treasure type they held in the past, hold now and will hold in the future, jewelry eclipsed *all* other treasure types.

70% of respondents owned jewelry as treasure now. About 57% did so five years ago and 47% plan to do so in the future. This contrasts with fine art (pictures and paintings) where only 49% own now. Past and future holding of fine are were both lower than jewelry.

Jewelry beat out all other alternative (treasure) assets in every time category (past, present, and future). Although precious metals tied jewelry at 5% for percentage of total wealth, precious metals' highest time category percentage was only 30% ("own now"), well below that of jewelry's 70%. Clearly, jewelry as a favored treasure has gained much ground, leaving the once venerable classic car (19% "own now") standing still as if stuck at a stop sign.

As a side note, there is a diamond ring setting known as "Past/Present/Future." The center stone (symbolizing the "Present") is the largest main diamond with two other smaller diamonds (symbolizing the "Past" and "Future") flanking the main center gemstone. This setting layout has remained popular throughout the years.

It's no coincidence that the most popular treasure is jewelry. Savvy investors have known for years that gemstones not only beat paper investments, if screened properly, but have significant intrinsic value. When was the last time you heard someone complain about diamond "upkeep," much less see a gemstone deteriorating? That's right, diamonds are extremely durable, timeless, and, combining that fact with how conveniently portable gemstones are, you have a natural born winner. As we've seen, about 70% of wealthy treasure investors own jewelry now, 81% among women.

In addition to the safety advantage of portability, jewelry can be easily moved in an emergency. Try that with real estate, large works of art or even classic cars under certain circumstances.

About 14% of senior managers of large companies and 11% of professional financial workers, entrepreneurs and senior manager of medium size enterprises hold jewelry as a treasure investment. These figures are expected to grow as more laymen, for lack of a better term, catch on to the value of treasure investments. Already, up to 8% of "other" professions have gotten the message by securing a portion of their wealth in treasure assets.[9]

When "Wynning" Art is Losing.

The last thing anyone wants when investing is major problems.

Glitches and minor setbacks are one thing. It's another issue altogether when your own actions spoil the deal in the form of a financial setback.

Back in 2001 Steve Wynn (Las Vegas casino magnate) became the proud new owner of Picasso's "Le Reve." Upon deciding to sell to Steve Cohen for $139 million, Wynn had the picture removed from its frame for inspection and verification. All checked out so the deal was done, at least on paper.

> *"Last year my boyfriend gave me a painting, a very personal one. I really prefer personal gifts or ones made by someone for me. Except diamonds. That's the exception to the rule."*
>
> Minnie Driver

Wynn was having friends (one of which was Barbara Walters) visiting from New York who wanted to see the painting. He had just moved the unframed picture from the lobby to his office with a few other paintings. As he began to tell the story of the Picasso's provenance in grand Wynn form with moving hands and body motion, a distinct ripping sound occurred. He had gotten too close to the painting due in part to his eye disease that affects peripheral vision.

The painting suffered a two-inch tear. Five hours to paint, a second to rip.

Although a New York art restorer attempted a repair, the end result was a major loss of value. The most Wynn could expect to get for the painting now was about $90 million.

Depending on the source, Wynn is said to almost be in the "500 Club" of the ultra-wealthy. His fortune places him at about the 512th richest man in the world.

His wife considered the entire episode to be a "sign of fate" and begged Steve to keep the painting, and he did.[10]

Keep in mind that this incident happened to a very famous person in front of several witnesses involving an extremely expensive and historically poignant painting. From these facts let your imagination wander and guess at what frequency this type of accident happens that we never hear about?

Diamonds are smaller and thus assumed to be more likely to get "lost," yet Yo-Yo Ma forgot his 266-year-old $2.5-million-dollar cello in the trunk of a taxi in 1999. Ma said he loved his cello and declared that "the instrument is my voice."

The cello was tracked down and recovered.

Both Wynn and Ma's experience goes to show that size isn't a determining factor. Nonetheless, it's much more difficult to "rip" a diamond or forget one in a car when it is in a secure container in your pocket. Better yet, insure the diamond and pay the low storage fee for a small security box and you'll sleep better at night.[11]

Museum Mayhem

The security that gemstones provide is almost never understood, much less appreciated.

Unless one wishes to intentionally destroy a diamond, being one of the hardest substances on Earth, they are virtually indestructible. We wish that was true for some of the following works of art that unfortunately met their match by being either damaged or, in one case, completely destroyed.

Who thinks keeping priceless Qing Dynasty vases on a low window sill near a flight of stairs is appropriate?

Antique curators at the Fitzwilliam Museum in Cambridge thought so.

Without any protection three Qing vases were showcased, out

in the open, then obliterated by a museum visitor who fled the scene. About a month later the perpetrator was apprehended. The relief was short-lived, however, as each vase was valued at between $400,000 and $500,000. The vases were heavily damaged with up to 400 pieces lying on the ground.

Qing vases are so valuable due to minute and intricate decorations that some are valued in the millions of dollars.

As mentioned, it's not often that one thinks of gemstones as a form of security too. Museums, offices, and even your own home can be dangerous places to store highly valued objects. At least a diamond can be hidden away when not in display.

A painting by Lucian Freud was sold for $33 million, the highest price achieved by a living artist.

So you'd wonder why someone would throw one of his paintings in a garbage crusher? Two porters did just that at Sotheby's in 2000. A Lucien Freud oil painting of plants made it to the Sotheby's storeroom where it was unpacked and mistaken as an empty crate. Before it was missed it was already on the way to an incinerator. This painting was valued at $180,000 and could have fetched more at auction had it not have been tossed in the trash.

Here is yet another saga of severe missteps in handling pieces of artwork. Having a diamond locked up in a safe brings much more piece of mind. If anything else, before any harm can come to the stone, the safe itself must be breached.

With all the hilarity that comes with the bumbling detective in a Pink Panther movie, here is another museum foible that led to senseless damages.

A British museum had the good fortune of housing statues from Greece that survived Turkish attacks in WWI, the Venetian invasion of Greece and a massive gunpowder explosion that blew the roof off the Parthenon.

The horrors began in the 1930s when the fine details of the statues were scraped off with steel wool. Restorers wanted to rid the statutes of yellow stains in hopes the original pure white glow would return. Vigorous rubbing was all it took to cause irreparable damage.

After the failed "exfoliation" attempt of the 1930s, the next assault came from a bunch of rowdy English kids on a field trip. 1961 was the year a centaur broke a leg after the fighting kids fell onto it. The crack was too deep to be fully fixed.

Can you imagine someone grinding your flawless diamond into the ground with their foot? Unlike the centaur statue, your diamond is highly unlikely to ever be put in harms way, or damaged even if someone attempted to break it.

After about two decades of peace, disaster struck again in 1981 when a workman dropped a skylight on the head of one of the statues.

More damage continued. A horse statue was the victim of thieves that were in search of lead in its hoof and the remaining statues were decorated with graffiti and otherwise vandalized.

These poor statues were no match for human clumsiness and simple disrespect while being held in one of the best museums in the world.

Imagine if you forgot a diamond in your pocket and subsequently sat on it. You'd still be in better shape than having artwork on display at your home or in a museum.

Diamonds are extremely durable. In order to "break" one you'd need to inflict some serious blunt force trauma directly to the diamond on the correct spot before it would shatter. In fact, the moment you made the mistake of sitting down, you'd most likely get "poked" by one of its many ridged edges. The diamond would hurt you before it would even be scratched.

So there you have it, a vase, statues and a painting all decimated under conditions that were supposed to protect these assets.

Great things come in small packages. When seeking alternative investments, stick with tried-and-true diamonds.[12]

World Markets Throw Curveballs

At times not even industry experts make the right calls on market direction.

Reports from several regions show that at times lesser diamonds, as graded by clarity and color, can show momentary gains to the temporary detriment to larger, higher quality diamonds.

Recently, at an international diamond show held in Hong Kong, there was weak Far East demand for perennially popular one carat or larger gems with VS+ (very slight inclusions) clarity ratings while IF-VS stones below the one carat threshold chalked up solid demand. In layman's terms, "lesser" quality diamonds took center stage while the proverbial curtain was drawn on higher quality stones.

Reports out of Hong Kong itself were typical for current investment grade stones. While general polished trading was reported as "slow" there was good demand for "triple EX goods, which continue to garner a steady premium over non-triple EX" stock. Interestingly enough, the report also stated, "more manufacturers are setting loose diamonds in jewelry to make better profit margins from the finished product. Dealers were encouraged by reports of strong gem-set jewelry sales in Mainland China over the Chinese New Year, while sales of both gold and gem-set jewelry remained weak in Hong Kong and Macau."

The above is not odd to hear since manufacturers capture profits rather than getting stuck sitting on loose diamonds. Slight aberrations do happen. Usually, loose gemstones enjoy a broader market due to their flexibility to be set as best determined by end users. A market adjustment such as this more often than not returns to normal in due time.

Meanwhile, in India, polished trading was also reportedly slow at the Hong Kong show. It was also rumored that several small companies were in the midst of financial hiccups. Diamantaires (diamond experts) made the news given supposed trouble receiving payments from overseas clients which squeezed liquidity. Currency devaluations also made the top of the list of worries for Diamantaires.

India also reported pear-shape diamonds less than one carat with SI clarity to be "moving well." Melee (small diamonds) stock scored stable status in the SI–I2 grade. In addition, the lower grade SI–I2's marked "steady demand" from 0.30 all the way up to the three-carat level. That is great movement for what is the lower level clarity range in all common carat weights.

Israel stood out with "stable" polished trading even though their appearance at the Hong Kong show yielded "okay" results."

US demand was also stable for Israel and, in contrast to India, clear diamonds form 0.50–2 carats in the VS – SI range yielded steady demand. That sentiment extended to triple EX goods too. Similar to India, the pear shape was popular.

Being aware of market gyrations and patterns will set you apart as an investor no matter what it is you buy or sell. The world economy is just that, a financial system that feels ripples from across the world whether surplus or deficit rears its head.

Not caring about VS clarity or a one-carat M-colored diamond upward price movement in India may not affect your specific diamond investment today, but rest assured that sustained market anomalies will get your attention "tomorrow."

Just like a connected stock broker, any successful diamond investor ensures that he or she is up to date on industry news that could influence gemstone demand or supply in the months or even years to come.

Stay connected and you just might be the next proud owner of a gemstone smartly higher in value by double digits this year.[13]

Real Estate Red Ink

Even private owners with a team of managers (financial or otherwise), personal assistants and other professionals end up losing large amounts of wealth in supposedly "less risky" ventures outside of "treasure investing."

Once assumed a perennially safe "millionaire maker," real estate continues to throw many for a loop, especially since the "Great Recession." Sure, one's home is not meant to be a cash generating investment, but some purchase and sale decisions seem to lack logic and rack up large losses in the process. A smart gemstone investment would have saved the following celebrities a boatload of cash.

Neither the famous Spelling name nor a popular reality show ("Tori & Dean: Home Sweet Hollywood") could save the loss of almost half a million dollars.

Tori Spelling and Dean McDermott let $450,000 slip through their fingers when selling their Encino, CA home. Despite the reality show being filmed at the Encino house, it sold for only $2.5 million in December of 2011. Public records show a purchase price of $2.95 million in October 2008. Clearly, the new owner was not swayed by the celebrity aurora or the history to the house.

Talk about loss, ouch! Imagine how many quality carats you could get for that half-a-million.

High-security and prestigious neighborhoods can't guarantee protection of wealth either as Britney Spears' real estate debacle illustrates.

On the rebound from the Federline divorce, she bought a

Beverly Hills home for $6.8 million in early 2007, only to sell it for only $4.5 million in Spring of 2012, a $2.3 million loss. After initially listing for $7.9 million, Spears suffered six, yes, six, price reductions in order to get out from under that estate. Just goes to show that judgment is usually clouded during emotional turmoil.

When was the last time you saw a diamond sold for such a steep loss? Sotheby's auctions have been pulling in major profits for gemstone investors and private sales have also been profitable. Real estate auctions of luxury properties can also do well if properly promoted to generate marketing buzz. Too bad Spears missed the boat on that one.

Hopefully she was wise enough to make the most of the upgraded diamond ring Kevin Federline gave her back in 2005. The ring was about 5 carats. Later in 2013, Britney broke off an engagement by returning a $90,000 ring (3.5 carats) to her manager boyfriend. In that case, the door swings both ways so good luck to the ex-boyfriend's "investment" as that is all he's left with when Britney handed the ring back. We can only hope he had the sense to buy a quality diamond that could have been a solid investment in his new bride to be OR eventually sold for limited loss in the unfortunate case of a break-up. It would be foolish to suggest that one buy an engagement ring strictly for the value of the ring. Nonetheless, given the high value of celebrity wedding bands, an objective and logical viewpoint would be to know what you're buying so as to avoid taking a financial "bath" on a major monetary purchase. All joking aside, celebrity marriages are usually short lived.

A prime example backing the need for common sense is the Jennifer Aniston New York purchase back in 2011. Being swayed by her heart strings, she sank $7 million into two units in 2011. No later than spring of 2012 she sold, losing about $500,000 according to a New York Daily News report. Her love for New York led to a big loss.

It would be extremely difficult to lose that amount of wealth in such a short time frame with the purchase of an investment-quality gemstone. Once again, know what you're getting into before committing your hard-earned money to any high dollar commitment.[14]

It is interesting to note that public records show Spears, Krasinski and Cruz all held their properties for about five-to-six years, yet Spears suffered a much greater loss on her residence. You don't see losses of this magnitude investing in quality gemstones. In fact, treasure investors back up their hunches with solid planning to eliminate losses. Their "exit plan" incorporates all known risks, trends, taxes, and more. For example, gemstone treasure investors who do well usually stick to a minimum holding period for about two years with capital set aside to sustain that period.

Best of all, methodical planning allows these investors to keep Uncle Sam's hand from grabbing too deeply into their pocket by holding their gem asset for at least one year. That pushes any gains on a future sale into the long term capital gains tax rate. This way the higher short-term rate can be avoided and provide the time frame to fine tune their "exit strategy." In general, a more profitable gemstone investment is possible when holding a bigger stone with top-notch color characteristics.[15]

Of course celebrities aren't the only ones absorbing losses. The obvious lesson is no one can depend on appreciably growing their net worth by tail-coating on their Hollywood elite status or supposed star power. Similar to expecting a lower grade diamond flanked by higher grade gemstones to maintain any meaningful value, one would be remiss to expect that celebrity status, gate-guarded communities, over-improvements and wishful appreciation hopes to guarantee prosperous real estate ownership.

Stories like this are too common these days. What was once thought of as safe investments are now fraught with risk. Granted, many of us don't purchase a home counting on it to be the star of our investment portfolio. However many have made the mistake of assuming residential real estate will only increase in value as time marches forward.

Alternate investments, particularly high-quality gemstones, have proven to be strong contenders of wealth creation year in and year out.

Expert Declaration: Diamonds are in Demand

Other luxury categories (treasure investments) naturally present competition to jewelry overall. Barclays *Wealth Insights* (2012) report mirrors current facts about diamonds' (jewelry) viability as an alternative investment. "Investment will be required to safeguard and nurture the diamond dream," declares a 2014 De Beers report.

Emerging markets like China as well as a slow but steady US recovery are sure to boost diamond demand looking forward in "real value terms," the De Beers report states. Couple this rising demand with declining supply from existing diamond mines and all is good for diamond investors. Any new mines are likely to be more complex and remote, thus supporting projections of a post-2020 diamond production decline.

Various sources of online research and sales for gemstones promote this geographic market channel to thrive. De Beers Group CEO Philippe Mellier presents the *Insight Report* as a supplement adding depth and detail to other industry information. Yes indeed, the multi-faceted world of diamonds is challenging while sparkling in spectacular fashion.

McKinsey & Company see diamond production slowing as

well as tapping out in some areas, which further proves growing demand will inevitably outstrip supply.

In an independent study RBC found that Chow Tai Fook, a leading retailer in China, could not help but take notice during the 2014 Chinese New Year as their retail revenue rocketed 32% higher. RBC states that the evidence is clear that China will "underpin diamond growth in the medium term, as penetration of diamond jewelry pieces increases…Consumer's desire for diamonds is high."

It's no surprise that, considering the world market, the US is more mature but still retains promising growth areas such as bridal, branded and diamond jewelry, all of which have performed particularly well in recent years. Again, at the retail level, China offers tremendous growth opportunities which can only help values at the investment quality tier.

For sure, consumer preferences have heavy influence upon diamond demand. Nonetheless, a competent investor executing proper due diligence can ride the retail wave formed by diamond lovers to new heights of profits. As emerging economies continue to post gains, consumer demand in the US will continue its five year trend of positive nominal growth at about 5% (2008-2013). Remember, this compound growth is for the industry at large (consumer) with much greater gains secured by investors as proven by auction news at Sotheby's and Christie's.

The dynamics of declining supply and ever increasing diamond demand will provide "value-creating business opportunities" enabling investment in branding, production and technology. With this value chain support from within the industry, investors will benefit from enhancement of the diamond's already rare and precious nature.

Real growth of diamond demand is even expected "under scenarios of volatile or weaker global economic growth." Better yet, previously discussed consumer desire for diamonds as a long time positive growth factor places gems above other natural resources and precious metals which have to appeal to the fickle whim of many sources of demand.

Another key factor to drive home the positive supply-and-demand trend for the foreseeable future is that there are no guarantees that mining companies will discover economically viable deposits to upset lingering supply. History stands as a great example backing the low probability of profitable new diamond discovery. Only 60 kimberlite pipes (nature's "birth canal" for diamonds) out of 7,000 sampled by geologists within the last 140 years were "sufficiently rich in diamonds to be economically viable." Of those 7,000 pipes sampled, only 1000 were diamondiferous.

Investing in diamonds has been a global market for decades. The strength of the Chinese market is further backed by a *Wealth Insight* study (2014) stating that there are more millionaires in Beijing and Shanghai combined than all of London. Credit Suisse, in their 2013 *Wealth Report*, state that "the number of Chinese millionaires (i.e. individuals with assets above US $1 million) to be 1.1 million in 2013, up 90,000 in one year alone."

HNWI (high net-worth individuals), those with investable assets over $1 million, have made China the fourth-largest conglomeration of such individuals in the world according to Capgemini, a global consultancy. Naturally, this fact alone sets the stage for "treasure investors," those serious about alternate investment options.

Back in 2003, diamond jewelry ownership in China was about 10%. Currently, US ownership is approximately 70%. Recently, a 20% rate of diamond pride is shown by the Chinese. This surge has come about due to urban Chinese women favoring fine jewelry over items such as designer handbags. Diamonds in particular were the most desired type of jewelry. History shows those who have already bought a diamond are likely to buy more diamonds for other occasions too. By 2020 well-to-do households and the mainstream consumer is predicted to be over half of urban households, according to McKinsey & Company.

Yes, savvy gemstone investors are cashing in on this swelling tide of diamond wealth. With that being said, it is always wise to secure the opinion of a diamond expert or broker as well as to pursue your own research in an effort to validate a business venture and investment in gemstones.[16]

Whether it's a friendly tip, industry newsletter, in-depth report or other source of information about investing, it is up to you to perform adequate due diligence.

As you've seen, the Wealth Insight from Barclays allowed much insight into where high-net-worth individuals favor placing their alternate (treasure) investments dollars. Much respect and admirable returns are earned from investment grade jewelry with quality gemstones being the common element.

Searching and heeding the advice of competent diamond experts will ensure that your financial venture into treasure investing has a strong foundation. Diamonds have become a welcome relief from once strong traditional investments. Backed by sound advice and realistic risk assessment, gemstones have proven a wonderful compliment to an investment portfolio. Better yet, current world financial events illustrate that gemstones have been responsible for counteracting portfolio losses attributed to struggling traditional investment vehicles.

The proof is in the pudding, as they say.

Colored Investment Grade Diamonds

Price records of colored diamonds have been broken in extravagant fashion, as witnessed over the last few years at auction.

Naturally private sales have mirrored this positive trend. Ranging from personal experience to reports obtained from Bain & Co., RBC, Barclays, Goldman Sachs and other prominent financial companies, the most valuable gems on the planet are natural fancy colored diamonds.

"20 years ago a 1 carat Fancy Intense Pink Argyle Diamond would have sold for approximately $70,000.00 per carat, today that same diamond would be worth $500,000.00," according to rarecoloreddiamons.com. It is now common for fancy diamonds to auction for over $1 million per carat.

Rarecoloreddiamonds.com's Rare Colored Diamonds Historical Price Tracing Systems is a tool for investors to view market trends as potential future value for rare diamonds. During the last 15 years economic cycles show that long term investment is the best bet for rare colored diamonds. Similar to securities and real estate investors, rare gemstone market predictions can be made and acted upon to secure shorter term gains if one is fortunate enough to assimilate industry information and accurately estimate price levels.

Today's price levels for one carat coloreds have plenty of upward mobility given that in 1987 a 0.95 carat Fancy Red Diamond was auctioned at Christie's for $927,000, in 1987! Visualize that. For a stone the size of your baby fingernail, almost $1 million was the investment the recipient happily made. For this reason, many experts recommend auctions as the preferred method of cashing in on your high earning investment grade diamond.

The earned popularity of diamonds as alternative investments has given rise to the financial markets taken quality gemstones seriously

"Real estate in your pocket" is what Europeans had called rare colored diamonds. The traditional "million-maker" real estate the world over has slumped in grand fashion and safe, portable, private, tangible diamonds have graciously stepped up to gain tremendous ground as the alternative investment.

Supply and demand is always a major influencing factor for pricing trends. Colored diamonds are not output in significant numbers from newer Canadian or Russian mines. Over the last several years De Beers has closed multiple mines. This imbalance makes all diamonds with special emphasis on coloreds as very strong investment options.

Live auction houses assist diamond liquidity, which in turn add to a gemstone's marketability. Minimum investment level for qualified investors are $20,000 at rarecoloreddiamond.com.

How rare are colored diamonds?

One tenth of 1% is quite a low number and that fraction is how scarce pink diamonds are. Want an investment quality pink diamond? Only a handful of that one-tenth is deemed worthy by high-net-worth investors, which basically represent the rare market. Fancy colored diamonds historically adhere to the 10,000:1 rule of thumb in mining. Nature makes it so. Typically only one carat fancy diamond comes out of 10,000 carats mined.

Fancy diamond color grades are described with words instead of letters as used to grade colorless diamonds. The standard, as graded by GIA (Gemological Institute of America), ranges from Faint to Fancy Vivid with Vivid being top grade of eight total grades. Colorless diamonds have color grades too, but use letters of the alphabet with "D" being colorless (best) and "S-Z" being light which is, ironically, of yellow tint. For a long time in diamond history a yellow diamond was the worst. Now Fancy yellows

> *"Praise, like gold and diamonds, owes its value only to its scarcity."*
>
> Samuel Johnson

put colorless diamonds to shame, considering the price per carat divide.[17]

At one time a chief engineer at Rio Tinto's Argyle Diamond Mine declared "Only 1% of our production is Pink diamonds. So for every 4 Olympic swimming pools of rocks we crash, we get half a bucket of diamonds, and within that half, only a tea spoon of pink diamonds."[18]

True investment-grade diamonds are categorized by color, clarity, cut, polish, and symmetry.

Traditionally nothing less than an "excellent" (EX) rating for cut/polish/symmetry were acceptable to investors. A "Fancy Vivid" rating for coloreds and "D" rating for colorless diamonds are the preferred color designations. Clarity perfection is known as FL (flawless) and IF (internally flawless). However you're still able to secure great returns (ROI) for "lesser" diamonds given how very rare top investment grade diamonds really are, especially colored.

For example, a D Flawless type 1 round brilliant at just a smidgen over one (1.03) carat with a thick girdle and no fluorescence marked on its certificate can bring over $22,800. Thick girdles commonly take up weight without contributing to the diamond's overall beauty, so some investors are put off by the fact that they're paying for fractions of useless carat. On the flip side, a spectacular diamond is stunning nonetheless, so other investors don't attribute much to a thick girdle. All depends on how critical the buyer is. The penalty, if any, for demerits such as thick girdles and other less desirable elements of a gemstone is more pronounced to lesser-grade diamonds.[19]

Regarding colored stones, clarity, cut, and carat weight are measured but not the defining or sought after characteristics. The hue itself, as well as its intensity and dispersion of color are main value factors.

You'd be correct to think a "clean" (high clarity) stone would be worth more, but many intensely colored stones benefit from that very depth of color "blocking" or otherwise "hiding" any defects such as inclusions. Even some surface blemishes may escape detection due to the saturated color of the stone.

So whether a blue, red, yellow, or other fancy colored stone, it is how deep and rich that color is and how evenly dispersed throughout the stone that further drives its value.

In addition, fancy shapes such as Cushion and Radiant match well with colored stones as a matter of fashion and flare. The reality is that round shaped diamonds are almost exclusively reserved for colorless (white) diamonds.

For more great details about colored stones, refer to the chapter in this book that delves further into these magnificent creations.

One Man's Treasure...

This is one investment you can really get a grip on.

One of many direct benefits of investing in gemstones is their

tangible nature. Portable, concentrated and seizure resistant, unlike real estate or large cumbersome works of art. Best of all this diamond investment can be "loaded" for self-defense, a win-win proposition.

These durable diamonds would certainly stand out during a 21-gun salute. If there ever was a 45 carat sparkling salute, this would be it. Yes, this is an actual newspaper ad that we'll affectionately call "Gunning for Diamonds."

Don't laugh, as this collection of carats will bring a pretty penny if the advertised clarity and color are true. G color and VS clarity is nothing to sneeze at. Many walk out of jewelry stores with SI grade yellow tinted diamonds every day believing they got the deal of the century. Like any set diamonds, assuming these are natural diamonds, it will be a bit challenging to assess if any faux diamonds are in the mix from among the amazing self-count of 2,000 that make up this gun handle.

A pilot test attaining a pass rate of 98.5% was used on loose small diamonds, utilizing a machine dubbed the Automatic Melee Screening (AMS). This Antwerp 2013 pilot, utilized by De Beers, is portable and scans both colorless and near colorless small stones quickly.

The Swiss Gemological Institute made ASDI (Automatic Spectral Diamond Inspection) is a fixed device with a small diamond screening rate of 3,000–4,000/hr.

Until these devices were unveiled, confidence at the consumer level was a concern. First generation machines focused on much larger gems and made small diamond screening ineffective due to cost. Despite the availability of the portable AMS, items like the advertised gun handle and other cluster-like diamonds that are already set inhibit the ability to efficiently reveal faux diamonds.[20]

> *"No thief, however skillful, can rob one of knowledge, and that is why knowledge is the best and safest treasure to acquire."*
> L. Frank Baum

Given the asking price of the advertised diamond gun handle, you should treat any declared value like a loaded gun, handle carefully.

Granted, the "value" is largely in the shear collection of diamonds as a gun handle in and of itself. "The whole is greater than the sum of its parts" rings true in this case, if nowhere else. And "beauty is in the eye of the beholder" is a sure fit for a diamond-encrusted gun handle. Also, if all those diamonds are closely "matched," there will be limited, if any, visual oddities such as color variances and/or "dead" spots due to heavily included stones.

True, this esoteric investment is a far cry from diamonds auctioned off at Christie's and Sotheby's. Giving credit where credit is due is warranted based on the fact that you're not likely to run across many creative carat creations like this. And if the $28,000 wholesale manufacture price is anywhere near reality you're in for sticker shock if attempting to replicate this rootin', tootin', and shootin' relic.

"Cluster" is a term used interchangeably to describe the setting arrangement and name for the small diamonds themselves. Officially, "small" diamonds ranging in size from 0.001, 0.18 carats are called "melee." Now deemed a somewhat derogatory term, melee's were once commonly called "Diamonds Chips." You can see why jewelers did not appreciated small diamonds being referred to "chips" as that implies lesser value. Who wants a "chip off the old block" anyway? Eventually the diamond industry won out and "chip" lost favor in the same manner the "I" in I1-I2-I3 now means "included", changed from the original "imperfect" designation.

Cluster diamonds have history reaching back to the 1800s when diamonds were discovered in South Africa. Late in the Victorian era, this discovery enabled affordable diamonds to be set in many more jewelry pieces of the time.

Over the years cluster settings have had a rollercoaster ride. They remained popular through the 80s, then waned in favor of the solitaire during the 90s.[21]

It's no surprise then that clusters are currently back in style today. That being the case, our friend "Don," the 45-carat-gun-handle seller, may be the one laughing all the way to the bank making good off the cluster popularity evident in the market today. Admittedly, no one is likely to say "I do" to a gun handle, but the cluster concept is back in style and a rising tide lifts all boats...err, diamonds.[22]

A Diamonds.net report indicates that overall melee demand in India was stable in the SI-I2 clarity range. Diamonds above melee size, particularly 0.30–0.50 carats, also demonstrated stability. Markets around the world change due to varying factors for melee and the trend toward cluster diamond rings stateside can only provide positive expectations.[23]

If you noticed, the ad was placed under the "Gun" category as opposed to "Jewelry" or even "Investment." One would think the best opportunity to sell would be under "Gun," yet you may see interest under another category. Amusingly, anyone seeing this diamond-encrusted wonder in public might forget about the gun because of their amazement at all the distracting glitter shining in their face.

For the right crowd these sharp shooting diamonds have appeal as an investment, albeit a niche appeal at that. Good advice would be to not let the sun's reflection off all those diamonds blind you to the reality of a limited resale market.

All in all, this unique gun handle gives "make me an offer I can't refuse" new meaning. In good humor, it all depends on what side of the barrel you're on.

Personal information was redacted for privacy in this ad, but if someone was interested we'd suggest they present "any reasonable offer," as the ad requests. Good luck and *Hi-Ho Silver*!

Soul Currency

For many years a leading Wall Street corporate finance expert said that your passion is your currency and that your fulfillment emanates from a greater sense of purpose.

As a child I related to gems and collected quite a few. Soon enough I became a gemologist (GIA certified) and owned jewelry stores. This led to gems, particularly diamonds, as investments.

Rev. Ernest Chu, of the aforementioned Wall Street fame, writes in his book *Soul Currency* that qualities such as insight and intuition are great resources of wealth and inner qualities we all possess to one degree or another.[24]

Rev. Chu learned during his time on Wall Street that he was gifted with the ability to process and sort through an overwhelming amount of information. Having just returned from an Israel diamond trip, I briefly spoke with Rev. Chu about "spiritual capital" and my sincere desire to help others achieve their goals.

Similar to Rev. Chu's gift of analyzing reams of financial data and coming up with key insights, I've been able to continually screen gems and recognize the opportunities they offer for financial abundance. One of the principles of *Soul Currency* is that what you bring to your work is a major part of that work. When you share the value of your talent, great things happen for not only yourself but for others. We all make choices with our money and I soon discovered that my talent in investing in gems could enable others to make wise wealth decisions too.

> "Next to sound judgment, diamonds and pearls are the rarest things in the world."
>
> Jean de la Bruyere

Trusted Gem Advisor

Whether it be an educated friend, financial professional, diamantaire, diamond broker, jewelry store proprietor or other reliable source, it is your responsibility to oversee the investment of your hard-earned money.

Opportunity abounds. Just years ago many were doubtful that diamonds could be capable of attaining the status of viable investment vehicles. Those in the financial arena now have to take notice that diamonds are actually leading the growth trend with, in some cases, double digit returns. Clients have been searching and found in gemstones of investment grade level a saving grace for meandering and limping traditional stores of wealth.

"Let us not be too particular; it is better to have old secondhand diamonds than none at all."

Mark Twain

Take what you learned in this chapter and apply it to your pursuit of wealth. You may not be financially independent yet, but with dedication, investigation and knowledge you will discover how "treasure" investing may best compliment your investment goals.

CHAPTER 3

BEFORE THE POLISH

WITH NATURAL BEAUTY in their pure and untouched state, rough diamonds have eternally had stand-alone value.

Upon the first discovery of diamonds, the entire world production was measured in pounds. In the 1800s huge mines in South Africa broke open the diamond market. Once only available to royalty and the extraordinarily wealthy, gemstones came within reach of those who thought they would never own a diamond.

Today man-made diamonds have become the accepted alternative for those unable or unwilling to invest in a natural diamond. Also, after the South Africa diamond rush, Australia, Russia, and Canada entered the diamond race. This led to added supply of natural diamonds only enhancing much broader and pent-up market demand for the middle-class economic strata.

Raw and Natural Appeal

In ancient India it was believed that altering gemstones would dilute their strength. Rough gemstones were attributed sacred powers.

As such, being worn in their naturally unearthed form was thought to preserve their inherent powerful energy.

Uncut, unpolished diamonds of the earliest jewelry dates back to 1074. At that time the Hungarian Queen's crown proudly displayed rough diamonds. Gemstones were celebrated in their natural form.

Rough diamonds are revered for their pure, untouched state and natural beauty. Their value lies both in their beauty and raw material and many do not know that actually it is the cost of the rough diamond that determines the price of a polished diamond.

Hollywood Gets Rough

In 2005, Diamonds In The Rough, a New York company, took on the mission of what can be called a rough renaissance revival.

The world seemed to have taken a detour from natural beauty in favor of cut and polished gemstones. The assumption was that cut and polished stones were somehow "better" than the natural state of gemstones, as if rough stones no longer made the grade. Soon enough, as is typical, trendsetters and the press took hold and over the years we've seen Hilary Swank, Demi Moore, Kelly Osbourne, Alicia Keys and others reawakening to the beauty of being "in the rough."

From the red carpet to public appearances, rough-cut diamonds have hit it big. Jennifer Lopez wore Diamond In The Rough gems on *The Late Show with David Letterman*, to the 20th Anniversary ICON Awards, on the *Tonight Show with Jay Leno*, as well as appearing in *Life & Style* magazine.

Katy Perry wore rough diamonds on the October 2011 Cover of *InStyle*, at the Paris Fashion Week, and to the 20th Annual Elton John AIDS Foundation Academy Awards Viewing Party.

Kelly Clarkson was seen wearing rough diamonds on Stage

at the 54th Annual Grammy Awards. On Fox's The X-Factor, Mary J. Blige showed off rough diamond flare and Minnie Driver was seen on the Graham Norton Show with a rough gemstone.[1]

"Rough" jewels have also graced the pages of leading fashion, lifestyle, and bridal magazines including *W*, *Elle*, *Harper's Bazaar*, *Martha Stewart Weddings*, *Brides*, *Elite Traveler*, *Town & Country*, and *Robb Report*.[2]

Rough Attraction

Modern jewelry trends are starting to come around, back to their origins.

Rough gemstones are never refined. The original and perfect form is unchanged. They say that no two diamonds are alike. That is true, diamonds are like snowflakes and fingerprints, none are quite the same. One must admit, however, that without a jeweler's loupe or other magnification source, not even an expert, in most cases, can definitely tell the difference between two gem quality polished diamonds of the same shape and similar quality.

The same cannot be said of rough diamonds. Very clearly and obviously from first sight, the difference is undeniable. Even the layman, the average person on the street, can see the uniqueness in person immediately. From a distance, the typical cut and polished diamond is the same as any other for the most part. Sure, size, setting and obvious glaring quality differences can be perceptible to the layman, but most of the time no discernable variances can be detected.

"Roughs" (short for rough gemstones) demand instant recognition due to their unique presence, unique form, sparkle and, in many cases, setting.

Given the varying physical diversity amongst rough gemstones, their shape is loosely described as "free form" (dodecahedron, octahedron, cube and dodecahedron: technical identified) and clarity is described as sparkling and degree of luster. Poorly cut polished stones can have "very poor" "fire" and "scintillation." Even their "polish" can be of low grade.

Like their polished cousins, uncut rough diamonds either have sufficient sparkle or not, naturally. You'll have plenty of competition getting your hands on a high grade rough gemstone. At one time fancy colored diamonds weren't even on the radar so to speak. The same could have been said for roughs, not anymore. Roughs, being untouched, are inherently worthy and in that fact is their gaining popularity and value.

It's amazing what a skilled artisan can do with a jagged looking raw gemstone.

Initial perceptions can be refined by working with the inherent characteristics of a rough diamond. Properly orienting a raw stone in a setting takes advantage of its asymmetric structure, turning a "lemon" into the juice of life. Once the setting, raw stone, and complimenting accent gems come together like a living piece of artwork, you'll be shocked at how out of this world a rough stone can really be. Its uniqueness alone will turn heads wherever you go.

Rough vs. Rough: Going Head To Head

A rough's internal sparkle comes from its unique shape, trigons, striations and complicated crystal faces. Also, what makes one rough more desirable over another involves "satin" and the nickname "glassies." Surface luster of the satin type, although often attractive, kills internal sparkle while a "glassie" has flat, planar faces leading to that "dull" look.

The asking price for a 1.96 carat "gem-grade cut able colorless complex crystal" was $12,500.

This diamond originated from the Orapa mine in Botswana with "no damage." Deep within its dodecahedral shape there are NO visible flaws or inclusions and its surface crystal faces are parallel. Clarity is "exceptional."

Contrast that with a 4.56-carat brown octahedral crystal at $2,210. This diamond crystal, from the Argyle mine in Kimberley Western Australia, has lustrous transparency, internal feather-like flaws causing "rainbow-like" reflections inside and NO damage.[3]

Size is only one factor and definitely not a determining one. As you can see, color, luster and clarity all play a role in market demand. And, to a certain degree, the mine from whence the stone came may work its way into the pricing formula.

A World Record, a Natural Masterpiece, and a Rough For You

The "Cullinan" graced the pages of the Guinness Book of World Records.[4]

At 3,106.75 carats this uncut rough was found in South Africa in 1905. Queen Elizabeth II came into possession of two of the largest of nine fragments of the Culinan.

The Queen's Imperial State Crown holds the second largest stone dubbed the "Second Star of Africa." On top of the royal scepter wielded by the Queen is the "Great Star of Africa," weighing in at 530.2 carats.

The "Dieu du Soleil" solitaire ring features a 12.41-carat yellow rough diamond accented with 0.61 carats of micro pave vivid yellow diamonds, hand-crafted in 18k yellow gold.

A unique band of 18k yellow gold is the setting to a 12.41-carat yellow rough diamond known as the Dieu du Soleil. Beautifully and creatively accenting this natural beauty is over half-a-carat of micro pave vivid yellow diamonds.[5]

With this new momentum of acceptance, many natural diamonds are skipping the cutter in favor of remaining rough.

There are many avenues to obtain that special rough diamond meant just for you. Having the means to secure a professional will assist your rough diamond search and purchase. A simple search for rough gem jewelers will provided multiple options.

A recent search of eBay produced some fine-looking raw beauties. Octahedron fancy canary yellows from Australia, gem-grade fancy champagne roughs, cuttable natural browns, as well as brandy colored stones round out the opportunities.

Arkansas Odds Favor Finding A Diamond

It's been said you've got a 1 in 10 million chance of finding a natural diamond. Those odds skyrocket to 1 in 1 billion if we assume a base diamond size of about 8 mm (greater than 2 grams).[6]

Impossible odds?

Not for a 12-year-old boy who in 2013 found a 5.16-carat diamond at Arkansas' Crater of Diamonds State Park. Fittingly enough, he named it "God's Glory Diamond." In case you're wondering, the State Park has a "finders-keepers" policy...the diamond is all his.

A park ranger stated: "This diamond is truly glorious. The *pear-shaped crystal* is complete, about the size of a jellybean, and it has a beautiful metallic luster. The diamond's surface features interesting notches that give it a one-of-a-kind appearance and tell of its *powerful and turbulent origins*, as magma brought it to the surface from deep within the earth."

The largest stone found at the park was 16.37 carats. It was colorless (white) and discovered in 1975.

The 5.16 carat find was honey brown and the boy found it while his father was in the process of renting tools for the search. Literally, the Boy Scout found the gem within ten minutes of his family's arrival at the park on their first visit.

Ten minutes?

Makes you wonder how many other park visitors passed up this "scuffed stone" in hopes of finding a bigger sparkling wonder. Or maybe they just weren't looking closely enough. After all, the diameter of this special stone was small enough to fit about six of them on the face of a coin the size of a quarter.

Colorless (white) and brown gems are the two colors in the top 32 finds listed on the park's website by size. Of the 31,476 total diamonds found since 1972, almost 82% were of the white/brown variety, and only 20% of those were brown.[7]

Based on the park's own published statistics, you might want to make your way to Arkansas and press your luck for a day.

Just think what your eagle eye can find if a young kid kicking dirt on a public access land stumbles upon a five carat diamond!

Mother Nature Knows Best

Rarity in nature is common, odd but true.

The more unique raw gems are, the more they reflect natural phenomena. Great works of art are unique in their greatness. A rough diamond left untouched by a cutting blade already has greatness inherently within itself.

Why mess with nature's best?

Rough gems that measure superior in factors such as shape, color, weight, radiance and natural appeal are worth showcasing as the most treasured jewels the world knows.

Could it be that despite all the technological means we have today to mine, process, cut, polish and display diamonds, they got it right the first time, 900 years ago?

True treasures are usually those you can't replicate yourself.

Naturally rough diamonds defy what we once considered the "perfect" diamond. "Cut," from what has been considered one element of the "4C's" of diamond grading, has been replaced by inherent shape regarding rough gems. Distinct features create character, and character is the most important "C" that had gone missing, until the rough diamond returned to favor.

Many naturally placed inclusions in raw diamonds, once seen as nuisances, are really the "life" and delicate distinctiveness that nature intended.

That's the way it was meant to be, naturally.

100 Year Diamond

It became the "Find of the Century," created instant buzz within the diamond industry and is a balance sheet altering event every stakeholder dreams about.

Lucara Diamond Corp.'s recent unearthing of the world's second largest gem-quality diamond makes 100-year history. About the size of a tennis ball, the 1,111-carat diamond came from the company's Botswana mine and is the largest of three impressive diamonds discovered by Lucara in 2015. The two other clear diamonds weighing in at 813 and 374 carats are of "exceptional" quality and also came from the same mine.

Shiny Stone Shockwaves

In the $80 billion diamond industry discoveries such as this spread serious shockwaves. As you would expect, Lucara has been inundated with requests about the spectacular stone. London's Natural History Museum wants to put the diamond on display while the Discovery Channel believes a documentary about the stone would be a stunning ratings success.

An offer of $40 million for the diamond was quickly rejected by Lucara's CEO.

Initial estimates of the stone's value have already reached upwards of $66 million. Nonetheless, Lucara is in no rush to sell. Given the fact that the Botswana mine just recently produced three diamonds ranging from about 370 to 1,100 carats the company is likely to strategically plan each step towards a possible sale in a deliberate manner. The possibilities are wide open. A private buyer, jeweler or group of investors may step up with an offer Lucara can't refuse—one never knows. Until then, generating further interest for the stones many include creatively displaying them.

In addition, the Vancouver-based company reportedly has no long-term debt. As such there is absolutely no pressure to let the shimmering 1,111-carat stone go for anything other than top dollar. News of this diamond discovery instantly boosted Lucara's stock about 32% which single handedly added $150 million of value to the company and wiped out the accumulated one-quarter securities value slide over the last year.[8]

Several other factors are likely to influence the value of this "100-year" diamond. Both Botswana and South Africa have long histories of producing high quality diamonds, thus any stone over the psychological 1,000-carat threshold is certain to attract worldwide attention. Lucara CEO, William Lamb, stated "…continued recovery of high quality stones…cannot be overstated…" referring to the 813- and 374-carat stones recently discovered as well as future prospects from the mine that has been operational since about 2012. Recall that Africa's Southern territory (near Pretoria) was the site of the "Cullinan" diamond, 3,106 colossal carats that became the centerpiece of the British Royal Jewels. The Cullinan, at its originally mined size, remains the world's largest diamond ever unearthed. Take note that this new Lucara 1,111 carat stunner has earned the prestige of being the largest diamond outside of the Royal collection. Further backing up Lucara's leverage was the July 2015 sale of 341 and 269 carat stones for just over $60,000 a carat.[9] Last, but not least, De Beers gave up its majority stake in the mine (Karowe, S. Africa) back in 2009 to Lucara for $49 million.

So, no matter how you cut it, Lucara can well afford to wait it out, which includes the option to do nothing, for the time being.

Carat Crusher Close Call

You may be shocked to learn that the second largest diamond in the world—almost never was.

One-carat flawless diamonds are rare enough much less those of gem quality of over 1000 carats, which is why Lucara almost, unwittingly, let the 1,111-carat beauty slip by. Thanks to the timing of an equipment upgrade the diamond was saved from the rock crusher. You see, the holes in the screener that lets gems drop through, escaping the crusher, was recently increased to accommodate stones up to 1,800 carats. Is it worth investing in a 3,000 "gem drop" hole size? Lucara is seriously pondering that question. The real question is how many more stones north of 1,000 carats will there be in this geographic area? "There's no real statistical numbers you can run on this," said Lamb. "It's an absolute anomaly. It's too far off the curve."[10]

With a bit of luck thrown in good fortune may continue to shine upon Lucara and the legendary Southern African diamond region in the years to come.

Chips Off A New Rock

Only time will tell what the ultimate fate of the freshly mined 1,111-carat rough diamond will be.

A hint may come from the Cullinan (unearthed in 1905) itself, which was cut by hand into nine major stones and 96 smaller ones. Graff Diamonds cut Gem Diamonds' 603-carat "Lesotho Promise" into 26 flawless diamonds along with a 76-carat pear shape that were assembled into a dazzling necklace.[11] Gem Diamonds' Lesotho operation in South Africa sourced the "Promise" and prior to Lucara's 1,111 wonder stone, "...held the record for the largest stone discovered this century..."

CEO Lamb did say that similar to the Cullinan and the Promise, Lucara's recent world-record-holding diamond find may end up with "...other offcut pieces as large as 20 to 30 carats each worth millions of dollars..." as well as one "...'significant' single polished stone."[12]

Prior to in-depth marketing efforts beginning, the 1,111-carat magnificent monster has to be sent to Antwerp just to be scanned since Lucara doesn't have equipment that can accommodate such a large stone.

From there it may move on to New York or remain in Antwerp, both leading cutting centers, for exceptional diamonds. The entire process from cutting to polishing to final sale may take years.

Perfectly Clear

CHAPTER 4

WHERE DO DIAMONDS HIDE?

I T'S AN AMAZING journey that has brought millions of carats of diamonds into the world.

This massive collection of stunning stones ultimately rings up $72 billion (USD) worth of retail value, every year. Behind the scenes, a "diamond pipeline" becomes a value chain that takes about $15 billion in rough stones, cuts and polishes them to boost value to near $24 billion before reaching the pinnacle of over $70 billion in total value.

Monetary value aside, where do diamonds really come from and how does this source make these minerals more valuable than the mere pebbles they initially appear to be?

Where in the World?

Diamonds are found the world over shining with amazing variety.

In fact, India was mining and trading diamonds during the dawn of commerce along the infamous "Silk Road" corridor to

Venice and beyond. Some estimates of India's diamond reign date earlier than 400 B.C. After dominating the diamond trade for hundreds of years, India slowly lost its advantage to Brazil, which continued the diamond trade legacy.

Since those early days, Africa, Russia, Australia, and Canada have all flexed their diamond producing muscles while marching forward into the diamond market of tomorrow.

Although world supply of gem quality stones is dropping, one never knows where the next mother lode will appear. The world has plenty of pent-up demand to last the long-haul.

Canadian carats have come a long way.

The tale of Canada's trail of diamonds goes back to 1899, about 90 years prior to the first exploratory drilling in the Arctic reaches of Canadian Territory. W.H. Hobbs, a Wisconsin university geology professor had a hunch. His hypothesis was simple. Ice Age glaciers of time gone by dragged stones discovered around the Great Lakes from Canada, the true source of these key minerals.

Despite geological backing and common sense application of science, it wasn't until the 1960s that De Beers took interest. Fast forward another 20 years and two other geologists picked up the trail of clues and dug deeper into the details. Where De Beers and others fell short, geologists Fipke and Blusson connected the dots of the proverbial mineral puzzle. The famous "Trail of Minerals" these geologists came across was no accident. After extensive and committed searching they discovered "dark red garnets, lustrous black ilmenites and green chrome diopsides." Diamonds were nearby, just not in sight.

They hit "pay dirt" at Lac de Gras (180 miles northeast of Yellowknife) during the freezing cold winter season of 1991. Their trail of minerals was so convincing they secured up to $500 million in financing from what is now BHP Billiton to drill exploratory holes. This venture unearthed about 80 gem quality diamonds from a kimberlite vein.

Canada was welcomed on the world diamond map. Soon after Canada sprinted into position as producer and marketer of high quality diamonds a new diamond leader in the developed world.[1]

It's interesting to note that the uninitiated assumes that the United States is a major diamond producer. Although New York is one of many worldwide diamond trading centers, only Canada can claim carat capital of North America, hands down.

> *"Diamonds are nothing more than chunks of coal that stuck to their jobs."*
> Malcolm S. Forbes

On the world stage of sourcing diamonds, the USA isn't even a road bump. However, Crater of Diamonds State Park in Arkansas is a very unique diamond-hunting experience. Visitors to the park get to keep whatever diamonds they find. Find yourself State side? Be sure to test your luck at this famous park, a true "solo-sourcing" diamond expedition.

Measured by value, the diamond power house producers of the world are undisputed.

Taken in aggregate, Africa controls about 50% of world diamond value output with the following estimated brake outs:

> Botswana: close to 25%
> South Africa: just under 10%
> Zimbabwe and Namibia: hanging on at around 5%
> Sierra Leone and the Democratic Republic of Congo: hovering near the 1% mark
> Central African Republic: barely holding on at 0.5%

Just behind Russia's solid position at one-quarter of world diamond value output is Canada striving to reach the 20% mark.

Reaching 20% was no small feat for our Arctic neighbors. Most impressive was Canada's dedication to marketing quality and conflict-free diamonds, which had a significant role revealing and impeding the "blood" diamond trade.[2]

Carats and Coal, Connection or Convenience?

Quotes abound connecting coal as the basic source of diamond. This subject is so ubiquitous you'll find many people, famous and not so much, have thrown their two cents into the hat.

> *"Perhaps time's definition of coal is the diamond."*
>
> Kahlil Gibran

This quote's reference to time hinges on fact while relating coal to diamonds is based upon a myth.

Forbes had it right linking work, which is essentially effort and energy, to the finished product of a diamond stone. Plenty of energy is transferred to the stone as it is created.

On the silver screen, *Ferris Bueller's Day Off* (1986) starring Matthew Broderick, included a comedic scene with Broderick's character making a quip about coal, diamonds, pressure and his friend's awkward demeanor.

Yes indeed, heat and pressure are critical elements required for diamond formation. So what can be said to debunk or support the still popular coal connection controversy?

Recall that myths become popular due to repetition, which re-enforces inaccuracies and half-truths which eventually become "facts" by assumption.

It is true: "no pressure, no diamonds." It is also true that coal itself forms as a result of pressure over time. However, when scientifically studied we find that coal originates from plant debris that assists in the formation of fossil fuels. This debris can end up buried, under pressure, up to two miles beneath the Earth's surface. Sedimentary rock is what coal really is.

Below Earth's crust is the mantle and continental plates where the carbon of diamonds reside. Some geologists believe this carbon was likely present and trapped during the Earth's formation.

Other scientists and geologists won't completely rule out coal's role in being at least a part of the formation process of a limited quantity of diamonds. They do, however, concede to the fact that the age gap between terrestrial plant debris and that of Earth's diamonds make coal an unlikely contributor to diamond development. Coal was considered a close cousin of diamonds given their common element of carbon. Although it is a fact that carbon is one of the most common substances on Earth, atoms of carbon are arranged differently in coal and diamonds.

Structural Formation Fundamentals

We've seen that Earth's earliest land plants most likely came to be well after natural diamonds already had formed, by about 100 million years.

Plate tectonics and topical events on the Earth explain about four ways in which diamonds were formed at or near the surface. Commercial diamonds are primarily found as a product of one of these processes.

Over 2,200 degrees Fahrenheit is "relatively cool" compared to Earth core temperatures of over an estimated 9,000 degrees, but just right for diamond formation. Graphite would be the result if this heat was turned up much higher, bypassing favorable diamond temperatures.

New York's Natural History museum equates the Eiffel Tower resting on a 5-inch plate as the pressure needed to make a diamond.[3]

Now that we have a grasp on pressures, temperatures and how

the passage of time is related to diamond formation, let's look at the processes that have these elements in common.

Diamonds, the Final Frontier?

Imagine waiting for the next "Space Diamond Express." As it hurls through space, we become more anxious by the minute waiting for its arrival here on Earth. What precious cargo will this meteorite bring? How many carats will we be able to harvest once it impacts Earth? Will the diamonds be colored?

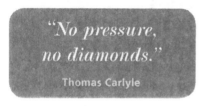

"No pressure, no diamonds."

Thomas Carlyle

As you might have figured, there is no such luck, but isn't it exciting to dream about a diamond-laden space rock bringing us riches from across the Milky Way?

Truth be told, these fast moving terrestrial rocks can contain diamonds, very tiny ones. The Allen Hills meteorite contained many diamonds according to Smithsonian researchers who cut a sample section from this space rock. The theory is that prior to impacting Earth, these meteors collided with other space matter. Asteroid collisions such as these involve powerful forces strong enough to create diamond in space and stuck to the meteorite. It is possible other spectacular events occur in space effecting rocks that assist in diamond formation.

A quarter-carat diamond is thought of as being quite small on one's finger. Imagine a diamond as small as billionths of a meter in diameter. That's what you call a Nano diamond. No matter their size, NASA researchers have found some meteorites containing large quantities of Nano diamonds. Although too small for commercial use, up to three percent of the carbon found in these meteorites have been Nano diamonds.

Popiqai and Meteor Craters in Siberia, Russia, Arizona, and the

USA, respectively, contained diamonds. 13 millimeter sized polycrystalline industrial diamonds were found at the Popiqai site while sub-millimeter crystals were all that Meteor Crater produced.

Impact sites of meteors on Earth have potential carbon sources such as dolomites, marbles, lime stones and other carbon-bearing rocks. Of course, coal is still considered a possible source by some researchers.

Asteroids that fall to Earth creating impact sites are known to produce diamonds on the spot due to the high velocity of impact. Mixing high temperature, an instant pressure spike, and unique source elements at the impact site yields tiny diamonds.

Volcanic Volatility

Interruption of stability, that is how diamonds come to be.

Whether it's asteroids colliding with terrific force or a meteor impacting the Earth's surface, the status quo is disturbed, change occurs, and a diamond is born.

Scientists believe that early in Earth's history there was significant chemical and physical upheaval that eventually settled and cooled down, allowing the proper environment for diamonds to form.

When the orderly chaos settled down, forming the Earth, many minerals including diamonds came to rest well beneath the surface of the Earth. This area, below continental plates, is called the mantle. A layer of the upper mantle, a DSZ (Diamond Stability Zone), is what is believed to be the resting level of most diamonds.

So how did minerals like diamonds, buried deep below Earth's continental plates, reach the surface?

A recent visitor (June of 2015) to the Crater of Diamonds State Park found an icicle shaped stone that turned out to be the fifth-largest diamond find in the Park at 8.25 carats.

At about one-half the size of a quarter, this dazzling white diamond was found in twenty minutes by a park visitor. The park is the only diamond producing area open to the public. Diamonds in this region reached the surface due to an ancient volcanic crater that has an eroded surface. The park is a rock hound's delight, given the 40 varying types of minerals and semi-precious stones to be found.

Oddly enough, the park was originally a farm in 1906, then turned into a failed mining operation and officially became a State Park in 1972. Dating back to the land's farm era, about 75,000 diamonds have been found, and it's been finders-keepers since the park took over.

The June 2015 diamond find was in the area of the park called the "Pig Pen," known for its muddy terrain after rainfall. Searching was made easier by the fact that the park personnel regularly plows the terrain, which helps loosen up the soil while jolting loose diamonds.

Back in 1924 the largest diamond found in the United States was at this site. Called the "Uncle Sam Diamond," it was about 40.25 carats.

Of particular note is the fact that Crater of Diamonds State Park is somewhat similar to the Kimberley region in Africa. Both areas hosted diamond finds fairly close in history (the late 1800s and 1906), farming land was common in both regions, diamond finds involved no "mining," much less any strenuous digging, and a few large carat finds are in the history books from each area.

It is no coincidence that lamproite is common at the State Park. Also, colorless, brown, and yellow diamonds are the mainstay of gem colors commonly found here.[4]

Diamond prospectors find the end result of stones disturbed from the DSZ. These "sleeping" diamonds were "torn" from the

DSZ by rare deep-source volcanic eruptions and pushed closer to the surface. When volcanic magma cools, kimberlite and lamproite "pipes" form into a prospectors dream.

Whereas coal is formed much closer to the Earth's surface, conditions prime for diamond formation are much deeper, 90 miles deep. These zones are not uniform in their presence. They are believed to occur in the mantle layer beneath a stable interior of continental plates.[5]

Clearly, then, carbon crystallizes under extreme circumstances to form a type of mineral that is not only unique but the hardest on Earth.

> *"A diamond, incarcerated in its subterraneous prison, rough and unpolished, differs not from a common stone."*
>
> Charles Caleb Colton

With this overview of how most diamonds are formed you can see why between 100 to 200 tons of ore must be mined, on average, to yield a one carat rough diamond.

Ore bodies, such as those of the Diavik Diamond Mine, are actually extinct volcano magma paths containing xenolith that are long ago inactive (extinct), which scientists call kimberlite pipes or veins. The Diavik open-pit mine resides in the Canadian NW Territories surrounded by the waters of Lac de Gras.

Subduction Zones

Closer to the surface than Diamond Stability Zones (DSZ) but much deeper than the common depth of plant decay that ultimately forms coal, are sub-ducting plates.

As "shallow" as 50 miles below the surface, these plates are fairly cool (390 degrees Fahrenheit) compared to inner Earth's intense heat of volcanic magma.

Plate tectonic processes capture rocks which are pulled into lower levers of the mantle and then return to the surface via subducting plates. Oceanic and continental plates that bump and rub into each other move trapped rocks when oceanic plates slide underneath their larger continental peers. This subduction zone scenario affects mantle stability as convergent plate boundaries collide. Obviously a descending plate is subjected to higher pressures and temperatures that become ideal for diamond formation.

A Brazil study confirmed the "bending" oceanic plate theory, given tiny mineral inclusions commonly found in ocean sediment and plate geology.

Dolomite, marble, limestone and other carbon sources such as offshore sediments of plant debris are needed for these tiny subduction zone diamonds to form. All this grinding produces diamonds which are too small for commercial use and very rare to begin with.

Eras Of Alluvial Action

Golconda was the region in India that held the first diamonds ever unearthed. This area was east of the Deccan Highlands and was famous for bringing us the Hope Diamond as well as other large high-quality stones.

Golconda allowed the sourcing of diamonds via placer deposits which come about from gravity separation of sediment that included an accumulation of valuable minerals, diamonds being "King" of these minerals. In Spanish, placer means "alluvial sand."

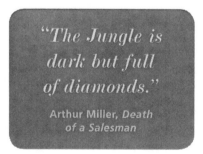

"The Jungle is dark but full of diamonds."

Arthur Miller, *Death of a Salesman*

Along the Orange River in Africa was a diamond find that led to a "diamond rush" in the late 1800s in the Kimberley region.

Sedimentary deposits can be found along coastlines and streams. It is not uncommon for eruptive deposits to be weathered and/or eroded to expose diamonds that naturally slip into secondary alluvial deposits.

Diving For Diamonds

Imagine you're snorkeling when your eyes catch a slight sparkle from below. You dive down and grab the object of your desire from amongst a vast field of similar objects.

To your amazement this "stone" turns out to be a diamond!

Legend? Lost treasure?

Hardly, but you'll need a lot more than a pair of flippers and face mask to free more of these gems from their submariner slumber.

Marine mining has been alive and well for about the last seven years off the South African coast in the Atlantic Ocean. Thanks to the original source (Orange River) there are millions of dollars' worth of diamonds that have been deposited on the sea floor.

Peace In Africa is one of multiple mining vessels off the coast of Namibia taking advantage of technological advancements to mine this substantial reserve, which is expected to last about 30 years.

De Beers is behind this "sea going prospector" that trolls up to 18 miles offshore sucking up stones.

> *"Like cats' eyes gleaming in the gloom, the precious diamonds rest."*
> Robert Leighton (The Duke of Brunswick's Diamonds)

The company is betting they'll get every penny of their investment back in under 15 years as long as the ship can capture about 20,000 carats every month.

The cargo ship to diamond hunter cutting-edge conversion cost around $140 million and offers the ability to search and suck diamonds off the seabed almost 400 feet down.[6]

That certainly gives "sea sparkle" a whole new meaning.

Diamonds and the Orange River date back to 1866 when what appeared to be an ordinary pebble was actually a diamond, weighing in at nearly 80 carats, found by a boy as he explored the banks of the river. A diamond rush ensued and the Kimberley region became famous almost overnight. These diamond discoveries were a harbinger of great fortune to come. Orange River-originated diamonds continue to place in the 95th percentile of overall gem quality.

Back to the Source

From the bottom of the ocean to the far reaches of outer space to the land in between, diamonds seem to be everywhere yet are often, metaphorically, out of reach.

Scientists and researchers are quite certain that the overwhelming majority of the diamonds mined were already in the Earth "in the beginning."

One can simply describe diamond formation as nature's "pressure cooker" that crystalizes carbon to form the most admired and respected mineral on Earth. How wondrous nature is to use molten lava as a "highway" to push diamonds within our technological grasp. Equally amazing is how certain regions of the world have been blessed with full mines of beautiful diamonds covering the spectrum of a rainbow.

Whether a streak across the sky, a glitter from the ground, or a sparkle from the sea, just remember that it could be a diamond that you see.

CHAPTER 5

GREAT WHITE DIAMONDS

THE HISTORY OF the Canadian diamond story has a few twists and turns, the most interesting of which involves Canada's long delay in participating in the world diamond industry.

Obviously many areas of Canada are well known for inhospitable climates and utter remoteness. It is no wonder, then, that it took almost an entire century to start mining diamonds since Professor W.H. Hobbs (University of WI, USA) first suggested, in 1899, that diamonds were likely to be found in Canada...somewhere. Professor Hobbs' hunch was based on earlier, but limited, diamond finds in the US that he figured were glacial based.[1]

It wasn't until the 1960s that Canadian diamond exploration began. About twenty years afterward, a major kimberlite (igneous rock containing diamonds) discovery was made. Then, in 1991, a diamond-bearing kimberlite pipe at Point Lake was discovered.

Low Mercury: A Great White North Reality

"Ice highways" are a reality in the frozen arctic reaches of Canada.

Literally, a Canadian diamond mine's very creation and continuing existence depends on frigid temperatures. Most mining locales have airfields, but it is trucks that perform the heavy lifting on the front-end, providing infrastructure and building materials. Ice highways are formed every year, stretching up to 200 miles and as wide as a football field.[2]

Covering nearly half a million miles of land, the Canadian NWT (Northwest Territories) is above the tree line, remote and barren. This is where cold is COLD, exposed skin freezes quickly. One second you feel your hand, the next it is numb.

Super frigid minus 50 degrees Celsius is not unheard of with minus 30–40 degrees being common. With or without wind, those temps are bitterly cold.

Located in the Lac de Gras region are the Diavik and Ekati mines. Geographically speaking, they are only 120 miles from The Arctic Circle.[3]

What's the chance for snow today? Oh, about 69%. And that's not just today, that forecast is accurate the entire year.

Of the various types of possible precipitation, it should be no surprise that snow dominates in Canada's NWT region. February is particularly cold. The majority (basically 100%) of the month is officially considered "frigid" in meteorological lingo. Daily highs are below 0 degrees Celsius on average during the cold season, November 23 through March 25. In January, a high of minus 16 degrees Celsius can be the coldest day.

Summer brings some relief. In July, highs can hover around 20 Celsius with lows near 11 Celsius.[4]

All these freezing figures contrast what is necessary for diamonds to form in the first place. The kimberlite "pipes" loaded with demands that every miner dreams of finding was once volcanic magma over 1,200 Fahrenheit. Without this heat, natural diamonds wouldn't exist. With that in mind, it is a bit ironic that frigid temperatures must be endured to free these now-cold carats from their once-molten magma resting place.

Terrific Times On The Tundra

Canada quickly became the new kid on the world stage of diamond exploration in the early '90s when Ekati, the first Canadian diamond mine, opened.

Operations at Ekati commenced in 1998 Northeast of Yellowknife, an area that is virtually frozen year-round. Meanwhile, Diavik, on a small island near Yellowknife (the capital of Canada's Northwest Territories), is expected to continue output until 2025 at an annual production of 10 million carats.

Victor, the first Ontario mine, opened in 2008 and is well known for exceptional rough diamonds that have commanded upwards of $400 per carat on the "rough" market.

In summer of 2006, Tiffany & Co. provided substantive construction funding for the Jericho Diamond Mine, which is close to 250 miles from Yellowknife. Several diamond deposits at Jericho have yielded stones as large as 56-carats and at least three measuring more than 100 carats!

These mines are but a few of Canada's many shining stars in the industry.

Godfather of the Canadian Diamond

Who would have figured that a rogue oil company geologist would be responsible for putting Canada on the world diamond map?

Chuck Fipke is best known for his part in the discovery of the diamond-rich Point Lake area. This find led to a diamond exploration rush which precipitated the Ekati mine opening and created the largest staking rush since the Klondike gold rush a century earlier.

Although De Beers geologists were already searching Canada for the proverbial "girl's best friend," Fipke, recalling the glacial declarations of Professor Hobbs, decided to look "upstream" (into Canada's NWT) using air support and a magnetometer.

It took eight years after Fipke's discovery for diamond extraction to begin. Canada became a world power in the diamond industry in just about a decade behind Russian and Africa.

"We took all the supplies and all the samples in ourselves," Fipke said. His sampling of the ground in Canada occurred by 1981. Fipke was down to his last funds and had the backing of goodwill from some friends and relatives who held down his "hardship" camps, as they were called. There was no helicopter support, times were rough for sure.

Besides ties to the oil industry, Fipke was a dogged gemologist who, with his fellow prospector Stewart Blusson, was "crisscrossing the vast frozen hinterland of Canada's Northwest Territories" in search of a most precious gem, diamonds.

Although an expensive proposition, floatplanes were a blessing in Fipke's early searching days. "They were living on beans and bacon," says Mike Vaydik, with the Northwest Territories and Nunavut Chamber of Mines. He says Fipke borrowed money for his barebones operation[5]

When his diamond discovery was official, the rush began. Floatplanes, helicopters and airplanes were worth "gold" due to excessive demand and much needed financing. Yellowknife Mayor Gordon Van Tighem summed up the magnitude of the rush as the largest North America ever saw.

Staking frenzy got so wild that lumber yards ran short of

wood, thanks to companies such as Slumber-Magic Adjustable Bed Co. This Vancouver-based company, like many others, had no mining experience to speak of, yet it was staking claims during the height of diamond fever. Brian Weir, a geologist himself, staked ground for miners during the diamond rush and spent over half a million dollars in yearly helicopter rentals.[6]

Learning from the past, going on a hunch, and being persistent earned Fipke a place in Canadian history. To this day Canadian diamonds are respected the world over.

All great things must...not necessarily end.

One could call it cashing out, but it's more like turning over a legacy and letting it prosper.

Dominion Diamond's chairman, Robert A. Gannicott, said, "Although the sale by Chuck Fipke of his interest in the Ekati project ends his financial involvement with Canada's first diamond mine, his contribution to its discovery and success goes well beyond that. The history of Canadian mining is full of stories of accidents of fate leading to discoveries but the discovery of diamonds in the Slave Geological Province is a story of years of dedicated technical work led by a focused technical expert with unwavering belief in the outcome."

The deal filled the Fipke bank account with $67 million, and effectively ended his stake in the Ekati mine that made him a diamond industry tycoon. $17 million was allocated to a buffer zone interest while the remaining $50 million covered Fipke's share of the core zone around and including the mine.[7]

Even with this multi-million dollar buyout, there was some squabbling to be had.

In early 2015, notices of civil claims from the BC Supreme Court (Vancouver) registry show Fipke as defendant in a $423,975 breach of a cost-sharing agreement. Guess who the Plaintiff was? Fipke's old diamond search partner, Stewart Blusson.[8]

Being a Canadian diamond pioneer came with many troubles. Nonetheless, mining will continue, and if Fipke's history has any say, a settlement is sure to be on the horizon. This just goes to show the complexity and detail that goes into a mining deal, including one's "exit" plan.

At less than half a million dollars, the alleged "breach" damages are but a minuscule drop in the net worth "lake" of both Fipke and Blusson. But that is between old business partners.

Canada moves into the future with the prize of a well-stocked mine, good wage-earning diamond industry jobs and national pride of a continuing legacy of world famous diamonds. What more could one ask from one of the most frigid and remote areas on the planet?

Buffet Maple Leaf Signed Diamond

During the Berkshire Hathaway stockholder's meeting weekend, Warren Buffett was selling diamonds, with a unique twist.

"The diamonds originate in Canada's Northwest Territory in which the company says miners and companies use the 'most environmentally friendly way to extract the diamonds.'" Buffett, playing the role of jeweler, sat behind the counter and sold out laser inscribed diamonds with his signature. You'd need magnification to read it, but the signature is genuine and on the girdle of the limited quantity of such diamonds sold.

Borsheim's of Omaha, NE was the location, a jewelry store Buffett's company owns along with two other chains, Ben Bridge and Helzberg jewelers.

Along with Buffett's signature on the diamond is a maple leaf guaranteeing Canadian origin. An inscribed identification number allows the proud owner to trace the diamond to the Canadian mine of origin.[9]

Buffett is also a fan of Canadian energy.

Being a "deep value guy" always in the hunt for long-term investments, his Berkshire Hathaway company had invested $500 million into Suncor Energy.

After selling several million shares that were up 20%, Berkshire still owns almost 1% of Suncor, which is a large Canadian oil-and-gas company.[10]

Is Buffett crazy for Canada?

One thing we do know is that he has always been a value hunter, investing for the long haul. Canada assets have intrinsic value, catching the value minded interest of one of the world's richest men.

The Fifth "C" is Key

Qualifications to become a "5th C" diamond are stringent.

First there is the Canada Diamond Code of Conduct. No "blood diamonds" to be found here. Tracking the history of a gemstone is a key and imperative element to ensuring quality. Tracing the roots of a diamond from "birth" is mandatory for all stones greater than 0.18 carats that are to be Canadian-certified. Flanking (side) stones used in many wedding rings are much larger than the 0.18 threshold monitoring size. Even a 0.20 sized stone is one-fifth of one full carat.

The Code Committee ensures laser engraving of logo and serial number. Thanks to the numbering sequence, all inscribed diamonds can be instantly traced with a first-of-its-kind website access portal. Containing extensive details and information, it's like having a diamond birth certificate.

This is a major contributor to customer confidence and a

trademark of competent service expected from a Canadian diamond outlet. Best of all, the beauty of the diamond remains intact despite the engraving. An added benefit is theft protection, similar to multiple VIN numbers stamped throughout vehicles these days. It will take a determined professional thief to keep a stolen diamond off the legal market due to the serial number. "Erasing" this inscription takes special equipment.

The Canadian Diamond Certificate is a "made in Canada" stamp of approval. With a Canadian diamond you are protected with not only the Canadian certificate but an independent grading appraisal and a unique identification number.

Of course, Canadian diamonds measure up to the average gem graded by the traditional "4 C" system of color, cut, and clarity and carat weight.

The Diavik mine is known as one of the world's richest mine. They call diamonds coming from this area "arctic treasures," as natural and beautiful as the pure environment around them. Yet another reason Canadian diamonds are coveted the world over.[11]

Further assuring the integrity of Canadian diamonds is the CanadaMark™.

This hallmark program was initiated by the Dominion Diamond Corp. Licenses are held by affiliated companies, manufacturers and approved third parties. The mark reveals the history and origin of polished diamonds from mine to retail.

CanadaMark™ ensures quality standards, an audited tracking program, a natural and untreated diamond, and assurance of a responsibly mined Canadian diamond.[12]

Queen Of Diamonds

In grand tribute to a coin integrating a genuine diamond, the Royal Canadian Mint issued the 2012 Queen Diamond Jubilee Gold Coin.

Each certified diamond is "locked" in the coin's rim and can been seen from either side of the coin in all its brilliance. The serialized certification lends authenticity to the diamonds weight and clarity, complimenting the 99.999% pure gold coin it is surrounded with. Retailing for about $2,000, face value is $300 Canadian dollars. Availability was limited to 1,500 world-wide.

On the face of the coin is a portrait of Queen Elizabeth II almost palming the diamond with outstretched hand. Yes, certified diamonds in limited edition Canadian coins are a testament to the significance of the diamond to Canada at large.[13]

Harry Winston: Diamond Magnate

From Hong Kong to Beijing to Paris to Beverly Hills, Harry Winston and his company get around.

Known as a jeweler to the stars, the House of Harry Winston once outfitted (on loan) Whoopi Goldberg in $40 million in diamonds for her Oscars appearance, as Queen Elizabeth I of England. Recently he designed a ring for Jennifer Garner, as has been the done many times over the decades for other Hollywood elites.

Mr. Winston's most grand gesture was to the American people, donating the Hope Diamond to the Smithsonian Institute in Washington, D.C. for all to behold. At over 45 carats, the Hope became the centerpiece of the National Gem Collection. A once former crown jewel was transformed into a treasure for the public.

Before donating the Hope, it was purchased by Winston in 1949, upon which it traveled through American cities until 1953 as part of the historic Court of Jewels exhibition. Raising money for charitable causes and offering precious gem education to the public were notable benefits.[14]

Today Winston jewelry salons cater to the luxury niche with

premier diamonds and timepieces in key locales around the world. In addition to the retail segment, Harry Winston Diamond Corporation holds mining assets. Being part owner of the Diavik mine, the Winston enterprise supplies rough diamonds to global markets.

In 2013 there was legal friction between joint venture partner C. Fipke Holdings Ltd. and BHP Billiton over its plans aiming to sell Winston Diamond Corp (Toronto based) the Ekati mine and surrounding exploration properties. Fipke's main complaint stated BHP's noncompliance with its "pre-emptive rights to buy assets under the joint venture," in addition to alleging that Harry Winston was complicit in the sale.

Reports indicated that Winston also was interested in BHP Billiton." Also involved was the Diavik mine.[15]

As is typical in the diamond industry, much was on the line. Eventually the sale progressed to the tune of $500 million. Continuing court conflict was averted with a settlement between the parties which included Fipke's original diamond searching partner and geologist Blusson who co-discovered the Ekati diamonds with Fipke. They both owned a 10% interest in the mine.[16]

The Ekati mine will remaining operating, producing fabulous gems for lucky admirers the world over. Ultimately this is what counts. In the world of high-stakes gem business, a few bumps along the road between "diamond kings" are to be expected.

First Nation Taps Into Carat Cash

The agreement signed in December 2014 sets the foundation for Gahcho Kue diamond mine operations to begin in 2016. Scholarship funds, jobs, training, and money was all part of the deal between De Beers and Deninu Kue First Nation.

Gahcho Kue is one of the world's largest and richest new

diamond mines under development globally. It has the potential to become one of Canada's major high-grade and long-lived diamond mines.[17]

South of Great Slave Lake in Fort Resolution (NWT) is where Chief Louis Balsillie leads the Deninu Kue First Nation band. "This is Akaitcho territory," chief Balsillie stated. The signing represents a meeting of the minds with De Beers on an Impact Benefit Agreement (IBA). Previously any rights to benefits were denied by diamond companies.[18]

Since gemstone mining ventures of this level involve immense financial commitment, the worst case scenario of expected carat output has been determined. In the case of Gahcho Kue, high-quality rough diamonds further enabled the project to move forward. Even with these relative certainties, De Beers' venture partner, secured with a 49% stake, is Mountain Province Diamonds. As a side note, Balsillie mentioned that talks are underway regarding Ekati and Diavik (Dominion Diamond Corp.) mine IBA's.

Resource development in Canada includes consideration for the duty to properly benefit the native people in unceded areas. Rights to land use obviously come into play. De Beers stepped up in agreement with the importance of the social commitment piece of diamond mining.

Benefits can be significant. There are four kimberlites, diamondiferous in nature, of which three have expected total carat content of 55.5 million. With production pegged at about 4.5 million carats a year, the Gahcho Kue mine has an expected life of 12 years. Mountainprovince.com revealed a feasibility study suggesting an IRR of just over 32%.[19]

Preliminary economic assessments (PEA's) are critical in determining whether a mining venture will pay off, usually quite handsomely. Although many factors are to be considered, an IRR

(Internal Rate of Return) basically calculates the yield on investment or the attractiveness of the project. It is an evaluation of sorts that allows ranking of projects by overall return by management.

Comparably, the Tongo project in Sierra-Leone reportedly had a "base case" pre-tax IRR of 23% with a 32% enhanced case return. The Liqhobong diamond mine in Lesotho (Southern Africa) was expecting 30% base return with a 45% upside potential.[20]

By 2020 some estimates place Gahcho Kue at up to 6 million carat output. World average US dollars per carat for rough diamonds is about $80. Australia (19% of world's total carats by volume, only 4% by value) has been placed at $15 per carat while the average realized Canadian standing is $110.[21]

The well-known Tongo fields have put out an impressive carat average of $248.[22]

Even though many financial forecasts are "forward looking" in nature, this one delivered on its original estimates.

In addition to concern for the surrounding environment upon the commencement of drilling and mining, the exit plan upon mine depletion of gemstones is also of prime concern.

As chief Balsillie stated, the Akaitcho territory of the First Nations is a social concern that mining companies in Canada must consider when calculating where all the benefits from the mining operation are to be allocated.

The Canadian government has always been keen on all facets of the diamond industry. Even in the arctic hinterland the concerns for monetary benefits, social issues, and nature itself all must be considered for any mining project to succeed.

Market Forces

Canadian diamond discovery was the final blow to the single-channel marketing monopoly of De Beers. After the Point Lake diamond news, severe strain on De Beers led them to announce the end of their efforts to control world diamond supplies.

During this period Nicholas Oppenheimer (former head of De Beers) stated that, "As new sources of supply opened up, particularly in Canada, it became evident that that role could not be sustained." By 2001 De Beers' rough diamond market share slid to under 60%...down from 80%.

With this new competitive environment Canada also became successful in vertical integration in the diamond industry. This includes mining, cutting, polishing, and ultimately retail distribution. The vertical business structure allowed for diamond sales to both manufacturers and retail outlets, which was key to multiple sales points along the diamond sales pipeline. So, from mine to retail shelf, the world benefited from "Made in Canada" diamonds.

Blood Diamonds: Barred By Branding

Blood Diamond (2006), staring Leonardo DiCaprio, revealed the deep corruption within the diamond trade in South Africa. These diamonds were soon labeled "conflict diamonds," given their direct relation to criminal activities of varying degrees.

Several years after Canada arrived on the world diamond scene with the opening of the Ekati mine, the "Kimberley Process" was initiated. This multi-national effort to stop conflict diamonds was whole-heartedly supported by Canada. The process instituted a zero tolerance policy to curtail illicit diamond trading.

By 2002 Canada passed the Export and Import of Rough Diamonds Act, ramping up import/export regulations of rough diamonds. A Canadian Certificate was now required for all shipments of Canadian-related diamonds which further supported the intent and purpose of the original Kimberley Process.

By stepping forward, Canada helped stabilize the diamond

industry with strict monitoring and branding of Canadian diamonds in an effort to differentiate themselves. Branding allows clear indication of a diamond's origin via inscribing logos (viewed under strong magnification) such as the polar bear, maple leaf, name of retailer, and even name of mine on the diamond's thin girdle. In fact, the polar bear logo on a diamond was the first to be marketed by Sirius Diamonds...giving no doubt you're holding a pure Canadian diamond. Soon afterwards logos like the snowflake, maple leaf, beaver, and others entered the scene.

The benefits of branding are clear: Quality, distinctiveness, prestige, and confidence in your diamond purchase.

Oh, Canada...

Canada's late start (30 years after Russia) on the world diamond stage has not deterred it from becoming the world's third largest (by value) diamond-producing nation, just behind Botswana and Russia.

Thanks to the hunch of a professor, the persistence of a geologist, and the marketing savvy of competitive diamond supply chains, Canada's diamond industry is here to stay and will surely play a critical role in the world diamond market.

CHAPTER 6

SUITS AND STONES

ORLD EVENTS OF late demonstrate that politics
has been anything but transparent.

Saying one thing while doing another seems
to be the playbook political representatives now
call their Bible on a regular basis.

From arranged marriages to ivory tower government propaganda to international spying to citizen oppression and everything in between, "politics" will always be around.

Turning a blind eye under the guise of being "politically correct" has come to an end in the diamond world for the most part.

Along with the crumbled monopolistic De Beers empire, "conflict diamonds" have been under constant pressure for almost a decade-and-a-half, thanks to proper political persistence.

Let's briefly investigate how the varying facets of politics have shaped the contemporary diamond trade.

Purposeful Politics

It was inevitable that the Russian and Canadian direct marketing of diamonds was instrumental in dethroning the De Beers virtual monopoly of world diamond trading.

Canadian diamond exploration began in the 1960s, yet it took over thirty more years for Canada to become a force to reckon with in the diamond industry. Now Canada proudly ranks as the world's third largest diamond producing nation by value.

As witnessed by outsiders, Canada appeared to become an overnight superstar in the world diamond market. In reality, Canada's rise to diamond prominence was the result of long-term commitment to geological surveys and review processes which effectively dealt with the most pristine and ecologically sensitive diamond laden areas in the country.

"Politics is the art of controlling your environment."
Hunter S. Thompson

Cooperation between four aboriginal groups, the Government of the Northwest Territories, and the Department of Indian and Northern Affairs allowed mining to commence with empathy toward fragile ecosystems and indigenous cultures. As a result, thousands of jobs were created thanks to government incentives, financial and otherwise, fostering economic development.

Eco Diamonds

Our environment, no matter how majestic in appearance, is fragile. Our resources and the environment they are found within are thought of as one in the same.

Natural resources are limited and must be treated with respect. Environmentally sustainable activities must be adhered to when using natural resources. Social responsibility is at the core of conservation and respect for nature.

At times various governments, companies, and individuals forget these guiding principles of respect.

Jewelers like Dawes Design in San Francisco are members of

groups such as "Ethical Metalsmiths," that strive for jewelry industry transparency. Being "green" paired with sustainability movement ideals drives the use of recycled gold and gems mined with responsibility. To keep these high goals evident and open, Dawes Design's tagline is "Sustainably Beautiful."

Although clearly a value-motivated effort, the Eco Diamond movement involves politically correct elements. For example, Satya Jewelers co-founder runs the Satya Foundation that supports women and children globally in the arts, wellbeing, and education as a 501c organization.

Project Ocean encourages "people to eat fish from sustainable sources only. So what does fish have to do with jewelry? For one thing, there are diamond "mining" ships off the coast of Africa that have their own level of safety and oceanic environmentally friendly initiatives. In the case of "Project Ocean," Stephen Webster jewelers (London) partnered with department store Selfridges to continue the Webster tradition of supporting sustainability efforts with a focus on the seas.

Metal refiner Hoover & Strong teamed up with socially responsible jewelry leader Toby Pomeroy in the launch of EcoGold, EcoSilver and EcoPlatinum. This new standard in fine jewelry history effectively "purifies" used scrap metals. Environmental sustainability comes about from these reclaimed metals.

Sylvie, of Sylvie Collections, stated, "No marriage is 100 percent conflict-free, but your engagement ring can be."

Ethical sourcing is a commitment written out on Sylvie's website in the form of the United Nation's definition of conflict diamonds: "Diamonds that originate from areas controlled by forces or factions opposed to legitimate and internationally recognized governments, and are used to fund military action in opposition to those governments, or in contravention of the decisions of the Security."

Having been born and raised in Antwerp, Belgium, Sylvie is a jewelry designer herself and has been at the heart of a major diamond trading center.[1]

What do you get when you mix social responsibility, the Kimberley Process, and GIA certified diamonds? Charity in the name of a great cause, autism.

Karen Simmons of AutismToday.com and a long time gemologist and jewelry store owner (the Gem Gallerie) knows that any society, any nation, is judged on the basis of how it treats those most in need. In addition to her own efforts of directing non-profit funds for the benefit of those on the Autism Spectrum Disorder (ASD), she has also backed charitable causes such as the HollyRod Foundation and several others.

Adhering to values, pronouncing taglines, and recycling used jewelry go beyond standing by a politically correct statement. It all starts with conflict-free gems coming from sustainable sources that enable great social causes in all areas of life.

Creating systematic change through action and dedication to diamond industry standards, such as the Kimberley Process, allows consumers the opportunity to "vote with their feet" to enable social change.

Our environment is nature itself. Preserving nature while responsibly utilizing the natural resources it provides is a great responsibility. Politics may be involved along the way, but it is up to all of us to ensure morality, common sense, and respect are our guiding principles safeguarding valuable resources.

Persevere and eventually "politics" will be forced to step down by popular demand.

Conflict Diamond Debacle

As eluded to in the refreshing discussion of eco diamonds, the United Nations included in its definition of "conflict diamonds"

the concept of areas of opposition against recognized governments, funding military action, and contradiction of Security
Council decisions.

"Blood" has been used to
describe conflict diamonds. Brutal
wars, armed conflict, and inevitably death spiraled out of control
in many African countries over
control of a natural resource, diamonds. Unfortunately the same
characteristics providing advantages
to legitimate investors by diamonds
are identical to criminals. The high
value, portability, conceal ability,
and selective untraceable nature of
diamonds are very attractive traits to
rebel groups in Africa in particular.

Long before the Kimberley Process
provided oversight and directives to
diamond trade the world over, civil
war was raging in Sierra Leone during

> *"I have nothing against diamonds, or rubies or emeralds or sapphires. I do object when their acquisition is complicit in the debasement of children or the destruction of a country."*
>
> Edward Zwick (Director, *Blood Diamond*)

the 1990s. The Democratic Republic of Congo, Liberia, Angola,
and Sierra Leone were the stages hosting diamond wars. Illicit trade
of diamonds for the purpose of fueling conflict and political power
grabbing was all too common prior to the United Nations mandate
over diamond trade in 2001 via the Kimberley Process.

"Blood" diamonds enabled bribes, threats, torture and even
murder in order to fund oppressive rebel forces. Such was the case
in the Western African nation of Sierra Leone, whose civil war
raged from about 1991 through 2000 in a power struggle to control diamond mines.

In 2003, neighboring nation Liberia gave President Charles Taylor asylum, ending Liberia's civil war. Prior to this action, Taylor was put on trial by the International Court of Justice at the Hague for his role in conflict-diamond trading during the late Sierra Leone civil war years. Terrorism and money laundering were found to be at play and a Taylor/Al-Qaeda connection illustrated the damage corrupt leaders inflict on local citizens and world security.

Collateral damage due to smuggling also ravaged surrounding countries while "polluting" the world diamond supply. This alternate pipeline filled with illicit gems also influence tax evasion and money laundering operations and at one time was estimated to be about as high as 20 percent of annual world diamond production.

Over the course of a about 10 years, up to 3.7 million people have died, primarily in Sierra Leone, the Democratic Republic of Congo, and Angola, strictly over the "blood" diamond debacle.[2]

Intergovernmental politics aside, armed conflicts have brought long term devastating effects to the Central and Western areas of Africa. Long before the obvious spillover into the media that brought our attention to the civil wars of the 90s, there were multiple armed conflicts dating back to the early 1970s in the same region. A large number of these conflicts revolved around diamond mining areas.[3]

It appears that for some time to come, Africa, UAE, Venezuela, and a limited number of other nations will remain a conflict diamond smuggler's best friend.

Kimberley Process

The Kimberley Process Certification Scheme (KPCS) continues to receive strong affirmation and support from around the globe in recognizing and eliminating the role of diamonds in armed conflict.

Enforcement challenges remain an obstacle for the Kimberley Process (KP), despite "tangible progress in breaking the link between the illicit trade in rough diamonds and armed conflict," said Mr. DeLaurentis, chair of the KP in 2012. At that time, the KP was reaching its tenth anniversary.

Interest was expressed in all stakeholders, including commitment from consumers, traders, and local producers for taking responsibility to ensure the KP remained relevant. Enforcement solutions extend to non-governmental organizations and the private sector alike.

KP Member States voluntarily participate in the process initiated in May 2000. Kimberley, a South African town where diamonds were discovered in the 1860s, was the location of the historic beginnings of this honorable process. An international rough diamond certification system (KPCS) took about three years to develop.[4]

As indicated on the PAC (Partnership Africa Canada; pacweb. org) website, those countries that choose to ignore simple diamond tracking rules put their country at serious risk of diamond embargoes as well as scrutiny of their motivations. In 2014, both Venezuela and the Central African Republic were under embargo per Kimberley Process rules. Furthermore, Security Council sanctions targeting the illicit trade in rough diamonds, particularly conflict diamonds was called for by the Assembly to the fullest extent.

Visits to Member States to review certification systems helped solidify settling any conflicts and consolidating peace. Participants were called upon to "submit consistent, substantive annual reports on implementing the Scheme and to improve its rules and procedures."

Success has been seen in troubled Zimbabwe after the African Diamond Producers Association certified that the country's operations in the East complied with the Scheme (KP). Nonetheless, the process is not perfect as mining companies in the area were denied acceptance by some KP participants. "Decisions made by the Scheme must be upheld and respected and its founding statute, rules and mandates must be adhered to." Setbacks have occurred given the arrearages of up to 21 Member States. This lack of financial contributions to the United Nations may put these members in jeopardy of losing voting status in the Assembly.

Progression of the KP revolves around all stakeholders which explains the reaffirmation of the "tripartite nature of the Kimberley Process forum." As such, civil society is more than welcomed in future plenary sessions.

Since its inception, the KP has made tremendous strides in curtailing violence, oppression, and armed conflict from continuing unabated. Much work has yet to be done to further ensure the original charter and mandates progress in concert with the ultimate goal of keeping peace through "clean" diamond trade.[5]

In Diamonds We Trust

Diamonds have represented security for centuries.

Whether used as collateral, an alternative investment, or as a secure concentration of wealth, diamonds have become more versatile as the years roll by.

Nations around the world have shown symptoms of financial collapse due to political missteps. Even the once venerable United States economy has been rattled by recession that traditional "security blanket" investments have not been able to fully shake off. Now, even laymen realize that the air has leaked out of the "full faith and credit" of many nations.

Where is your safe haven?

Diamonds are much more than pretty stones. If a political storm were to hit tomorrow, causing dire civil unrest, could you truthfully say that you're confident in the security of your assets? With diamonds there is nothing stopping you from immediately picking up and relocating while you wait the storm out.

They still say "diamonds are forever." It may not be too long before the new motto is, "In diamonds we trust."

The Political Voice Heard Round The World

Since its first step onto the diamond market world stage, Canada has been a fervent supporter of ensuring integrity and stability in the diamond industry.

Seeing a need for advocacy, natural resource governance, and human rights protection in Africa, Canada established Partnership Africa Canada (PAC) before the Kimberley Process became official. The horrors committed in Sierra Leone and the lack of international interest to intercede was a driving force behind the PAC initiative. PAC helped expose conflict diamond links and was nominated for the Nobel Peace Prize by members of the US House of Representatives and Senate for efforts to halt the conflict diamond trade.

What do Venezuela, United Arab Emirates (UAE), Lebanon, and the Central African Republic all have in common?

They are all on the "Diamond Watchlist." This list tracks countries that have shown perennial issues related to the abuse of the diamond trade that never seem to be solved. Concerns in this regard are an advisory to consumers, the retail trade, the media and others that must be voiced given the lack of integrity in some countries that "still fail to meet the tests of adequate regulation, good business practice and common decency" of legitimate diamond trading procedures.

As was the hallmark of PAC's beginning, a spotlight and persistent pressure must be ingredients in the recipe for guidance and ultimate compliance of these nations. Allowing rough conduct only erodes confidence in the diamond market overall.[6]

Of particular interest has been the rise from virtual obscurity to a major diamond trading center that is now Dubai. Obviously being famous for oil reserves will not last forever, so the alluring profit of illicit diamond trading has been more than tempting. With laisser-faire government policies of the most limited scrutiny, as well as a 50-year tax holidays for companies, the UAE (United Arab Emirates) is a boon for those seeking to revalue and/or disguise diamond origins.

Sitting as a geographical crossroads between the "old world" and "new world" of the diamond industry, the UAE is capitalizing on this newfound power play. A unique opportunity indeed. It is suggested you take additional caution with "KP certificates" from Dubai. Originally set to track value and origins of all rough diamonds the loophole, and Dubai's recent specialty has been to mix origins and values amongst parcels passing through the UAE trading center. So just like a magician putting a dove in a hat and pulling out a rabbit, one never knows where a Dubai "KP certificated" diamond really came from, a legitimate or "blood" diamond mine.[7]

Now you've witnessed why the diamond industry as a whole announced a zero tolerance policy towards what are known as conflict diamonds.

The Export and Import of Rough Diamonds Act was passed by Canada in 2002, which ramped up "Kimberley Process" import and export regulations of rough diamonds by requiring a "Canadian Certificate" for all shipments of diamonds. Clearly this helps to counteract the persistent and clear violations of other diamond mining and trading countries.

With significant pre-planning, substantive ethics, goodwill, and positive politics, Canada sprinted to world diamond prominence and along the way helped create a true competitive market for diamonds that has benefited consumers worldwide.

PAC is also part of the Diamond Development Initiative which aids the diamond industry with improvement and regulation.

It was once said that all politics are local. At the end of the day "politics" always has and always will influence the diamond industry. It's up to you to judge what policies and conduct displayed by world countries is worthy of praise or closer scrutiny.

CHAPTER 7

"OSCAR" LOVES DIAMONDS

J UST LIKE AN attention-grabbing movie trailer, the shorter the better.

When it comes to Hollywood, long introductions spoil the experience. So let's get right onto the red carpet and into the action...

All Hail Queen Whoopi

Imagine yourself decked out in more than $40 *million* in diamonds, all at once!

That's how Queen Elizabeth II of England appeared at the 1999 Oscars. To be exact, Whoopi Goldberg (acting as the Queen) was adorned in diamonds on loan from the House of Harry Winston.

Well before Whoopi dressed up as Queen, Mr. Winston, following the lead of image-conscious Hollywood, set up shop and began loaning diamonds to celebrities for major events like the Oscars.

Speaking of Harry Winston, another one of his Hollywood elite designs graced the finger of Jennifer Garner.

Flanked by two emerald shaped stones (baguettes), Garner's beauty weighted in at about 6.1. The main stone is of the radiant/cushion variety, and is reported to have cost Ben Affleck a cool $1,200,000. The center stone weighs in at a very respectable 4.5 carats.

> "I never worry about diets. The only carrots that interest me are the number you get in a diamond."
>
> Mae West

Before revealing more traditional Hollywood "rocks," here is one of the most recent and creatively designed rings Hollywood has seen in some time. It gives a new meaning to "creative carats."

Ashlee gleefully tweeted the engagement news with a captioned photo of Ross stating: "My baby love and I are ENGAGED!!! Hallelujah Hawaii!!!!!"

Sure, Pete Wentz's engagement offering of a 4 carat Asscher diamond with pave surrounding stones was nothing to turn one's nose up at Ashlee Simpson's new ring from Evan Ross set the bar high with a unique setting patterned after the Marquise center stone.

Ross, son of legendary Diana Ross, chose Neil Lane to create this very unique and clearly one-of-a-kind setting to fit Ashlee's personality.[1]

Now, we will take a look at what the "who's who" in Hollywood is favoring in precious jewelry when it's time to say "I do"…

Top "Rocks" Rank High in Hollywood

A diamond's beauty never fades, as Hollywood jet-setters can attest to.

Before we jump into revealing the "top rocks" stars flash on the red carpet, let's take a quick glimpse at what those of us on the other side of the velvet rope, the fans, are sporting on their ring fingers.

An online poll indicated that the average center stone size for engagement rings of one carat made up 31% of the respondents with a ¾ carat size stone coming in at 19% of responses.

Jumping up to 1¼ carats resulted in a nosedive. Only 7% of those polled said that size was average for their geographical region.

This is not to say that a smaller stone is less worthy. In fact, the survey showed a slight popularity increase dropping in size from a ¾ stone to ½ carat. At the ½ carat mark, 20% of respondents stated that size to be average for their locale, a 1% increase over ¾ carats.

A clear, clean, and classy cut diamond of 1¾ carats was below average as far as ownership is concerned, based on poll results. Both ¼ carat and lesser sizes outranked the 1¾ carat stone by three, and one percentage points respectively.

So, if your zip code is somewhere beyond Beverly Hills, like way beyond, then feel proud to be "keeping up with the Jones'" with a ¾ to one carat diamond. You'll have plenty of company at that size stone, 19% claimed this to be typical. Combining one carat and ¾ carat stone statistics puts you in strong position, 50% of fellow diamond buyers are with you. Add to that those with a ½ carat stone and you're in great company, 70%![2]

If you fancy a gemstone for more than looks keep, in mind that usually the bigger the better rules when it comes to investing in diamonds.

No matter what size sparkler you're after, take note that celebrities, investors, and everyday people are on to something. According to the Rapaport Diamond Index, diamond values have been inching up the charts steadily since the 1990s. A definite historical trend.[3]

Now, without further ado, here is the rundown of ravishing rocks you can expect to see on Rodeo Drive.

Over 2 carats:

Really? A 2.5 carat "rock"?

Yes, it's true. There is nothing to sneeze at with this beauty designed by Red C Jewelers. The center stone is haloed by numerous complementing diamonds worth an estimated $65,000.

Also, the band incorporates similar diamonds found in the halo. We trust tennis player Ryan Sweeting knows that true "love" means not keeping score when he proposed to Kaley Cuoco.

Bernie Robbins Fine Jewelers was the source of this next 2.25 carat Princess shaped stone.

Basketball player Hank Baskett chose this 18K white gold setting that includes up to 60 assorted diamonds under and around the Princess main diamond. This spectacular $50,000 sparkler was proudly worn by Kendra Wilkinson.

3 Carats:

Leave it to Ellen DeGeneres to twist tradition into something to catch the eye of Hollywood.

The Neil Lane design rotated the marquise shape with spectacular results. At 3 carats, this $100,000 stone proves great things come in small packages. Ellen combined the horizontal center stone with a platinum engagement band for Portia de Rossi.

Here are other stones at the 3 carat weight with well-known owners:

At $55,000, Jionni La Valle got "Snooki" a Princess-shaped main stone with an eternity band encrusted with diamonds. With the center stone at 3.02 carats, the ring's total carat weight comes in at 5.

Next, at the 3 carat level, is Katherine Heigl's pear-shaped stone from singer Josh Kelley. The centered pear is surrounded by multiple other diamonds, which has become popular.

An attractive art-deco inspired ring now rests on Scarlett Johansson's finger.

Journalist Romain Dauriac found favored flare by placing three round diamonds in a row on a diamond-encrusted face-plate. Bucking tradition with an Art-Deco design led to serendipity and a happy Scarlett.

Scarlett's former hubby, Ryan Reynolds, put a traditional round solitaire on her finger. The "twist" was the eye-catching gold-entwined band resembling vines weaving together in a circle which compliments the continuous visual flow of the wedding band itself.

Kevin Jonas also got on the three-carat bandwagon when presenting Danielle Deleasa with a cushion cut ringed with a halo of pave diamonds, all 210 of them. The double shank platinum band was designed by Angela Arabo, Jacob & Co.

In the spirit of the late Princess Diana, Javier Bardem put down $34,000 for a sapphire surrounded by 12 diamonds. With a simple band, it is similar to what Kate Middleton now wears.

Last but not least, in the three-carat category, is Hugh Hefner. His choice of engagement ring was a $90,000 round solitaire at about 3 carats for Crystal Harris. Although she called off the wedding, Hugh let her keep the ring.

3.5 Carats:

Oval-shaped diamonds have been seen on celebrities like Naya Rivera, the *Glee* actress. The Neil Lane 3.5-carat solitaire was from her dream guy, Ryan Dorsey.

A round Neil Lane Collection came from Jason Trawick, Spears' agent, now ex. With a diamond-encrusted band, the 3.5 carat round solitaire reportedly cost $90,000. Britney Spears promptly returned the ring when the engagement ended.

4 Carats:

With the eye of her art consultant hubby, Will Kopelman, Drew Barrymore was bestowed a four-carat radiant shape diamond with diamond-covered band. He picked it out at Graff Diamonds.[4]

Joel Madden (singer) worked with Neil Lane to give Nicole Richie a great surprise — a four-carat round diamond with pave encrusted octagon surround setting. Can you imagine the most majestic engagement ring?

French banker Olivier Sarkozy mixed surrounding sapphires with a European-cut diamond And Mary-Kate Olsen loves the 4 carat creation from Cartier, vintage 1953.

Purchased from Sotheby's auction for over $81,000, the 16 sapphires and main diamond are atop multiple petals inlaid with small diamonds.

The "rope" band is simple, yet adds to the majesty of the entire design, purely poetic in nature.

5 Carats:

Moving on up...

A diamond-encrusted band has two rows of micro-pave diamonds designed by Neil Lane. Professional wrestler David Otunga presented a five-carat center stone to Jennifer Hudson.

Neil Lane also had his hand in designing Jessica Simpson's five-carat round shaped ruby center flanked by equally-sized pear diamonds. A yellow gold band was the setting for this unique and stunning stone pairing that Eric Johnson chose for Simpson.

Pears seem to be popular with Simpson. Prior hubby and singer Nick Lachey also had proposed with a pear center stone, partnered with pears on each side.

Country Carats for Underwood

Ottawa hockey player Mike Fisher found a flawless yellow diamond for Carrie Underwood for their engagement. This five-carat super stone is surrounded with white diamonds. Micro-pave diamonds make up the cluster setting with a platinum band designed by Jonathon Arndt.

Estimated value varies with close to $1 million possible given this diamond. Expert David Mamane says this dazzling diamond rates as VVS1 in clarity, nearly flawless.

The pear shape comes out again in great fashion to compliment a round center stone. A split-shank is covered in diamonds, including two rows on the side.

Amber Heard's engagement ring from actor Johnny Depp is a round diamond center stone surrounded by smaller diamonds and flanked by two larger pear-shaped diamonds. The entire split-shank setting is covered in diamonds from the top to two rows of diamonds on the side.

Depp made Amber Heard proud and has even worn the diamond himself, joking that it was a bit big for her.

6 Carats:

Even more marvelous is Jerry O'Connell's choice of a six-carat yellow diamond paired with yellow gold band known as the "yellow-on-yellow" design. The band hugs four rows of micro pave diamonds. Rebecca Romijn gracefully accepted the engagement ring. Micro pave's popularity is proven.

Vintage inspired settings add magic to a ring. That is clear from the six-carat sparkler on Jessica Biel's finger from longtime boyfriend and mega pop star Justin Timberlake. Unique aquamarine side stones flank the cushion cut center. Surrounding the main stone are two rows of round diamonds of differing sizes.

Musical minds think alike.

Adam Levine's recent pop-like music style is chart-topping, as was Timberlake's. Both artists went "old school" with vintage settings for their sweeties. Levine's choice of a 1930s-era engagement ring setting is just what Victoria's Secret model Behati Prinsloo loves.

Princess shape stones still make the grade in Hollywood. Nicky Hilton was at Lake Como, Italy, when James Rothschild proposed with a six-carat to his "Princess."

7 Carats:

"Lucky #7" seems to be popular with a few well-known celebrities. George Clooney, Marilyn Manson, and Ryan Reynolds all selected seven-carat stones when they proposed.

Once thought of as the eternal bachelor, Clooney finally found "The One." Clooney chose a stunning ethically mined emerald shaped stone. Set in platinum, and tapering the main emerald stone, are two tapered baguette diamonds acting as perfect complements.

After two decades of dating, Clooney shocked the world and popped the question to Amal Alamuddin. She seems to be his match, being intelligent and stunningly beautiful, and now she has a ring to resemble how they fit like the perfect couple.

Clooney and his *Ocean's Eleven* movie series co-star, Brad Pitt, appeared to be on the same page. Pitt presented Angelina Jolie with an emerald-shaped diamond too. Both their brides' fingers are long and slender, adding to the beauty of the emerald's rectangular shape and fittingly appropriate. Great choice indeed.

Word has it that jeweler Jean Dousett estimates Clooney's investment in love at around $750,000.

Another member of the "7-carat-club" is Ryan Reynolds, who had the pale pink oval diamond set on a super thin rose gold band. Blake Lively was thrilled to accept this Loarraine Schwartz creation with many small diamonds set in the band.

8 Carats:

Witness the amazing emerald, or two, or three, or…

Rapper Future "stacked" the ring's band with an 8 carat center emerald with several others to boot.

Two emeralds immediately flanking the main stone weigh in at 2.5 carats each. Total carat weight is a whopping 15 carats.

How could a gal not be ecstatic? Designed by Avianne & Co., the ring is estimated at $500,000.

With a simple gold band, Jennifer Aniston received a radiant-shaped eight-carat sparkler from Justin Theroux.

8.5 Carats:

Designed by Jason of Beverly Hills, Dwayne Wade's engagement surprise to Gabrielle Union reached for the $1 million threshold. At 8.5 carats, the cushion shaped beauty sat on a simple band.

At an estimated worth of $4 million, Marc Anthony gave Jennifer Lopez a blue diamond 8.5-carat beauty. Neil Lane assisted Marc to secure this very rare stone.

10 Carats:

This Valentine's "I do" was worth a cool half-million.

At about 10 carats, the huge heart-shaped stone came from Taylor Kinney.

Despite Lady Gaga's colorful nail art, the ring stands on its own in spectacular style.

Combining Valentine's Day with a celebrated champagne toast, was enjoyed by the cozy couple.

"Happy Life" says Gaga.

"Gold-on-gold" is the unofficial description for yellow gold paired with a fancy yellow diamond. What a fitting moniker.

Such a combination is attractive to say the least. Even the band included yellow diamonds.

Seal presented a 10-carat oval-shaped diamond to Heidi Klum on a glacier!

Although the marriage ended, the stone was about 10 carats, estimated at $150,000 and designed by celebrity jeweler Lorraine Schwartz.

Michael Douglas proposed to Catherine Zeta Jones with a 10-carat "old school" marquise.

Ever lose your ring?

Jenny McCarthy did, within months of getting it.

The 10-carat yellow sapphire and diamond engagement ring was picked out with the assistance of her son, Evan, with now husband Donnie Wahlberg leading the way, of course. Newport Jewelers owner Daniel Arik guided Donnie during the custom design.

Actually the ring was only missing for a short time frame. While at a hotel, they "lost" it in the bed sheets.[5]

Grace Kelly, who passed away in 1982, was well known for the 1950s films *To Catch A Thief, Dial M For Murder* and *High Society.* Flanked by two diamond baguettes, she wore a spectacular Cartier emerald shaped diamond of almost 10.5 carats.

Prince Rainier III of Monaco originally proposed with an eternity band of diamonds and rubies. Realizing that her peers expected much more in an engagement ring, the Prince quickly upgraded to match, thus the larger Cartier Emerald cut set in platinum.

12 Carats:

Melania Trump's engagement ring from real estate developer, Donald Trump, is a 12-carat emerald cut diamond center stone flanked by two diamond baguettes. It is reportedly worth $480,000.

12.5 Carats:

Smaller than her sister's ring from the now ended marriage with Kris Humphries, Khloe's 12.5 carats is quite large. Khloe Kardashian's cushion shaped diamond came from basketball star Lamar Odom for $850,000, now that is a large investment in the future for sure.

14 Carats:

Hillary Duff's hockey playing former hubby dug deep for a gorgeous and glimmering 14-carat stone.

He proposed in Hawaii, but don't worry, this "ice" won't melt. It was a Princess shaped stone estimated at $1 million.

Avril Lavigne's ring was a huge pear shape stone from musician Chad Kroeger. Weighing in at 14 carats, it is reportedly worth $350,000.

15 Carats:

For $8 million Lorraine Schwartz led rapper Kanye West to a gorgeous 15-carat rock for Kim Kardashian.

Kanye was hands-on selecting and setting up the proposal. He rented out a baseball stadium which had the Jumbo-Tron lit up for the occasion. For ambiance, a 50-piece orchestra was on hand as well as all of Kim's friends and family. Yes, down on one knee, Kanye presented the flawless, colorless cushion-shaped whopper.

The ring also had a diamond encrusted band.

16 Carats:

Working for close to a year on his vision, Brad Pitt used Robert Procop to design a "stand-out" ring without typical tricks using different colored diamonds. The ring's stones encircle Angelina's finger with 16 carats (total stone weight) of glory.

The four-carat emerald shaped center stoned ring was the culmination of seven years of dating. The flanking emerald shaped stones decrease in size along the band to complement Angelina's slender fingers.

17 Carats:

Half-moon flanking gems grace Mariah Carey's finger next to the huge light pink emerald shaped center stone.

The uber-exclusive Jacob Arabo design includes 58 small intense pink diamonds as halo and band accents. The rarity of pink diamonds make them a costly proposition. The ring is estimated at about $2.5 million.

Each half-moon diamond is about 3.5 carats. The center stone beauty is just over 10 carats.

Nick Cannon has been the America's Got Talent host and is the happy husband, with a slightly lighter wallet.

18 carats:

Jay-Z dealt with renowned Hollywood jeweler Lorraine Schwartz when he was thinking of investing $5 million on a ring for Beyonce.

"Putting a ring on it" was how her beau blessed her with an 18-carat wonder.

Notoriously private about their relation from the beginning, we do know the ring is considered flawless and that at times Beyonce wears a fake ring in public to hopefully avoid theft.

Musical festival producer Pasquale Rotella made sure his bride Holly Madison's ring was a work of art.

Pink and yellow diamond "flowers" run down the sides of the ring into the band in an art-nouveau style, very striking indeed.

In collaboration with jeweler Alan Friedman, Pasquale had a "hidden" owl engraved on the rose gold in between two of the flowers since the couple has a special affinity for owls.

The fancy yellow is a wonderful cushion cut.

And now, two of the most sensational "rocks" ever seen out-and-about in Hollywood:

24 Carats:

Of course, as you'd expect, Paris Hilton is a diamond diva.

Her honey parted with about $4.7 million for this a stellar stone but gained a 24-carat emerald-shape diamond to die for.

He had to throw in a Cartier eternity band for her too, since Paris complained about the heavy stone being "too much" at times.

Surely the prongs holding that monster in place are inspected by a jeweler every year at a minimum.

33 Carats:

In 1968, actor Richard Burton paid $305,000 for a ring at the Sotheby's New York auction that was part of the estate of the late Vera Krupp. The ring is now called "The Elizabeth Taylor Diamond", even though she passed some years ago. Formerly, the Asscher shaped stone was known as "The Krupp Diamond".

The 33 carat monster pre-dates the 1920s. It was a fifth anniversary gift from Burton, husband number five, for Taylor.

At $3.5 million, two baguettes flank the main stone and are almost hidden out of sight given the magnitude of the Asscher shaped center stone.

Taylor "was the "custodian" of the ring, as she preferred to characterize herself with respect to the ownership of her enormous collection of jewels."

As the prized possession of "the internationally renowned Hollywood celebrity," Taylor wore it on all occasions which was cause for it to become part of her identity in due time.[6,7,8,9]

Neil Lane: Hollywood's Elite Designer

True to Lane form, his hand-crafted rings are "vintage-inspired yet contemporary in style, celebrating Hollywood's glamorous past and your remarkable future."

Lane's childhood fascination with objects of desire and beauty led him to painting and later to architecture and art. His stone and metal jewelry creations celebrate love in unique ways that celebrities have come to appreciate.

Ellen Degeneres, Ashlee Simpson and Jessica Simpson, Jennifer Hudson, Naya Rivera, Nicole Richie and more have all trusted Lane to design works of art to wear on their finger. One look is all it takes.

You've heard the jingle, "Every kiss begins with Kay." Now experience Neil Lane's one-of-a-kind bridal collection at Kay Jewelers.

Try out the Design-A-Ring feature and you'll be that much closer to your piece of legendary Hollywood jewelry.[10]

What's On Your Finger?

Despite the impressive size of those larger Hollywood rocks, a good quality gemstone of "only" ¼ carat is still a quality stone if it has amazing fire and sparkle.

That's the unique beauty and nature of diamonds. With the proper cut, clarity, and color, any diamond can look like a million bucks!

"I love diamond facials, they leave me glowing and refreshed."

Fergie

For those that must have size AND quality, you'll be hard pressed to find a quality stone that ranks high in each of the jeweler's "4 C's" (diamond rating scale) without spending a small fortune. It is not uncommon for quality one carat stones (loose) to go for over $10,000, and that's without the band, pave stones, flanking, or other gemstones in the setting.

As you'd expect, since diamond popularity keeps growing, prices rise to the occasion in true Hollywood form.

Remember this: anyone can have a piece of the proverbial Hollywood "rock."

We saw celebrities such as Brad Pitt, Ryan Reynolds, and others not only invest significant money but also their time in the process of discovery. Time is equally distributed to all of us. Just like a celebrity that seeks out a jeweler's expertise and makes time to get educated, you too can budget your time wisely in the creative process to ensure that your loved one is surprised by something special that sparkles.

You may be surprised to learn that Jennifer Love Hewitt's engagement ring had a 0.5-carat center stone.

Believe it.

Brian Hallisway creatively gave Jennifer a "flower" ring, minus the color, yet a beautiful creation. The diamond center stone was raised slightly with 10 other similarly sized diamonds surrounding it to create the appearance of a flower.

Hewitt's ring is very reminiscent of a Victorian cluster ring of the 1800s.

Here is what folks on the Glamour.com wedding blog had to say about the news of the average ring being almost exactly one carat:

"mstaco7" Apr 27, 2011:

"I'm just like zlie17, mine is WAY below average but I love it because of the super unique setting that we chose. My center stone is 1/3 carat marquis, with 16 side stones that bring it up to about 0.6. Still, I wouldn't trade it for the world because I love it and I know my fiancé worked really really hard to afford the beautiful ring he bought me. :)"

"Lisamorri" May 29, 2014:

"Oh my, I guess I am really below average. My promise ring was 0.18 carat and no engagement ring (we couldn't afford that)…My 10th anniversary ring was 0.25 which we upgraded to a 0.50 for my 25th anniversary. I guess we just don't have the kind of money most people I see posting do. The 0.50 is an F color, VVS2 and Very Good cut. it cost $1250.00 (which I thought was a lot to spend."

"zlie17" Apr 27, 2011:

"way below average. but I'm ok with that! because i have a really unique ring"[3]

Sounds like a few of these ladies are very happy despite having a ring size "way below average." One liked hers due to its uniqueness. Another happy gal appreciated her hubby "worked really really hard to afford the beautiful ring he bought me."

Remember the section on Hollywood "rock rankings"?

You'll recall the Prince of Monaco, under outside pressure, bestowed Grace Kelly with a larger ring. He originally planned to give Grace an eternity band.

A comeback is apparently in the making of the simple and timeless eternity band.

Quite some time ago Joe DiMaggio presented Marilyn Monroe an eternity band with 36 emerald shaped diamonds.

A similar return to popularity is seen with the Asscher shaped ring made wildly famous in the late 60s and 70s by Elizabeth Taylor.

Gwyneth Paltrow's ex-hubby, Coldplay front man Chris Martin, proposed with an elegant Asscher shaped stone on a double pave band.

Also, a haloed Asscher (five carats) was Jessica Alba's engagement ring, whose band also included diamonds.

We've seen celebrities with center stones from ½ carat to double digit carats wider than the finger they're on, rings with over 200 pave diamonds, custom creations, and investment grade fancy colored stones.

Styles of diamonds lose the spotlight, then become popular all over again, as the Asscher, Cushion, Emerald, and eternity band prove.

Be creative and you too can secure a piece of the Hollywood diamond dream.

Royal Rocks

Queens, Duchesses, Princes and Princesses all come and go. It's the jewelry that is passed from generation to generation, remaining a virtually permanent reminder of the past and promise for the future.

Garrard, jeweler to British royalty, designed the Duchess of York's 18K white and yellow gold ring. Surrounded by 10 "drop diamonds" was a deep red Burmese ruby chosen to highlight the Duchess's signature "fiery" red hair.

Prince Andrew's choice of gemstone is said to have set off a flurry of ruby sales in many areas of the world.

As expected, Garrard Jewelers is responsible for creating one of the most famous engagement rings in the world.

Prince William and Kate Middleton are treated like royalty around the world and akin to Hollywood stars in the US. It would be naïve to think that Kate's ring, once Princess Diana's, is only a second thought to those that get close enough to her.

The 18 carat stunning sapphire takes on an age-old yet always fresh cluster setting. The big center stone almost acts as the sun with "rays" of diamonds acting as a halo.

Royal Stars?

A rough and tumble footballer (soccer player) would hardly be thought of as "royalty."

Considered a spokesperson, actor, model, businessman, and one of the best known athletes in the world, David Beckham certainly is treated like royalty where ever he goes.

Back in 2007 when the Beckhams moved to Los Angeles, Tom Cruise, their new neighbor, threw a "Welcome to LA" party for Victoria and David.[11]

Victoria was a success in her own right before meeting David. She was a popular member (dubbed Posh Spice) in the pop group Spice Girls.

A yellow gold setting with a three-carat marquise diamond was Victoria's original engagement ring from David.

Since that time many "upgrades" came her way. The first of which was an eye-popping pear-shaped beauty.

David, having played for over six teams during his successful career, had plenty of cash rolling in from endorsement sign-ups. The Beckhams' net worth is estimated at over $350 million. Victoria's sapphire upgrade is super spectacular and dwarfs Kate Middleton's.

There you have it. The Beckhams have the money, the popularity, and the fame to be considered "elite" and "royalty" almost by default, according to fans and friends alike.

Cultivating a Diamond Culture

How long does it take to change a 1,500-year tradition? Oh, only about thirteen years.

"Arranged" marriages dominated Japanese culture for more than a millennium. Courtship, seduction, romance and prenuptial love that occurred prior to an American wedding was virtually taboo overseas. Japanese wedding ceremonies consisted of sharing rice wine from the same wooden bowl.

There was no "you may kiss the bride" moment or emotional Hollywood enhanced whirlwind of love or "boy wins girl" moment of truth.

Enter the dazzling diamond...

Soon enough Japan became the second largest market for diamond sales, specifically engagement rings. In fact, from postwar until 1959, diamonds were not even permitted to be imported to Japan, but by 1981 about 60% of Japanese brides wore diamonds, up from 5% in the late 60s when the power of campaigning for diamonds focused upon Japan.

It certainly helped that back in America Hollywood starlets wearing diamonds on the big screen and at publicized events turned the cultural tide in favor of diamonds. Moviegoers were beginning to see that, unlike a Hollywood mansion or Rolls Royce, a small but spectacular diamond allowed them to own a piece of that silver screen dream.

Hollywood Catches "Yellow Fever!"

Has the creative combination of yellow stone and band reached your locale?

There is now doubt that the popularity of yellow hued stones have gained a level of respect once only held for red, pink, blue, and select other fancy colors.

Surrounded by clear diamonds, a wonderful canary colored yellow diamond is sported by Kelly Clarkson. Her beau, Brandon Blackstock, trusted jeweler Jonathan Arndt to guide him in the right direction when choosing the best engagement ring which is similar in design to Rebecca Romjin's ring. Four rows of micro pave diamonds really make this ring stand out in spectacular fashion.

Yellow has become the new color of commitment and the hue to say "I do!"

Heidi Klum's ex, Seal, bestowed her with an oval canary yellow diamond and Carrie Underwood's flawless fancy yellow cluster ring was designed by famous Jonathan Arndt.

Yellow has arrived and is rapidly advancing as one of the more popular center stones.

Jonathan Arndt: Jeweler Extraordinaire

One doesn't need to be a Beverly Hillbilly to serve the country crowd.

In fact, just the opposite is true.

At the Country Music Awards (CMA) Red Carpet Jewels, Carrie Underwood wore a 31.67 carat flawless diamond known as the Signature Jonathan Arndt Trinity Ring. This $14.8 million ring was all radiant shape featuring a flawless canary fancy vivid yellow center with a duet of flawless D color radiants.

Don't forget to accessorize with a $9.2 million pair of earrings of 23.92 carats, also designed by Arndt.

Carrie also showed off what "elite" jewelry is all about with Arndt's "Museum Collection." No less than flawless diamonds made up a staggering 298 carat diamond bracelet, $23 million and it's yours.[12]

Jonathan Arndt Gallery of Jewels sought the finest jewels the world had to offer for their star studded client list that includes Elton John, Steven Spielberg, Celine Dion, Keith Urban, Miranda Lambert, Reba McIntyre, and Kelly Clarkson.

You can see the perfection within Arndt's designs showing through his love affair with jewels. Arndt's gallery is "invitation only" with six locations worldwide.

Arndt's Gallery has jeweled the Oscars, the Golden Globes, the

Emmys, the American Music Awards, the Billboard Music awards, the Grammys, and many other international red carpet events.

Arndt is proud to have teamed up with the CMA. Blake Shelton, another Arndt Gallery client, had custom "hidden" black diamonds in his band.

Carrie Underwood was right on the money with Arndt designing her engagement ring, and she isn't alone. Heck, Arndt even designed a diamond "A" charm for Carrie's dog.[13]

Diamonds on the Silver Screen

Gentlemen Prefer Blondes first appeared in 1928 as a silent film. The lobby poster depicted a man on bended knee offering a ring to a surprised woman. By 1953, a film adaptation of the stage musical by the same name was made famous by Marilyn Monroe with her rendition of the iconic song "Diamonds Are a Girl's Best Friend."

Diamonds Are Forever, starring Sean Connery as James Bond, hit the silver screen in 1971 with great success. Interestingly enough, the advertising slogan "A Diamond Is Forever" was actually used by De Beers back in 1947 and was recognized about fifty years later by *Advertising Age* magazine as one of the most recognized and successful tag lines of all time.

> *"Good news is rare these days, and every glittering ounce of it should be cherished and hoarded and worshipped and fondled like a priceless diamond."*
>
> Hunter S. Thompson

In 1984, Madonna's hit song "Material Girl" hit the airwaves on MTV. It was clearly an inspired homage to Monroe's infamous "Diamonds Are A Girl's Best Friend" scene in *Gentlemen Prefer Blondes* more than three decades earlier.

Other notable diamond-related films include *Blood Diamond*, *The Pink Panther*, *Titanic*, *A Fish Called Wanda*, *The Bank Job*, *To Catch A Thief*, and *Flawless.*

Songwriters and artists who often rubbed elbows with the Hollywood crowd also got on the "diamond train."

The James Bond film featured the catchy tune "Diamonds Are Forever" sung by Shirley Bassey. Paul Simon had "Diamonds On The Soles Of Her Shoes" and former Bob Dylan flame Joan Baez sung "Diamonds and Rust" in the 1960s.

No one can forget the infamous Beatle tune "Lucy in the Sky with Diamonds." No doubt, a few lyrical lines from that hit hint at the wonder of diamonds: *"Look for the girl with the sun in her eyes"* and *"The girl with the kaleidoscope eyes"* in particular are great clues.

Not to be outdone, Miley Cyrus recently appeared in a cover of "Lucy in the Sky with Diamonds."

And so it goes with diamonds. Very stunning, popular and within reach, even if you thought you missed the chance to be a movie star.

CHAPTER 8

CARATS ARE KING

T HEY SAY "EVERY dog has its day." So does every diamond.

In fact, diamonds have had their months, years, and decades of continuous popularity.

Not even the deepest of world economic crises have been able to subdue a sparkling diamond. From the poorest of Developing World countries to the richest nations on Earth, diamonds have provided a means of wealth, prosperity, opportunity, and security.

From the far reaches of the Arctic Tundra to the Ocean off of Southern Africa, diamonds are like a global gift to the people of the world. All the world is truly a diamond's stage.

In The Beginning...

Good things come in small packages. As one of the world's major resources, it can be easy to forget how magnificent a mineral as small as a diamond can be.

The greatness of a diamond's global reach had humble beginnings.

India has the distinction of being the first in the world to record diamond mining as far back as 800 B.C. Belgium became the center of cutting and trading of diamonds, but not before Venice controlled the diamond cutting niche in 1330 A.D. By the mid-18ᵗ century, Brazil surpassed India's output. When the late seventeenth century rolled around, De Beers, a name ubiquitous with diamonds, was formed, which forever changed the diamond industry.

About 20 countries mine diamonds. Eight of those (Botswana, Russia, South Africa, Canada, Angola, the Democratic Republic of Congo, Namibia and Australia) produce the majority of diamonds.

Large-scale mining in Africa commenced in 1870 at the Kimberley Mine after a prospector rush. A little known fact occurred several years prior to the "rush" on the banks of the Orange River where a boy, curiously looking for colorful pebbles, found a 21 carat diamond.

By the 1960s, Russia was in the diamond game and in the late 1990s Canada put itself on the map with a diamond discovery so sought after that a frenzy not seen since the gold rush ensued.

Today, diamonds are a global phenomenon that have captured and held the world's attention. They are used in industry, jewelry, and as investments.

So what is it like around the globe with diamonds today? Let's explore...

Airlines Aren't Alone... Diamonds Have Hubs Too!

How do millions of carats move efficiently throughout the world?

Long-term-hub giant Antwerp remains a top six diamond hub. Across the world the primary hub for US corporations is in New York. Dubai is home to the fastest growing hub in the world with a high of about $45 billion turnover per year. Tel Aviv, although "only" $27 billion in turnover, is quite a diverse hub. While serving about 3,200 companies involved with diamonds, Tel Aviv covers all aspects of the industry. New York and Hong Kong hubs tend to spotlight polished diamond.

Frozen Tundra Thaws Out a Diamond Monopoly

Today, as is true in many areas of the world, ALROSA (Russian mining company conglomerate) independently distributes its rough diamonds to the world market. This was not always the case. Back in 1963 the first sales contracts between the USSR and De Beers group were signed. In 2009 this cooperation was brought to an end as it was contrary to European Union competition laws by decision of the European Commission.

The fall of De Beers' Central Selling Organization (CSO) led to a large door opening to true market competition.

Historically the "late" discovery of Canadian diamond reserves was the final blow to the single-channel marketing monopoly of De Beers. After the Point Lake (Canadian) diamond news, severe strain on De Beers led them to announce the end of their efforts to control world diamond supplies. During this period Nicholas Oppenheimer (former head of De Beers) stated, "As new sources of supply opened up, particularly in Canada, it became evident that that role could not be sustained." By 2001, De Beers' rough diamond market share slid to under 60%, down from 80%.

Nonetheless, as was true during the De Beers monopolistic reign, about 65% of rough diamond sales channels are via long term contracts which do provide innate market stability.

Also, per absolute value and per carat metrics, ALROSA and De Beers remain producers at the top of the profitability mountain. This is especially noteworthy given the fact that ALROSA, going against the industry norm of about 1%, sells about 20% of its production through short term agreements. Be aware that "leftover" gems, those that fall outside typical size ranges, over-whelmingly make up the short term market.

Many say the best thing to come out of De Beers was the mem-orable catch phrase, "A diamond is forever," which was a simple yet powerful way to grow the diamond industry.

Diamond Model: Supply and Demand

Diamond production scenarios fall under increasing, stable, and decreasing outputs.

Up until 2018, rates of diamond supply and demand are fore-casted to differ. From then on, limited capacity and depleted mining stores set the stage for a predictable and ever-widening gap with demand outstripping supply expected to last into 2024. Of course this estimate bars any unexpected market shake-ups.

Intensifying demand could become reality if diamond engage-ment rings capture more interest in countries such as Africa, Russia, and Latin America. Minus this wildcard, strong fundamentals in developed and developing countries will bolster robust growth.

Setting aside India's diamond manufacturing sector red ink, sustainable long-term growth appears positive given steady rupee value and overall economic fundamentals.

Demand prospects could be cut short depending on Europe's continuing economic recovery. Officially in a state of "stagna-tion," concern is that a bogged down GDP has become a plateau, not the typically low point of a normal economic cycle.

The US retail market leads the world. The US region has come a long way since posting declines linked to the "crisis" period sparked in 2008. Diamond jewelry markets in China, India, and the US are expected to remain the largest worldwide.[1]

For further cues to the leveled-off European market,

"Euromonitor" has emerged as a source for investigating niche luxury and high-income patterns for emerging markets.[2]

Financing Facets

Selling billions of dollars in rough diamonds a year makes De Beers the largest supplier of the durable gemstone by value. This fact endures today, just as it did decades ago when De Beers reigned over the diamond industry with a virtual monopolistic "iron fist."

On the topic of politics and diamonds, the subtopic of eco-diamonds highlighted jewelers' efforts to become transparent via social responsibility in the form of recycling metals.

A Kimberley Process (KP) goal, mandated by the United Nations General Assembly, is to eliminate the illicit trade of diamonds through strict gemstone tracking rules. In the name of transparency, many nations have come clean while others, such as Venezuela, continually resist the verification of diamonds mandated by the KP.

Despite a past history of monopolizing diamond trade, De Beers has recently announced plans of reform with transparency as a core element. The spotlight is being pointed on "sightholders," De Beers' customers that buy about 90% of mined output from the company. Financing stability is behind this motivation for more transparency.

Sightholders play a vital role in the diamond industry as cutters, polishers, and channeling. They are also a fairly small group of coveted "customers" of De Beers, about 80 sightholders exist. Most are established in well-known diamond trading centers such as India, Israel, and Antwerp. After being approved by De Beers, these "customers" buy rough diamonds at "sights," which are regular sales of gemstones.

With bank based financing showing signs of slowing in the

diamond industry, De Beers wishes for sightholders to acquire more equity in their companies as well as "present their accounts according to international standards." In fact, a recent rough price decline was blamed on lack of liquidity when Antwerp Diamond Bank closed to new business.

The goal is to ensure everyone (sightholders) are on the same level regarding financial clarity, as several sightholders confirmed some banks "were shunning the diamond trade."[3]

Rallying Roughs Pinch Polished Profits

Free market theory is easy to understand. By keeping artificial restrictions at bay, people, products, and services dictate demand and supply, which influence price.

Perplexing complexity imposed on a free market is where trouble starts. Most of the time, it is the market participants themselves that caused the economic train to skip the track.

Storm clouds have been brewing over the Indian government and bankers due to the irrationally of elevated rough diamond prices. At its core, there is an overvaluation of rough stones to the detriment of diamond manufacturers and ultimately polished diamond margins.

> *"There's a difference between a free market and free-for-all market."*
>
> Bob Menendez

At the macro level, the diamond industry seems to be in a bit of a bind reflecting the theory of "irrational exuberance," coined by Alan Greenspan (former US Fed Chairman) about 18 years ago. Diamond industry lenders have enabled over-financing, while diamond manufacturers, especially in India, have been more than willing to participate.

Elementary supply and demand reality applies, too many dollars chasing too many rough stones causes too large of a margin between rough and polished stone prices. Polished diamond prices suffer as a result due to a flooded diamond market.

At the most basic level, millions of honest workers in India are on the brink of hardship based on the reality of significant job losses. Apparently, good people are being forced out of business by irresponsible banks.

Could this diamond dilemma be a bubble about to burst?

Seeing the writing on the wall, De Beers has already tightened up financial requirements of their sightholders by insisting their own equity ratios by increased. No more large bank loans became the standing order to sightholders wishing to remain associated with De Beers. Unfortunately, this logical move will put some sightholders out of business. But that's not the worst consequence. Speaking of the industry at-large, many legitimate diamond manufactures striving to remain in the game have been forced to copy competitors' loaned money grab to sustain ever increasing rough diamond prices. This unsustainable escalation has driven many manufactures to operate at perpetual losses, borrowing more money to pay interest on massive outstanding loans.

> *"The most important single central fact about a free market is that no exchange takes place unless both parties benefit."*
> Milton Friedman

Dire long-term industry effects are plummeting polished prices, job losses, stagnant industry growth, and negative diamond industry reputation. Short-term excess financing artificially inflates rough stone prices causing negative reverberations throughout the industry.

Interestingly enough, the rough stone market squeeze being applied upon manufacturers is literally forcing exchange without compensating benefit. "Freedom" vanishes when the menu has only two options, swallow unsustainable debt or shutter your doors immediately. Either way, a going-out-of-business sale eventually transpires. Simply letting the diamond manufacturing sector remain caught between a rock and a hard place only defeats overall industry sustainability. Financing unprofitable actions is not how free markets thrive. Millions of Indians' "daily bread" depends on stable diamond cutting operations unfettered by front-end profiteering at the rough stone market level. When one speaks of the diamond "value chain," all links must remain profitable in order to benefit the entire industry.

Although it is true that the manufacturing sector "suffers significant problems," as International Diamond Manufacturers Association (IDMA) president Maxim Shkadov declared, all stakeholders are keenly aware of the issue at hand. The diamond industry has seen its share of short-term setbacks and spectacular surges within its own niche market cycles.

With India ceding manufacturing volume to China, other regions such as Europe, North America, and Southeast Asia saw reduced shares while specializing in the high-end store niche.

Transparency does exist through trade networks and price lists from parties such as Rapaport.

The diamond dream is surely alive. Containing unsustainable practices will ensure the dream continues.[4]

Retail Rankings

On the retail front, diamonds in the half-carat and under lost 2% of pricing power. Between the 2 and 4 carat range, there was no effective pricing maneuvering.

Pricescope's peek at retail sales, which included "over 450,000 diamonds" examined in their database revealed an aggregate month-after-month price increase for April 2015. This all came about despite industry pressure from rough diamond supply increases leading to worries of dilution of polished stone prices.

Retail store reports showed 2% price gains for the half-cart to one carat weights and the four and over carat range.[5]

Outside the realm of retail, savvy investors search for avenues to capitalize on diamond value trends. Diamonds as alternative investments have become popular as of late, evidenced by mega-auction houses Christie's and Sotheby's. There is no direct comparison between fancy diamonds selling a few hundred thousand dollars per carat and a "common" one-carat stone pricing out for a fraction of that. Investors use general market news to supplement market sentiment.

Millennial Money

With a record fine jewelry purchase level averaging $434 per household in 2014, it is no wonder total jewelry sales in one of the largest consumer nations (USA) reached almost $69 billion. Amazingly this sales level was achieved despite a drop in sales during the US Christmas holiday season, which normally is counted on by retailers to make up the majority sales for the years.

Trending toward more online purchases, the Millennials, not baby boomers or Gen X'ers, are driving this growing jewelry demand. Spending less per piece has been counteracted by higher quantity of jewelry purchases.

Millennials (20-35) have certainly been doing their part to boost the economy. Outpacing the average household by 28%, the 25-34 age group has proven their attraction to fine jewelry according to Edahn Golan, industry analyst. Their "US Jewelry

State of the Market Report" included new data of demographic breakdowns confirming Millennials' command over the latest upsurge in jewelry purchases.[6]

Asian Diamond Persuasion

Of the developed countries during the economic "crisis" (2007-2009), Japan beat out the United States and the World, but with a bit of shame.

At -3.3% (GDP CAGR) during the "crisis," Japan was at the bottom of the proverbial barrel of developed countries per Bain's analysis.

It wasn't until the economic phases of "Rebound" (2009-2011) that Japan statistically pulled ahead of "world" Gross Domestic Product (GDP) Compound Annual Growth Rate (CAGR). Japan continued to keep itself above the economic waterline, based on Bain's short-term outlook for global economic growth.

Surprisingly, the US (world epicenter of the "Great Recession") outpaced Japan every year (2007-2015), which encompassed all phases (from Crisis to Growth) of the global economic cycle.

China reigned over the entire world during that same eight-year period with a stellar average GDP CAGR of 8.4%. During the "crisis" and "rebound" phases, China produced highs of 9.4% and 9.9% respectively, clearly dominating over the well-known consumerist nation that is the US Eking out a meager high of 2.7% during the "growth" phase, the US was playing catch-up. Even during the "growth" phase China stood head and shoulders above the "world," ranking at 2.9%. The closest competitor to China was India at 6.3%, followed by Japan ranking at 3.9%.

Bain's analysis clearly shows that over the span of eight years representing the five global economic phases ("crisis to growth"), developing countries showed up developed countries by a large margin, the largest of which was 12.7% during the "crisis" global economic phase. Upon reaching the "growth" phase eight years later, that margin was reduced to about 6.2%, still a healthy advantage. At that phase Japan had edged out the EU by a 0.6% margin.

These numbers prove to diamond industry insiders, as well as casual observers, undeniable evidence of opportunity and revealing trends.[7]

In decades prior to this most recent global economic cycle, the expansion of cultural boundaries literally opened the door to diamond trade in Japan in an amazing way. After World War II and up until 1959, diamonds were not even permitted to be imported to Japan. By 1981 about 60% of Japanese brides wore diamonds, up from 5 percent in the late 1960s when general diamond industry advertising campaigns included Japan.

Despite modern day Japanese monetary policy earmarked as "expansionary" in nature, the yen became devalued, offsetting overall growth. No matter the currency exchange rate or internal monetary policy strife, once a culture of diamond acceptance takes root, future gemstone purchasing expectations soon become reality. After all, Japan is known as the "Third Pillar" within the developed world market for diamond jewelry. Japanese tax pressures affecting luxury-goods sales have only slowed demand growth to a moderate level in 2013.

Japan was part of the De Beers marketing machine plan during the second half of the twentieth century. Western Europe and the US were also part of this three-phase process to bolster polished diamond demand. Generic marketing was the first phase which successfully promoted diamond jewelry in general.

A refinement taking place during the second phase shifted focus to an affinity for diamonds themselves. China and India were included in this marketing push.

Currently downstream players (retailers and middle-market players) were recruited to execute the third phase in an effort to solidify spreading responsibility in replacing phase one generic marketing with a branded approach. De Beers' own "Forevermark" brand is a prime example. "Moments in Light," "Natural Brilliance," and "A true promise will never be broken," are slogans and campaign-related taglines of a promotional origin.

Maintaining demand and supporting growth led to the sale of the "Hearts on Fire" proprietary diamond to Chow Tai Fook, a Chinese jewelry giant. Rio Tinto tapped into Chinese consumer tastes by engaging jewelry manufacturers and designers from China with its "The Fashion of Diamonds" initiative in 2014. This push highlighted the value of Argyle diamond mine stones backed by Rio Tinto.

With China's jewelry retail markets becoming "democratized," hard luxuries are no longer the domain of the wealthiest citizens. China's middle-class is a force of growing support to diamond retailers. Once the impact of new anticorruption measures pass through a short-term gestation period, all looks well for the Chinese for years to come. Adding to their position as a world leading jewelry producer will be China's manufacturing niche to the detriment of the US and Europe's top end market in particular. In 2013 it became clear that China is now a formidable global hub of jewelry manufacturing, having captured significant industry revenue growth.

China's middle class growth has provided so much steady steam for the country that continuously high GDP percentages provide a solid foundation supporting Chinas as the main engine of diamond jewelry industry growth.

Some regional buyers reported mixed results, yet common sentiment backs positive results from the 2014 Fall season Jewelry & Gem Fair in Hong Kong.[8]

Chinese Carat Craze

The free fall hit in the summer of 2015.

For about two decades China's economy was booming at an annualized GDP increase of about 10%. Good times were expected to last until at least 2018, according to some expert estimates before a slowdown of any significance would crash the party.

Prior years had seen large increases in the Chinese stock market. It only took weeks for about one-third of that value to melt away during the summer heat. As is typical in any market run up there were those that jumped in too late in hopes of catching the bandwagon to riches. Crumpled up "ticker tapes" are all that's left telling their tale of woe.

Despite world-wide economic uncertainties, tangible assets, especially diamonds, are riding. In fact, diamonds remain the bright spot amongst the doom and gloom emanating from the securities sector.

"Smart money" in China took an early exit from once popular traditional investments in search of alternatives. Being keen on market trends, savvy investors saw the sparkle of diamonds to be a harbinger of a prosperous future.

Although seeing a possible buying opportunity in the works, money manager Huey-yuan Yang admits that the "market continues to be very expensive." His "buying-on-dip" inclination is a stock tactic that has burned brokers before. Betting that Chinese policy will prop up the market is a long-term gamble prone to a volley of volatility which undermines free market philosophy.

It only took one day for the Shanghai Composite Index to plunge 8.5%. Thus far, of the total one-third market loss, about 15% occurred in one month. These losses are the most this particular index has seen in six years, which is just past the tenure of beginning of the latest Chinese run up of the market.[9]

Perhaps you've heard that Chinese tycoons have a preference for perfection.

Diamonds are allowing them, and other investors, to scratch that itch. Despite the staggering popularity of colored stones, Sotheby's was able to provide a seller a 230% return for a colorless (white) diamond. The seller had acquired the pear-shaped 75-carat monster in 2001 for $4.3 million, then sold it in 2015 for a cool $14.2 million.

Bigger stones do attract attention. Fancies (colored diamonds) are very expensive the larger they get. As large auction houses have proven over the last several years, the collecting habits of investors has even upped the ante for white diamonds, which have taken a partial back seat to colored stones in the sales record department. Although some Chinese men have just begun to overlook the "feminine" history of diamonds, many Chinese investors covet and dominate the flawless (defect-free) white diamond market.

Following years of market enthusiasm, the Chinese have joined in the love of fancy stones, particularly pink and blue. Even the Chinese upper-middle class have saved up to join the diamond craze, which has assisted the rise in asking prices.

The elite are even calling in to bid via telephone. Upon the gavel falling at Christie's auction of "Princie," the over-the-phone bid was the winner, at $39.3 million. Said to be from the infamous Golconda mines of India, the stone was named after a fourteen-year-old Prince of Baroda. Back in 1960, this same stone was auctioned off for $1.3 million.

This major Chinese stock market drop has finally grabbed the attention of anyone who had once thought China escaped the 2008 recession many other countries suffered. Chinese fence sitters and bystanders now realize their mistake. Even across the world in Miami, USA, a radiologist and design collector wishes he would have invested in diamonds much sooner. He described the jewelry he's since collected as "miniature sculptures." Years ago he thought of jewelry as, well, just jewelry his wife wore, not part of his net worth. Looking back he figures his jewelry has "probably done better than anything else I've bought."

Founder of RapNet, Martin Rapaport, says concentration of wealth and portability of diamonds is very appealing to many. Once again, with all the economic woes and uncertainty concerning politics, people are on edge and their paper currency and stock certificates are not soothing those worries.

Under a hypothetical situation Rapaport calmly states, "If the world gets a computer virus and suddenly you need to move $10 million in 48 hours, gold will set off metal detectors and too much cash gets cumbersome." He continued, "But you slip on a $5 million ring and a $5 million necklace and you've got no problems." Point taken, who wants to try negotiating with TSA agents about the stack of cash you're trying to get on the plane or the weight of multiple gold bullion?

Rapaport tells the tale of a billionaire friend turning $1.1 million into a small portable nest egg. Looped around the safety of his wife's neck was his friend's "quick getaway" plan in case his fortunes shifted and he needed to leave in a rush, for whatever reason. In the style of a Roaring Twenties' strand, he had 100 single-carat diamonds strung together. How creative, very portable, very condensed, and very smart for the intended purpose.[10]

Asian persuasion has turned to stone, in a most spectacular way.

According to the Natural Color Diamond Association (NCDIA), New York and Geneva were common focal points for natural colored diamond sales. Now Hong Kong is seeing plenty of action, thanks to major auction houses. At the Magnificent

Jewels and Jadeite Autumn Sale of 2014 and throughout 2015, Sotheby's of Hong Kong made several proud sales. One record-setting stone was "only" 8.41 carats, yet brought in $17.77 million USD. This stunning stone was a pleasing purple-pink hue.

With a more educated market, private buyers are taking control of their future. Sitting by waiting for the next market crash to wash away their equity portfolio is apparently not going to cut it anymore. Asia's super rich on no longer the exclusive buyers of the special stones we call diamonds.

Diamonds have truly gone global, not only in mining operations, but now accessibility to global investment in the stones themselves, whether that is auction houses, diamond center "sight sales," or strictly private transactions behind closed doors.

Established in 2014, the Fancy Color Research Foundation (FCRF) had indexed fancy stones appreciating an average of almost 20% from 2006 to 2014. The Diamond Prices Index showed white diamonds drumming up an aggregate 62% return during the same period.

As a further testament, Asian markets have found in diamonds the Chinese segment accounts for 40% of all fancy sales per FCRF numbers. Pink diamond values in particular are said to now be driven by the Asian market. This niche cultural popularity has also obviously lifted the fancy market world-wide.

In addition to Asian men preferring more masculine colors in the fancy hues their diamonds to personally wear, Asian investors are not scared away from white diamonds as investments, bucking the trend in many other countries. White diamonds in Asian culture can be both gifts and investments.

Diamintel, global supplier of exquisite natural color diamonds, has seen their 50% revenue from Europe and the United States give way to 80%, all from Greater China.[11]

Around the world the "refugee mentality" is alive and well.

A few years ago National Jewelry Institute President Judith Price captured the sentiment of many. "If there is a problem, people want to feel like they can escape," she stated at an international diamond dealers conference in New York City. Referring to the instant security that portability provides in dismal economic times, she mentioned that with jewelry "you can slip it in your pocket and walk away."[12]

That was a few years ago. Today we see turmoil increasing with the once venerable growth of China stumbling. The world economy has much to do with many citizens becoming uneasy. Even the ultra-rich are turning a cold shoulder to some of their once beloved "treasure" assets. The "Blue-chip" paintings, seen as prime alternate investments, are now seen more and more as a liability of sorts in case of emergency. An unforeseen "emergency" could be a fire or disaster of another sort, such as a failing economy or even distrust in the presiding government.

Professionals in the jewelry industry within Europe and the United States have seen contemporary art collectors doing something odd in their world of paintings and sculptures. As an offset of risk, these collectors are buying into tried-and-true gemstones. As a result, jewelry that was once seen as strictly as ornaments are now accepted as works of art.

Just as shrewd countries are not likely to put all their eggs in one basket when it comes to budgeting and trade partners, neither are some citizens with their hard-earned wealth. The niche "prepper" libertarian crowd, although a small group in the United States, is an example at the most basic level. Recently the Asian populous has realized they must consider a paradigm shift regarding economic news. After all, the world has witnessed the implosion of the Greek fiscal status where banks were put under order to close for days at a time while rationing fund withdrawals of customers. Of course, heavy borrowing and spending patterns in the virtually bankrupt United States are a world problem if that situation continues to deteriorate.

Did you realize that Henry VIII had his jewelers embed his initials in his jewelry?

One might wonder what the King had to worry about, but the point, common to contemporary circumstances, is that "hard" assets are where the value really resides. In more ways than one, diamonds are a universal "hard" asset, no doubt about it. Selectively shifting assets into gemstones is becoming seen a wise decision.

So now we see the downside of decades-long import demand by China. Store housing commodities in an effort to drive its economy eventually ran low on steam. South African exports, due to China's slowdown, have slid in decline to as much as 32%. Balance has been disturbed. The "reset" process will take time for transition to occur and there will be risks.

Call it coincidence, but it appears the Asian gemstone market, all the way down to the private investor, is attempting to create their own light at the end of the tunnel.

Once a hedge, diamonds have become a mainstream investment.[13]

Rounding out the facts of the Chinese economic condition, it is apparent that a major correction is working its way past an overheated growth phase.

Not many countries have seen the investment levels that China has, 49% of GDP. Although amazing, that credit binge pushed debt to about 250% GDP, up about 100% in the last seven years. Eerily similar to the recession that severely oppressed the United States economy, much of China's credit was in the real estate sector where unsold home inventories sit at record high levels.[14]

Credit hang-overs have one remedy, time. Most likely, double digit economic growth in China is a past memory.

They say every cloud has a silver lining.

As investors around the world have proven year after year, the shining safe haven of choice is the spectacular diamond.

Global Trends

Combining trends with investments can be a bag of mixed rocks, you never know what you'll get.

Swimming upstream seems futile, unless integration in the diamond industry is your aim. In the name of efficiency, control, profits, and stability, major retailers are consolidating vertically along the diamond value chain.

Seeking economies of scale, companies are integrating retailing, polishing, and manufacturing as the diamond industry strategically consolidates. Taking steps to offset a possibly prolonged credit squeeze, large companies with financial resources are side-stepping scarce liquidity that is debilitating to smaller players, especially in China. Chow Tai Fook has secured cutting and polishing sites in Botswana. Signet Jewelers (specialty jewelry retailers in US and UK) has also set up cutting and polishing stations in Botswana. Tiffany & Co. has also made inroads in vertical (upstream) integration. Signet acquired Zales jewelry stores, covering the horizontal expansion horizon. Downstream Asian players gained exposure after Chow Tai Fook acquired Hearts on Fire, a branded luxury diamond from the US.

Smaller diamond retail chains need to watch for the online threat posed by Alibaba, Amazon, and Blue Nile. As consumer trust deepens, online diamond dealers are capitalizing on tremendous opportunity to expand upon wider inventory and transparency. Not having to concern themselves with high brick-and-mortar costs, these online companies can take advantage of developing a strong online sales channel.

Yet another retail trend is dubbed "diamond recycling."

Certainly not your local pawn shop, high-end retailers have jumped at the chance to repurchase stones from customers. De Beers is assessing this retail model with the International Institute of Diamond Valuation (IIDV), a standalone venture.

Reselling is what recycling is all about and reinforcing in-house brands provides a path for customer loyalty. There may even be an upside for the investor as this model provides liquidity and transparency.

Vintage (recast) jewelry is gaining US popularity and polished diamond recycling is up to $1 billion.[15]

Diamonds of the Future

Sparkling stones have always garnered attention, but none so much as diamonds.

World economies and local business cycles have always had an effect on gemstones. The beginning of the 2008 financial crisis ultimately allowed diamonds to prove their true toughness as an alternate investment and are still going strong.

Asian middle class income growth is providing a major engine fueling diamond purchases and during the latest crisis recovery many developing nations are turning in impressive GDP growth. These trends prove disposable incomes are backing not only the very beauty of diamonds but the increasing acceptance of their inherent value.

No forecast is flawless, and neither are all diamonds. What can be said is that by the numbers, the global community has shown respect and trust in the great momentum diamonds have brought to nations around the world.

CHAPTER 9

SPECTACULAR
SHAPES

G IVEN THE WORLDWIDE availability of diamonds today, it's hard to imagine a world without them.

By the 1650s, "Mazarins Double" and "Triple-Cut Brilliants" were the creations of Cardinal Maxarin which are now known as the popular round shape. You'll hear the terms "brilliant" and "round brilliant" as descriptors today too.

We'd have to travel back in time to witness history being made as the Archduke of Austria gave the first engagement ring to Mary of Burgundy. The year was 1477. And, of course, it was a diamond ring.

Residing in the Tower of London is the Koh-I-Noor, a diamond theoretically believed to have the longest known history dating back to 1304.[1]

It has been said that whoever owned the Koh-I-Noor ruled the world and some suggest that it may date from before the time of Christ. Often thought of as an elongated round diamond, the Koh-I-Noor was oval in shape.[2]

The Shape of Things to Come...

Cut...shape...what's the difference?

Well, that depends on whether you're a consumer or a diamond professional.

Saying "cut" to the average person (consumer) makes them think of the "4C's" they often see on brochures, online and highlighted in point-of-purchase displays in jewelry stores. They think of "cut" in terms of the shape of the diamond such as round, oval, rectangular, square, etc.

> "The soul is placed in the body and it is like a rough diamond. It must be polished within, or the luster of the soul will never appear."
>
> Daniel Defoe

When a diamantaire (diamond expert) hears "cut," a grin typically spreads across their face upon visualizing the sheer beauty of a well cut stone. "Cut" in this instance is how the stone's facets are planned out and the degree of accuracy and craftsmanship therein. It's the way stone's facets are arranged regardless of the basic shape of the stone.

For instance, one could have a heart-shaped diamond with a poor cut grading on its GIA certificate while a round diamond may be graded excellent. At the same time a Princess (square, or nearly so) shape diamond could receive a good cut grading.

So we can have many different shaped diamonds with varying cut grades. And while each natural diamond is as unique as a snowflake, many diamonds can have the same cut.

When you think about it, it all becomes clear.

Though extremely difficult to analyze or quantify, the cut of any diamond has three attributes: brilliance (the total light reflected from a diamond), fire (the dispersion of light into the colors of the spectrum), and scintillation (the pattern of light and dark areas and the flashes of light, or sparkle, when a diamond is moved).[3]

Very simply stated, shape is to outline as cut is to facet. So a shape can be faceted in a variety of ways, or cutting styles. The brilliant cut is most common and includes 57 facets (58 if a culet is included, not pointed).

At times you'll find jewelers using the terms shape and cut interchangeably, preferring "cut" when describing a diamond's shape so as to be congruent with the "4 C's of diamonds" sales literature and presentations.

Shimansky is correct. He's essentially speaking about a "perfectly" cut diamond's appeal, which makes up a large part of its overall beauty. One could also say that personal preference and popularity is the basis for our attraction to a particular shape of diamond.

> *"The beauty of a perfectly cut diamond lies not just in its exquisite aesthetics, but in the way it makes you feel."*
>
> Yair Shimansky

Now that you know shapes from cuts, let's explore the many fascinating shapes of gem quality diamonds. Going forward, be on the lookout as we'll use "cut" and "shape" interchangeably too.

Old Mine Shape

Most people will give a big blank stare if asked to describe an "Old Mine" diamond. Not to worry, you're not alone.

Surprisingly enough, the Old Mine shape is the distant "relative" of the most popular diamond today…the round (sometimes called "brilliant") shape.

Before modern laser technology, all diamonds were cut individually by hand.

Despite being considered strictly antique jewelry by the contemporary crowd, Old Mine diamonds are vintage, one-of-a-kind gems you won't find anywhere else. Ring settings were made after Old Mines were cut, thus adding to their truly one-of-a-kind stature.

What represents love between two individuals better that a truly unique diamond?

The fact is that the heritage of an Old Mine shaped diamond lives on in the wildly popular round diamond of today.

Emerald Shape

Remember Nick Cannon bestowing Mariah Carey with a unique light pink emerald diamond? This rectangular stone is the epitome of class and sophistication, a very stunning choice for the Hollywood jet-setting crowd.

The emerald shape is, overall, less costly than the popular round and princess shapes for similar size and quality gem. The step-facet (opposing the brilliant-facet cut of round diamonds) cut of the emerald diamond appears to the viewer as a "hallway of mirrors" visual effect. The step cut usually has beveled corners, with rows of step cuts that reflect off of each other.

This gem is very transparent, meaning that its clarity needs to be of higher grade to maintain visual appeal. Any lesser clarity step-cut gem would allow too many imperfections to be seen by the naked eye.

Clearly, then, if you favor the emerald cut, its clarity grade had better be on the high end, lest inclusions and imperfections disappoint anyone when observing this diamond up close.

They say leaders choose the emerald shape as well as those who like to impress others. Is it any wonder Paris Hilton has a $4.7 million 24 carat emerald?[4]

Asscher Shape

Coming to true prominence during the Art-Deco era and known as the "square cousin to the emerald," the Asscher shape diamond has been seen back in the spotlight thanks to Ashlee Simpson, Jessica Alba, and Gwyneth Paltrow.[5]

Quite often, squared emeralds are commonly referred to as Asscher-cuts, which are known for their angled and cropped corners, giving the gem a timeless look.

At the Royal Asscher Diamond Company, diamond cutter Joseph Asscher introduced the "revolutionary" Asscher-cut in 1902. Despite its fan-fare introduction, the Asscher shape has not been as popular in modern times...even with the Taylor name and a high-profile burglary linked to this gem.

Two Hollywood actresses owned the same Asscher gem. Vera Krupp (the original owner had her Asscher ring stolen only to be reunited with it in short order due to FBI involvement).

Interestingly enough, Richard Burton purchased *The Krupp Diamond* at Vera Krupp's Sotheby's estate sale auction for about $305,000 (now estimated value of $3.5 million) in 1968...gifting it to his wife, Elizabeth Taylor.

Despite its lagging popularity, the Asscher shape still enjoys a celebrity factor familiarity since it's known as *The Krupp Diamond* and *The Elizabeth Taylor Diamond.*

Hollywood elite aside, the Asscher has caught the eye of many Avant Garde diamond enthusiasts, art deco stylists, and vintage ring admirers. Its architectural-like cut radiates a super shine due to the "hallway of mirrors" effect, similar to that of emerald-shaped diamonds.

In 2002 the cut was slightly refined, leading to attention diamond marketers just love.[6]

The Asscher diamond has endured for more than a century by adhering to a basic but intriguing cut style.

Princess Shape

Living life to the fullest and setting trends are supposed characteristics of princess shape owners.

The princess diamond was developed in the US during the 1980s and rose through the ranks of popularity, just below the round diamond, seated at number one. Tradition has always favored princess and brilliant (round) shapes.[7]

Princesses are shaped with 90-degree corners, yet they are anything but square in a fashion sense. In fact, the more perfectly square, the more valuable!

A great tip is to find a princess cut that appears perfectly square upon quick glance, but not so much when actually measured by a jeweler. "Off-squares" come with varying discounts. You can also mount a less than square princess cut by offsetting it relative to the band. Another visual trick is to mix-and-match by flanking your princess with other gems, throwing off a discriminating eye that would otherwise detect a "rectangular leaning" shape.

Admirers respect the flexibility of the princess and should know that inclusions are less visible due to unique cutting and polishing techniques. This fact alone increases perceived value of the gem. On the flip side, beware that a princess cut tends to reveal lower-grade diamond color more readily than other diamond shapes.

One big factor in cutting cost, and thus promoting popularity, is that about 60% of the princess's original weight remains after cutting.

Best of all, contemporaries and traditionalists alike have nothing but praise for the princess!

Round Shape

As measured by popularity, the round (brilliant) shape is the queen of diamonds.

Only the princess shape is even in the same popularity race.

"The Knot" research revealed that up to 53% of center-stones in engagement rings are round and about 75% of all diamonds sold are of the round variety.[8]

"Brilliants" are on a stage all their own.

Sure, other diamond shapes have rounded or otherwise smoothed-out corners, but none have the fluid and continuous form of a circle like the brilliant. Some say the "endless" nature of a circle represents eternity, thus driving the demand for this shape of wedding ring.

Great sparkle emanates from this ring in brilliant light due to a classic 58 facet cut. The "fire" from the refracted light demands attention from across a room. "Rounds" are used in earrings, rings, pendants and other forms of jewelry.

The brilliant cutting style has been around since the 1700s. Slight enhancements took effect in 1919 by Marcel Tolkowsky. However it was cutting maverick Henry Morse that perfected the round brilliant in the 1860s.

Brilliants are more expensive for two major reasons. First, the cutting process leaves much less of the original stone than any other cut, and second, their popularity further creates price inflation. But don't fret, brilliants retain value quite nicely.

They say faithful, traditional team players are the type of people that choose brilliants.

The appeal of the brilliant has reigned supreme at the "pole-position" of popularity.

Heart Shape

When speaking of love and diamonds, "Ya gotta have heart," as they say.

So who would have expected rude-and-crude rocker Kid Rock to choose the most sentimental and dreamy of all diamond shapes when proposing to Pamela Anderson.

Balance and symmetry is the name of the game when shaping a heart out of a rough diamond stone. The heart shape's appearance dates back to the 1500s and is obviously ideal for Valentine's day, Sweetest day, engagements, and other memorable events. Hearts are especially favored for pendants and "steal the show," so to speak.

In the 1960s, the Trillion variation came out featuring a brilliant cut. Another variation, the Trilliant, morphed from the radiant shape and became a triangle. This three-sided wonder appeared in 1978.[9]

The Millennium Star, a 203-carat pear diamond, had a "sister" stone, the Heart of Eternity. At 27.64 carats of fancy vivid blue, the Heart of Eternity is one of the most well-known heart-shaped diamonds in history.[10]

Of all diamond shapes, the heart is the most demanding shape for a cutting center to undertake. No one said love from the heart comes easy.

Pure romantics realize the heart shaped diamond is as close to fairy tale love they'll ever get from a diamond.

Obviously a true symbol of love and romance, the heart shape has earned admiration in diamond history.

Cushion Shape

Hold onto your bridal bands, brilliant lovers…the cushion shape's got what it takes.

Once Marcel Tolkowsky created the "cushion brilliant" the cushion-cut would never be the same...literally. You see, originally, step facets were utilized to cut a cushion shape. Then Tolkowsky experimented with brilliant facets (cutting technique of round diamonds) and the rest is history.

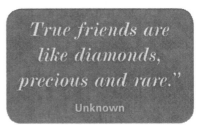

True friends are like diamonds, precious and rare."

Unknown

This new cutting technique allowed the cushion shape to refract more fire and brilliance, which naturally attracts more attention.

The cushion is an "oldie but goody," with some estimates dating this shape back to the 1750s.

Cushions are square or rectangular in shape. Their rounded corners are reminiscent of a vintage version of round diamonds while giving the "soft" visual appeal of a "pillow," hence "cushion." This stone is easy on the eyes evoking what some call a "comfortable" feeling.

Eco-minded diamond lovers will be happy to know that much of the original stone is preserved by diamond cutters forming a cushion shape since limited cutting is required to round the corners. Thus you keep more carat weight.

Jessica Biel (Timberlake), Jennifer Garner, Khloe and Kim Kardashian, as well as Holly Madison have cushion cuts. Kevin Jonas and Dwayne Wade also invested in cushions for their sweeties.

Of historical significance, the cushion shape is that of the infamous Hope Diamond.

So if you're looking for a little bit of "brilliance" in your cushion, opt for the "cushion brilliant," you won't be disappointed.[11]

Oval Shape

Prince Charles boosted the oval shape's popularity tremendously when he bestowed Princess Diana with an oval sapphire engagement ring. They were married in 1981.

About 21 years prior to that fabulous wedding, the "oval brilliant" cut was modified, which also boosted its popularity. The 184 carat Victoria, cut in 1887, is a notable oval brilliant.

Much earlier, in 1304, was the first mention of an oval shaped diamond thus making the oval shape likely to have the longest known history. Residing at the Tower of London, the Koh-I-Noor (oval diamond) has this historical distinction of tenure.[12]

Ovals can be made narrow or wide to complement the wearer's finger. Good news for those with short or stocky fingers: an oval shaped diamond makes a finger look slender and slim.

Another famous oval that now resides in a royal collection is the Beluga by William Goldberg. This flawless color D stone became the largest such oval in history after several months of shaping.

Now in the hands of a private collector the Pink Muse is a world-class pink hue with vivid color. It was whittled down to 8.9 carats from the original 40-carat rough stone.[13]

Shield Shape

One famous "shield," the Guinea Star, was in the *Guinness Book of World Records* for "highest price ever paid for a rough diamond." Discovered in the Republic of Guinea, it was also the largest diamond ever found in a Western African country back in 1986.

A pear, heart, and shield shape came out of this world-famous rough of 255 carats. All stones were "magnificent D Flawless diamonds." The incomparable Guinea Star weighed in at 89.01 carats and is known as a Modified Shield-shape.[14]

Similar to a trillian and kite-shaped cuts, the shield shape cut mixes brilliant and step-cut facets.

It has seven sides with the longest being those joining the two sides below that meet to form the shield's point.

Rare diamond characteristics such as being flawless, colorless, and of perfect symmetrical cut earns the "Star" name. The Guinea Star is in the company of the "Star of America" (Asscher-cut), "Star of Happiness" (radiant-cut), and "Star of the Season" (pear-shaped) diamonds.[15]

Although not necessarily considered popular by sales standards, shield shapes are quite the diamond to behold and are rightfully worthy of recognition.

Radiant Shape

Known as a hybrid of the brilliant (round) and elegant emerald-shaped diamond, the radiant has a 70 facet cut which radiates shine superbly. That's 12 more facets than a brilliant!

Henry Grossbard is credited with the radiant shape in the 1970s, which can be of rectangular orientation, near-square or square. If you appreciate the combination of fire (brilliant) and sophistication (emerald/Asscher), the radiant will do the trick for you.

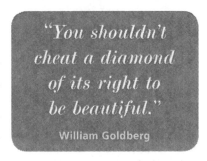

"You shouldn't cheat a diamond of its right to be beautiful."
William Goldberg

However, do be aware that the color of a radiant will be intensified due to their many facets. That could be not so good with a lower-grade color diamond.

Pear Shape

A most famous pear diamond made its way to Saudi Arabia. Known as the Taylor-Burton diamond, it was auctioned for $3 million to jeweler Henry Lambert.

Rumor has it that Richard Burton bought the Cartier ring in an effort to calm a bit of friction in his marriage to Elizabeth Taylor. At $1.5 million, the 69-carat rock was stunning. Too bad the couple's enormous screen appeal didn't transfer to their marriage, which ended soon after and was the reason this pear diamond was auctioned off.[16]

Like the heart shape, a pear's symmetry is most important given that its shape is like a teardrop. Poorly cut diamonds, particularly hearts and pears, will surely lose sparkle.

Pears are typically worn with the "top" being pointed toward the end of the finger. The effect of this setting is akin to a marquise diamond, fingers appear longer.

Aesthetically pleasing, the pear shape is an intermediary between the round and marquise which are flattering stones in their own right.

"Brilliant" pears came about in the eighteenth century, with their initial appearance being recorded in the 1400s.[17]

Marquise Shape

The marquise's history stems from an accomplished and intelligent woman.

It is said the voluptuous contours of the marquise shape resembled Marquise de Pompadour (aka Jeanne Antoinette Poisson), King Louis the XV's mistress. Having a keen sense of the arts and gaining the admiration of the Queen, Marquise (the mistress) certainly had much activity to keep busy. Being named after the mistress in 1745, the marquise shape has been popular ever since.

Like the heart and pear shape, marquises can be tricky to cut. Lack of symmetry immediately translates into a dim stone. Expertly crafted angles of a marquise give the appearance of a stone larger than it is. This is due to how the angles work in tandem, leading to the impression of size.

Forgetting its name is easier than one might suppose. That being the case, some default to simplistically calling it the "football" shape.[18]

On rare occasions you'll see a marquise set horizontally, contrasting traditional alignment with the fingers. This setting choice cancels out the marquise's ability to compliment slender fingers, while at the same time gaining attention with the unique appearance.

A Cut Above...

The shape of a diamond is the first visual element that influences our preference for one diamond over another.

All natural diamonds originate "rough" by nature, yet are expertly transformed into wearable works of art.

History shows that diamond shape popularity shifts with the times. Like the person wearing them, diamonds are unique, precious creations holding deep emotional meaning.

From the eternally popular round and princess cuts to hearts, pears, and emeralds, diamonds always hold a special something for their lucky owners.

Be bold and express yourself with a shapely diamond you can call your own.

CHAPTER 10

DIAMONDS AND DOLLARS

T HEY SAY BEAUTY is in the eye of the beholder.

There is merit to that saying and it's true, undeniable, in fact, that no matter how one defines "beauty," diamonds are a glowing, living example of loving splendor in and of themselves.

Have you had the pleasure of encountering a diamond's eye?

It's marvelous!

True to all diamonds, the eye is always wide open for all to see, beauty. Diamonds have nothing to hide. The eye is up-front-and-center and on top, proudly gazing right back at you. The collage of colors seems to be a show especially for you.

Looking deep into a diamond's eye reveals its inner beauty, beauty that beaconed you from across the

> "The beauty of a woman must be seen from in her eyes, because that is the doorway to her heart, the place where love resides."
>
> Audrey Hepburn

room. The doorway to the heart of diamond is always open. You're free to explore how valuable diamonds are and how fittingly they symbolize love itself.

Behind the inherent beauty of diamonds is the value they naturally command.

Like prized parcels of real estate, no two diamonds are alike, aside from the common glowing beauty they display. Whether lakefront cottage, mountain chalet, or grand cityscape view, each holds its own unique and magnificent value. No two views are exactly the same.

And so it is with diamonds, yet most majestic. A view to a diamond promises and delivers beauty. These magnificent stones abound with special surprises only possible from each and every discrete diamond.

> *"Nowadays people know the price of everything and the value of nothing."*
> Oscar Wilde

Price is not value, in any sense of the word. Price is applied while the value diamonds have earned, the world over, is respected, bar none.

Where does this sometimes mysterious value come from?

Going Beyond the "4 C's"

Since *bang for the buck* equates directly to value in many endeavors, when specifically speaking of diamonds, you can place your bets on never going wrong with the basics of geometry.

Of the numerous characteristics making a diamond the spectacular stone that it is, remember that cut should not be compromised. Cutting stones involves angles and accurate angles affect light refraction and reflection. Everyone knows that diamonds live to be lit up with light. Light makes diamonds come alive. That sparkle gets attention, even from across the room. People are fascinated by glittery things, yet diamonds deliver so much more than a rainbow of rays.

This guidance on cut comes from the fact that putting lipstick on a pig, as the saying goes, can only cover up so much. For example, a colorless diamond with a "D" color rating (very clear stones have been nicknamed "Super D") can be overshadowed by a poor cut which "robs" the diamond of its potential to utilize light most effectively. A diamond with a top-notch clarity grading cannot be fully appreciated if the light that could have helped show off that crystal clear clarity is too dim.

And that's the key. A well-cut diamond is a supremely wonderful manager of light. It guides the flow of light in and out of the diamond like a smooth flowing river runs effortlessly to the sea. Any light "leaks" ruin any chance for a diamond to return a spectacular sparkle.

Gemologists speak of "symmetry" and "polish" when the topic of cut is mentioned. Many "Excellent" diamond cut gradings come with an "Excellent" or "Very Good" polish grade. Be advised that a "Very Good" symmetry and polish grade, as compared to "Excellent," is not detectable with the naked eye, so your "bang-for-the-buck" value can be maximized in this regard. It is possible, with a trained naked eye, to ascertain a "Good" polish rating, however. Sometimes cut is downgraded due to a lesser quality polish. Polish and symmetry reflect the craftsmanship of the cutter, skill and care.

"Polish," as you'd imagine, refers to the surface condition of the diamond. It's the "fit and finish" dimension. "Inclusions" are internal to the stone and affect a clarity rating. The "wear and tear" on a diamond affects polish and is usually the culprit of flaws due to the cutting process. Great polish, like a great cut, is beneficial for light's interaction (permeability) with the diamond, resulting in a lovely luster.

Polish grade can be altered by polishing time, polish wheel quality, and the graininess of the diamond dust used for polishing. In addition, pits, scratches, polish lines, nicks, abrasions, and "burns" can all combine to nix an otherwise top polish grading on a particular diamond's certificate.

No matter how complex they appear to be, things such as engines are actually very simple devices. Engines are really air pumps, with a mass of accessories attached. Diamonds are quite simple too, at least in concept.

Diamonds are directors of light.

Think of it like the early computer acronym GIGO, Garbage-In-Garbage-Out. There is no need to be dazzled by the seemingly endless array of computer statistics these days. Computers are simply data processors. We input most information into our data devices. To be direct, a poor diamond cut is going to guarantee only one thing, a dull-looking diamond. If the cut is poor enough, even a layman will be able to sense, at first glance, that "life" is missing from the sad stone. "Garbage" cut yields "garbage" light performance.

Light performance is most altered by the cut of a stone. Diamonds refract light best when the angles of the cut are optimal. Of course, cuts also dictate the proportions of a stone which also greatly affect light performance.

Bottom line, to ensure the best value, cut is critical.[1]

Light It Up!

Light Performance can be further detailed by several parameters.

"Sparkle" is a commonly accepted term concerning diamonds. When a diamond is moved, sudden flashes appear, as if bursting out of the stone. This is sparkle.

Equal distribution of light reflecting from the stone is coined

"Symmetry." Intense, bright light that emanates from the diamond is commonly called "Brilliance," and that spectrum of vivid lights making up the color of the rainbow is an awesome "Fire" in all its glory.

These four distinct light characteristics can be graded separately. When combined, a light performance grading scale is achieved. Measuring these light parameters is the specialty of equipment from companies such as Sarine Technologies. Their scale has four tiers ranging from "low" to "ultimate." The advantage is obvious. For the untrained eye, one is likely to be fooled by a "flashy" diamond.

> *"The hardness of a diamond is part of its usefulness, but its true value is in the light that shines through it."*
> B.K.S. Iyengar

With light performance test results you can be confident that all aspects of how a diamond caresses the light it touches is the best it can be.[2]

Staying In Shape

Commonly mistaken for "cut," shape is usually the first diamond characteristic to attract us.

Traditionally, round and princess shaped stones have been very popular with the masses. More and more you'll notice emerald, oval, marquise and even pear shapes coming out.

The ubiquitous "4 C's" have used the term "cut" to describe a diamond's shape for so long that the average consumer pays little, if any, attention to the value added by a diamond's cut.

As you'd expect, shape is a personal preference. Sometimes you'll hear any diamond shape, other than round, being called "fancy." Jewelers even refer to round shaped stones as "brilliants."

Each shape has its pros and cons which allows one to choose

what best fits their desires. Mounting options allow different shaped diamonds to be set with each other sharing the spotlight or one shape as side stone(s).

Up to a 30% premium has been charged for a round diamond over a princess shape with other stone characteristics remaining similar. It has been reported that up to 75% of all jewelry diamonds are round. Although popularity does equate into price, much more of a rough stone is sacrificed during the cutting phase for a round diamond than that of a princess.

The right combination of shape, clarity, and other diamond value factors can turn up wonderful surprises.

A recent random online diamond sale search offered an $18,000 discount if you paid via wire transfer. The heart-shaped diamond was almost six carats with a list price of over $603,000.

> *"Everybody wants to be a diamond, but very few are willing to get cut."*
>
> Unknown

Claiming "D" color was icing on the cake next to a clarity grade of "Internally Flawless." The $18k discount is enough to buy a nice new economy car.

Better yet, it's nice to see a heart-shaped diamond making waves at the top of the value scale. Can you imagine the premium this stone would demand had it been a round brilliant cut? Deals are out there, you just have to look.

Cut: A Matter of Degrees

Shape is not cut and cut is not shape, even though these terms are used interchangeably in jewelry stores around the world.

Always remember that a great cut reflects great craftsmanship.

Color, carat weight, and clarity are all initially inherent in a rough stone upon its removal from the Earth. Cut is the only parameter of a diamond that depends on human hands.

The manner in which a stone is cut dictates how the diamond directs light. This fact is the most significant factor behind a diamond's beauty. Many resellers, however, make stone buying decisions based off of the initial "glitter" factor.

You know the phrase, "All that glitters is not gold." Similar reasoning can apply to diamonds, with a twist. Just because a diamond glitters doesn't necessarily ensure its cut is good or proper. A poor cut allows glitter to act as the equivalent of "fool's gold"; you may be momentarily distracted by the color or clarity of the stone, but that's all it takes for you to forget about the sacrificed sparkle, brilliance, and lack of fire a properly cut diamond displays.

Light paths in round brilliant cut

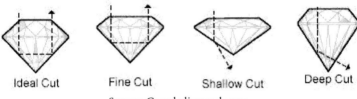

Ideal Cut   Fine Cut   Shallow Cut   Deep Cut

Source: Canadadiamonds.com

As you can see by the simulated paths of light rays within a diamond, deep and shallow cut stones are detrimental to light distribution. Overall beauty and value suffer. Light leakage and loss leads to dim and sometimes dark diamonds. Viewing a stone such as this will have you wondering "who turned out the lights," at best. At worst the diamond will appear "dead," especially when compared to other stones of good cut proportions.

So how can you detect a "leaky" diamond?

With enough diamond gazing experience and a little education behind you, it is fairly easy to detect that something is "off" about poorly cut stones. Especially when at jewelry stores, be observant of similar stones around your target diamond as a beginners guide to picking up on irregularities. Especially as a

> *"The cut is the most important factor in the value of the diamond. You can have two diamonds of equal carat size, color, and clarity, one cut to ideal proportions and the other not, and the value between the two may be as much as a 50 percent difference. That is why it is always important to look at the stones and compare them."*
>
> Kyle Hain

newbie, however, you must always keep in mind not to jump to conclusions. All diamonds are unique and therefore can't really be compared at first sight. Ultimately nothing replaces an expert independent evaluation of a stone.

No one is telling you not to buy a diamond if it looks good to you, since at the end of the day beauty really is in the eye of the beholder. However try to back up the impression you have of the "glitter" you see.

One way is to check the "numbers" of the stone. Just like classic muscle car enthusiasts "check the numbers" to ensure the engine, drive train, and other components "match," you should do likewise with a diamond. The "numbers" are verified measurements of the stone's angles that relate to proportions. Without these figures, you can't really be sure the diamond's apparent brilliance is due to a high color grade or a great cut. Compare what you see to color grade and don't be fooled. A bright "white" color and brilliance are not the same. Only a well cut stone can display true brilliance and other good cut traits such as symmetry and fire.

An observant and educated consumer will be able to notice a poorly cut diamond only after knowing the numbers and ensuring other factors such as color and clarity are not so detrimental as to be equally as damaging to value. Some jewelers will group stones by price, quality, or other tiered methods, all the while being upfront about it. Others live and let live, allowing "buyer beware" to rule the day. Be prepared.

Many years ago GIA's William Boyajian revealed that many years of research led to the belief that there is no ideal cut diamond. The California Institute of Technology collaborated.

This came as a shock to many industry players. Over the last 90 years it was taken as gospel that an "ideal cut" was the best option for those seeking the most brilliant diamond. The infamous Tolkowsky cut has long been assumed the ultimate for diamonds. Variations on this cut, favoring a larger table (top of diamond) have been noted as having more brilliance. GIA's research found that no particular set of numbers universally guarantee the best brilliance.

So what are the details behind the idea of "ideal"?

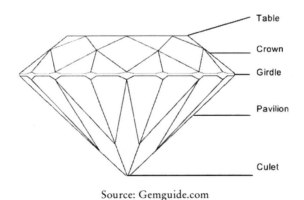

Source: Gemguide.com

Diamond Design, published by Marcel Tolkowsky in 1919, illuminated his work on light behavior theory. Basically this physicist and member of a Belgian diamond-cutting family presented his opinion of balance, between dispersion and brilliance of light. His "ideal" cut angles and proportions are set out below:

34.5° Crown Angle
40.75° Pavilion Angle
59.3% Total Depth
53% Table Diameter
Girdle Edge: Extremely Thin

Appropriate depth percentages vary per diamond shape and desired cut. Not all buyers want or need the most ideal cut.

Grading reports can show measurements in millimeters and percentages. Obviously percentage allows one to quickly assess a stone's depth to width comparison, which then allows rule-of-thumb checks. For example, a princess shape with a depth percentage of between 75–78% is likely to result in an attractive diamond while the common round diamond of 65% or greater is excessive.

Brilliance and thus value are affected by the depth percentage, but the story doesn't stop there. Where said depth lies is the other side of the coin. Once light passes through the table and crown, it must navigate the pavilion precisely in order to reflect back up an out of the table. Think of a light ray as a Ping-Pong ball. The "ball" must bounce off the pavilion facets on the inside of the diamond in such a way as to exit the table and hit the viewer's eye, just right.[3]

Theoretically, a virtually nonexistent "knife-edge" girdle gives a clean appearance while allowing for precision cutting. In reality, such a super skinny girdle has led to many chipped and broken diamonds due to the required pressure during setting to a band. However, a very thick girdle resulting from a less than ideal cut opens the door for wasted carat weight as well as girdle finish, affecting cut grade in a negative way.

Sure, Tolkowsky's "ideal cut" produces a beautiful diamond, just not necessarily the most brilliant. Further, this ideal renders the stone with a smaller table, giving viewers the impression of a smaller stone, no matter the true carat weight. Known in the industry as the "faces up" factor, many observant customers are likely to pick up on this and assume all is not on the up and up, no matter how the sales person attempts to explain the logic. Especially in Europe, larger stones are appreciated, which makes a "ninety-pointer" for one carat (100 points) prices an issue.[4]

The beauty of brilliancy includes internal and external light reflections entertaining the eye. Scintillation also teases the eye by alternating these reflections off polished facets.

GIA has also investigated Weighted Light Return (WLR) as a "calculated numerical factor." WLR, based upon proportions of diamond cuts, was determined for over 20,000 combinations. Similar to the challenge presented against the long held "ideal cut" numbers from Tolkowsky, the thousands of cut combinations showed that the "ideal" stone was not always the most stunning in appearance.[5]

Clearly cut is how well the gem has been shaped, not the shape of the gem.

This basic concept relates directly with the fact that, even though the round brilliant cut supposedly returns a very high percentage of light, this alone does not ensure a brilliant diamond. Despite being cut and facetted accurately, a stone with poor symmetry can ruin quality by misdirecting light exiting the diamond. This misdirected light can be most detrimental to scintillation and fire, which are two crucial light elements a diamond admirer needs to see.[6]

Whether a diamond will be full of life with light or dull and dead is a matter of measured degrees. Minute differences of dimensions alter the geometry of the stone, which can help or hinder how light interacts within the stone's interior and finally the rays' exit trajectory.

Following are some finishing details about a stone's cut to

aid your appreciation of diamonds. Take note that fancy shaped stones (those other than round) will have slightly different parameters that define excellent cut proportions.

One would suspect that a very large table sounds great. Not so with diamonds. Tables more than 65% are considered very large, which has consequences on the reflectivity of light. Table percentage is a proportion of the average diameter of the diamond. 60% is considered standard, a good table size. "Ideal" runs down as low as 53%, which is bordering on the small side. Just like too much water trying to push out of a miniscule hose, light needs a big enough table to enter and exit a diamond in order to display stunning scintillation, brilliance, and fire.

Same goes for the depth of the stone. Brilliance is lost ("leaks") when a stone is too shallow or deep. 60% depth is a standard but not carved in stone (no pun intended). Rounds range in the 57–63% range.

Between the crown and pavilion is the girdle. There are eight girdle size grades, of which only two are considered "acceptable," "Thin" or "Thick." The extremes to be avoided are, well, graded "Extremely Thin" and "Extremely Thick." As mentioned earlier, a very thin girdle can make mounting the stone challenging and can even chip the stone. Too thick and the consequence is useless weight and a black mark on beauty.

Don't discount turning a diamond upside-down.

This action may get a weird look from a jeweler, but there is a method to every supposed madness. Think of this heads over heels maneuver as being equivalent to checking under the hood of a car with a mirror in hand. You might be surprised what you may discover on the underside. For example, a novice consumer has a much better chance of detecting a damaged culet by looking at it directly versus staring down through the stone's table. Better to go right to the source.

Culets can chip and even break off, leaving the upright view (face up, looking down through the stones table) and showing a dark spot resembling a black hole, unsightly to say the least. Depending on the extent of damage, you might miss this if only performing a cursory top view of the stone.

Not all diamonds have culets. Those that do may be pointed or too large, which is another waste of carat weight. Sure, not much, but demerits can add up quickly. Recalling how important angles and proportions are, a burdensome culet certainly affects the stone's pavilion and light dispersion characteristics.[7]

Prior to GIA adoption of cut grade, AGS labs had their own standards. The AGS system was numbered, with the "ideal" cut being "0" and lesser cut quality being assigned anything between "1" through "3." AGS had also further delineated cuts into tiers of "00" and "000." By 2005, GIA used a word grading system for cut grading but only applied it to round brilliant diamonds. The five GIA grades range from "Excellent" to "Poor."[8]

Don't sell yourself short, cut is critical.

Coloring by Letter

Transparent or colorless diamonds once ruled the roost over value.

Colored stones, specifically tinted yellow or brown, were essentially worthless for the most part, key word being "were." Primary colors such as yellow, pink, and blue are very popular nowadays, known as "fancy-colored." **Nature's gift of mixing nitrogen and carbon atom substitution gives us the wonderful beginnings of colored diamonds.** Many of these colored stones have been setting records at auction houses for many years. For a time "chocolate" (brown) colored stones gained in popularity among the masses. See the chapter covering colored stones for more intriguing details.

The various colorless grading levels are almost undetectable to the human eye. The exception would be two diamonds in different grading groups being placed right in front of you, such as a "whiter than white Super D" and a slightly brown or yellow tinted stone. Gemologist grade stones using a "Mother" set as a base and even then under controlled lighting conditions.

Stones free from impurities reaching the rare strata of absolutely colorless would be a sight to behold. No tint can be discerned and such a stone is almost impossible to find in reality, but scientifically possible. Chemical and structural perfection is a high order to attain. There have been many diamonds graded as flawless, yet you'd be very lucky to be in the company of such a rare specimen. Tremendous value attaches to stones that come close to the perfection benchmark.

Diamond color grading starts at "D" (colorless or "white") and ends at "Z." Lower quality colorless diamonds lie on the tinted (yellow) end (towards "Z") of the spectrum. You can expect about a 15% price reduction for a stone that is outside the colorless range of D-F. An untrained eye can't tell the difference between a diamond outside of the top colorless range of which "F" represents the boarder grade.

When attempting to estimate a stone's degree of colorlessness, it is best to attempt doing so in natural light. True, this is not the technical assessment as would be conducted by a gemologist, but it is closer to the reality of where the diamond will be seen when in your possession.

Clarity and color are sometimes confused by novices. A very poor clarity diamond can be identified with relative ease by the average person who employs a bit of patience. Color, especially in the lower grades, determines the hue of light returned by the stone.

A tinted stone is not unclean. It simply has what can be said to be a film or haze when the color grade is at the bottom of the scale.

Color is an overall attribute of the stone while clarity refers mostly to intermittent and localized internal structural defects.

The standard that exists today backing the color grading scale came to be in 1953.

Richard Liddicoat, known as the "Father of Modern Gemology" was the architect of GIA's D-to-Z system that came about due to his search for a consistent standard for polished diamond quality.

Liddicoat was not pleased with customers being led astray by commercially tainted promises of "extra, extra, extra River Stones." The terms "river" and "top Wesselton" were used in the old diamond grading scheme that eventually had to be replaced.

The reasoning behind changing to the alphabet-based grading system was two-fold. First, there were no popular grading associations. Second, consumer appeal could be disengaged by starting the color grade with "D." Especially in America, consumer's common connection with the letter "D" was a failing grade with "E" being "excellent." Not a perfect replacement, but it worked.

A few years later this color grading system set the stage for GIA diamond reports.[9]

Clearing The Air

Clarity is to cleanliness as cleanliness is to clarity.

Diamonds did have a place in religion and royalty in ages gone by, but that is not the angle we're aiming at. The cliquey rhyme assists in driving home the point that a clear diamond is a separate characteristic than the color grade.

Gas, bubbles, cracks, and scratches all contribute to the development of defects that harm a diamond's value. Clearly the absence of these intruders is directly proportional to the higher value of a diamond. A "clean" stone is a clear stone and a very clear stone is rare.

Defects are of two types. "Blemishes" are surface in nature while "inclusions" are internal. Both types can occur during the growth of the diamond in crystal form. Some blemishes can come about during or after mining.

A poorly cut stone impedes a diamond's light transmission, which in turn devalues the stone. Inclusions, if bad enough, can also affect light traveling through a diamond. These defects are specific to each stone in their number, size, and location. Numerous inclusions are the most detrimental and value-degrading. Carbon spots, minerals, and cracks are common inclusions.

It is possible for some blemishes and inclusions to be polished out during the manufacturing process, location permitting. Stones heavily burdened with inclusions are not even worthy of marketing for retail purposes and are called "Boart." These stones are ground into diamond dust and usually used as grit for polishes.

> *"Great virtues may draw attention from defects, they cannot sanctify them. A pebble surrounded by diamonds remains a common stone, and a diamond surrounded by pebbles is still a gem."*
>
> Robert G. Ingersoll,
> *The Great Infidels*

Grading varies per gemological institution. GIA grades diamonds anywhere from "Flawless" to "Included." Jewelers commonly use a microscope or loupe to examine diamonds for clarity. Loupes take a bit of getting used to, but are well worth the money and time to master. Magnification standard is 10x, yet 20x can be used to aid in exposing many a flaw within a diamond. Many chain diamond retailers sell diamonds at the low end of the clarity grading scale such as "SI" and "I." This is to be expected given the extreme expense of flawless diamonds to the average consumer. It would behoove you to invest in a diamond of at least "VS" clarity. Doing so will not only secure you a fairly "clean" stone but avoid the naked eye visibility of inclusions found in low grade "SI" stones.

It is true that the clarity of a diamond is not as much of a value influencer as cut. However, markets change due to buyer income, demand, desire for larger versus "cleaner" diamonds, and many other factors. With that in mind it is still advisable to reserve buying an "I" graded stone in smaller carat sizes given the obvious visibility of the inclusions to almost anyone who peers at the diamond for more than a few seconds.

Ever wonder what variance is allowed in diamond clarity grades? It is legal in many states for a reported diamond's clarity to be one to two grades off. That means a diamond labeled "SI" could be of only "I" quality. Of course the same is true. The seller could be declaring a diamond to be an "SI," yet a new gemological certificate you get after the sale could come back with a "VS" clarity grade.

Following big auction house (Sotheby's; Christie's) jewelry sales can be educational. Only a few record-breaking years back, Christie's auctioned off a $36-million-dollar diamond that was far from being at the top of the grading charts. This deal proves that although you can't skimp on clarity at high-end luxury gem sales, there is room for quality stones that are less than perfect.

Counting Carats

Over time it seems the general public has become fixated on size.

How often do you see large diamonds that just don't seem to

be that impressive? As we've learned, the cut of the stone is the number one influencer over diamond value. No one wants to get stuck with a tinted stone with numerous inclusions, but these factors can slide a bit in quality before the total value of the diamond is substantively affected.

Nonetheless, many times people sacrifice all important cut and its close supporters, clarity and color, for as big a diamond as they can get. It must be the erroneous assumption carried over from Real Estate that the bigger the house, the more valuable it is. Could it be ego, image, or just plain misinformation?

"Carat" originated from the ancient use of the carob seed as a constant and efficient determination of a stone's weight. One carat is a fifth of a gram, or 200 milligrams. Ancient lapidaries used the carob seed to balance their scales due to their very uniform weight.

Both rough and polished diamonds are weighed to two decimal places. Carats are further divided into points with one carat equaling 100 points.

Weighing a mounted diamond introduces a bit of complexity, but is not difficult to understand in theory. Be aware that estimating the weight of a set diamond takes a trained eye as your measurements must be extremely accurate in order for the formula to generate valid results.

Volume of the mounted stone must first be determined. Then figure the product of that calculation with the mineral's specific gravity followed by the product of the resulting figure by a set factor.

For instance, a mounted Pear-shaped diamond's weight is determined by with this formula:

$$L \times W \times D \times S.G. \times .0018 = \text{carat weight.}$$

"S.G." is specific gravity. For a diamond, it is 3.51. For emerald shape diamonds, you simply replace the factor of ".0018" with ".0025" and so on, depending on what the applicable "Dimensions to Carat Weight" chart shows for the shape of diamond you have.

Of course, no layman is ever likely to crunch these numbers, but it is useful information that can easily be verified on the internet. A little time with the good ol' thinking cap on you can verify a jeweler's estimate of a stone's weight in their own case prior to a gemological report, which can take many days of delay to get. This can be to your advantage as you can quickly estimate whether the asking price is within reason. Time is money.

> *"A diamond doesn't lose its value due to lack of admiration."*
> African Proverb

You can even change out the S.G. figure for other gemstones. As a comparison to diamonds, quarts have a specific gravity of "2.65," Rubies and sapphires come in at "4.06" with opals as low as 2.25. Fun stuff!

When you're certain of your stone's weight, you must be aware that, holding all other factors constant, diamonds are not priced linearly. So a two carat diamond will be much more expensive than a similar one carat stone. This jump in price is known as an exponential increase and is usually a shock to novices stumbling upon this reality.

When speaking of the "ideal cut," it was noted that a penalty is paying one carat prices for a "ninety-point" appearance stone. This certainly can be an issue of concern and brings up the point of price breaks. Seeking out diamond purchases where the carat weight is just under half carat increments can yield good deals. You may even be able to score a dual bonus by getting a reduced price for that "ideal cut" stone that is actually just under that carat

increment pricing scheme. Since the one carat strata has historically been a psychological benchmark, you can get a stone close to
that mark for less money while no one being the wiser. It is quite
difficult for the average person to notice the difference between a
0.90 and 1.00 carat stone in real life.

Adding to the confusion, there have been half-carat stones
worth more than a one-carat diamond. Size is only part of the
diamond value equation, which can be a tricky business, as much
art as science. "Linear logic" is not an accurate measuring stick
in the diamond industry.

Throwing yet another wrench into the works are the numbers from the spring of 2015 Sotheby's "Geneva Magnificent
Jewelry" auction that brought in a record-setting $160.9 million,
the highest ever jewelry sale total.

At $1.8 million per carat, a Fancy Vivid pink diamond sold
for over $16 million. This fabulous 8.72-carat stone also has his-
tory on its side. Napoleon Bonaparte's niece, Princess Mathilde,
was supposedly a former owner. Similar to the Krupp diamond,
there is no chart or "4 C's" plug-in to figure exactly how this
value came about.

Even rubies are breaking records. The winning bid was $30.38
million, equating to $1.2 million per carat, which was twice the
pre-sale estimate. This price level was the highest ever Ruby
price at auction.

The day following the Sotheby's auction in Geneva was the
Christie's sale that saw a 5.18 carat GIA-graded Fancy Vivid
pink go for over $2 million per carat.

Meanwhile, back to colorless diamonds, an Asian buyer
snapped up a "D," 55.52-carat Pear shape for $162,000 per carat.[10]

No matter what the carat price, it's as true today as it was
hundreds of years ago, great things come in small packages.

"Rough" Value Rules the Roost

"Roughs," as they are affectionately called in the industry, literally create the very beginning of the diamond value chain.

Most gem-quality roughs are bought by manufacturers (stone cutters and polishers), leading to traders and retailers who present these stones for sale.

Fairly recent attention on roughs has proven the appeal of these stones to celebrities and fans as well. A rough diamond's captivating natural beauty traces back to the era of Roman rule. Today we are back to breaking conventions by replacing cut diamonds with roughs as the focus in diamond rings. Everything from earrings to cuff links are incorporating roughs to show off their shimmer.

As you may expect, polished diamond sale prices heavily influence rough stone value fresh out of a mine. You might think that basic mine operation overhead coverage would dictate minimum rough value, but, as we learned in the chapter about rough diamonds, that is not always the case.

What other factors guide rough diamond value?

Our global economy significantly impacts diamond value at any given moment. You may not be personally concerned with the political or socio-economic climate in countries across the world, but you're likely to feel the effects. Good old supply and demand are obvious influencers on diamond prices. In fact, several years' worth of demand figures have proven that diamond prices, particularity for higher-end stones, are likely to continue increasing. Backing this trend is the overall diminishing supply from worldwide mines without enough new stone sources scheduled to come on line to cover reduced output.

On the subject of celebrities, our chapter covering Hollywood and diamonds revealed the great and growing appreciation the

Hollywood crowd has for fancy colored stones. After evidence of the record prices fancy stones have been commanding at famous auction houses (Christie's and Sotheby's), the Hollywood crowd was more than willing to mix and match with colored diamonds. This publicity further vaulted fancy stone value as middle-America began opening their wallets for a piece of the colored dream.

As of late many of these same stars are stepping out to embrace diamonds in the rough, literally. Foregoing cutting and polishing leaves the natural stone as mined, a unique mount for a ring.

The world has since realized that the rough-to-mount route retains inherent value, a diamond is a diamond after all.

Rough stones hold their own when it comes to value.

Even back in the fall of 2013, per-carat values for colorless roughs went as high as $66,000 and the mid to high $50,000 range was common. Size did matter concerning total value, however a 55.57 carat rough raking in almost $3.2 million stood up well to an 82 carat stone going for $4.8 million. Note that the 55-carat stone yield was $57,000 per carat, compared to the 82-carat stones at $59,000 per carat. That $66,000 per carat beauty weighed in at 78.69 carats, clearly blowing away the slightly larger 82-carat stone. Size takes a diamond only so far up the value ladder.

An extreme example of an excellent concentration of wealth and value comes from Gem Diamonds Limited's Letseng mine in 2014. Two colorless ("white") roughs, both over 160 carats, were likely to bring in up to $8 million each, according to Citi Financial analysts. One quickly sold to a partnership for about $9 million.

The mine, in Lesotho, South Africa, is known for originating four of the world's 20 largest colorless diamonds. One is a Type II while the other is Type I.[11]

A reputation such as this certainly does wonders when it comes to assigning value to roughs. The Letseng mine has raised the bar for quality stones in modern times as did the Golconda region in India back in Biblical times.

Reverse engineering has been used to accomplish some amazing feats throughout history.

Towards the end of WWII, the Russians duplicated a United States B-29 Superfortress so authentically that the same faults and breakdowns occurred with their replica that were common with the original they copied. Reverse engineering can also be a life saver. The medical community is fortunate enough to have been able to take viruses and other biological threats, dissect them, expose their weaknesses, and develop anti-bodies or other defenses against them. Consumer goods are also taken apart and put back together by competitors in order to build a "better mouse trap."

With all this reverse engineering going on within many disciplines, it should be no surprise that a simplified version of the concept has been applied to valuing rough diamonds.

"Valuers" utilize international market knowledge and technical expertise to estimate rough diamond value. The trick is applying this information precisely since, at any given moment, market data can change, and usually does in the dynamic world of diamonds.

Working back from "polished" value, expected yield and market expectation, aids valuers in their quest to accurately determine a starting point for rough valuation. Like snowflakes and people, no two diamonds are alike. Further, the growing importance of diamond types on value stones must be precisely sorted to ensure a proper starting point for valuation.

Many miners depend on Antwerp, Mumbai, New York, and other major world diamond centers to sell roughs to manufacturers. Additionally, in-house facilities may be utilized to sort and value mined stones. What may seem like a pile of light-colored pebbles to the uninitiated is money in the bank for a diamond miner.

Miners like Dominion Diamond Corporation are customer-centric. By tailoring to customers' (manufacturers') needs, all parties profit from a deal. It's a two-way street. Stones are sorted into parcels which are further tailored to meet specific customer demands. By limiting broadly varied parcels, a premium can be charged for these uniquely tailored parcels. Again, both the customer and miner benefit from this scenario. By selling some stones direct to the manufacturer, Dominion Corp. fills a market need for up to several dozen preferred purchasers.

Regardless of a specific customer request, miners' stone quality is assessed based upon each mineral specimen and its characteristics.[12]

Over time a mine will have enough data pooled, allowing predictions on what is called run-of-mine (ROM) production. Overall an aggregate ROM and typical parcel ROM will show a value expected composition of output stones.

Quality of stones produced from mines soon becomes known to manufacturers and the industry at large. To set supply and demand aside and take into account the global and local economies, politics, consumer trends and other such factors, the technical quality of roughs can be priced anywhere from about $35 to several hundred dollars per carat and above.

> "Rough diamonds may sometimes be mistaken for worthless pebbles."
>
> Thomas Browne

Reminiscent of the Indian Golconda era, Merlin Diamonds (Australian Stock Exchange) are but one contemporary example of high value stones recognized for their crystal-clear clarity and "super" white color nature. Similar to Canadian diamonds, which hit the world by storm upon their introduction, any stone characteristic that is unique offers the opportunity for branding, loyalty, and a solid value proposition.[13]

Rough diamond quality varies per producer country. There have been up to 19 rated countries ranging from poor to gem quality. Remember that the overwhelming (up to 80%) majority of all rough stones mined are below gem quality (stones suitable for jewelry). Industrial use remains the mainstay of diamond market demand.

There are stones of lesser quality than what is commonly known as industrial diamonds. Unheard-of except for industry insiders is the Crushing-Boart (or bort) category. "Borts" are essentially diamond dust formed from crushed stones, which are ironically used for diamond polishing. Varying in opacity, these stones of imperfect crystal structure are fairly dark, shard-like in appearance, and sub-par in quality. These are very popular as an abrasive industrial grit as well as effective when used in drill bits. Up to 75% of Crushing Bort comes from the Democratic Republic of Congo.

An interesting side-step in history involves De Beers and the US Justice Department. Shortly after the commencement of WWII, rough diamonds surged in value anywhere between 30 to 60% after pre-war annual increases of about 5%. Of course this was an unprecedented increase in "value." The Justice Department accused the Oppenheimers (De Beers fame) of dumping "boart" on the US market for insane profit. Allegedly millions of these inferior carats were sold at profits as high as 1,000%! Originating from the DR Congo region, estimates pegged net profits for De Beers at nearly 114% during 1943. Attempting to bring a South African company to justice proved impossible for the Justice Department during the 1940s.[14]

Value determinations must also take into account that those gem quality stones get shaped and cut, which leads to waste. Rough stones must be analyzed for deformations, inclusions, and basic shape so that post-cutting will yield the best possible polished result.

A rough in overall "good" condition will still likely loose almost 50% of its gross weight after cutting. That means a one-carat rough may be lucky to retain half its carat weight after polishing is complete. A rough in "bad" condition is not so lucky. Such a stone could wind up weighing only 0.35 carats from its original one full carat. Crystalline structure is key for cut planning.

You can easily find websites that provide rough as well as polished diamond value "calculators." Whether dubbed value finder, calculator, price estimator, or some other catchy title, you must proceed with caution. Nothing can substitute an in-person examination of a stone by an expert gemologist.

At the professional level, software algorithms sift through literally millions of possible rough stone cuts with the goal of returning the best value.

Unavailable many years ago, cutting software allows manufacturers, cutters, and others financially fit enough to pay the price of admission 3D analyses of their prized rough stones. An integral diamond calculator is included. "Advisor" is the most widely used software. Users can dictate diamond shape, clarity, carat weight, and symmetry as priority upon which the program offers prime cutting options.

Diamantaires love the inclusion scanning option and other parameters that assist in yield maximization of their on-site tenders and rough diamond bids.

Sarine Galaxy is the vendor as well as provider of other diamond systems. Users love the system's ability to provide optimum results when measuring the "4C's" with the inclusion output mapping data function.

Theoretically, this advanced software will permit less rough-to-polished diamond waste. One would hope a portion of realized savings flows through to the customer. Either way, this software is yet another piece of the diamond valuation pie, in that making the most of every stone cut helps retain inherent value.[15]

Supposedly originating from the infamous Argyle mines of Australia, here is an example of two typical rough stones.

The two stone had a "buy now" price of $1,150 and $11,500, respectively. Both were purplish in color and declared "natural" stones as well as "very rare." They also were assigned identical clarities of "SI" and as far as possible treatments, "none" was declared.

At $1,770 per carat, the smaller 0.65 carat stone was trumped by the larger 2.25 carat stone, whose asking price was $5,111.

So what is the cause for such a large gap in carat price?

Since these were rough stones yet to be cut, that factor was not even in consideration. The stone descriptions did not indicate their type subcategory. The larger stone description did claim a "very rare intense purple color" and oddly enough lists a return policy in bold letters simply stating "if item found other than as per details within 7 days."

> *"Praise, like gold and diamonds, owes its value only to its scarcity."*
>
> Samuel Johnson

The smaller stone was also stated as being very rare and pink-purple in color.

Without having any idea of the color intensity, or what kind of possible inclusions await inside the stone, one would be gambling to purchase any stone online site unseen with such a short return policy as the larger stone is burdened with.

Certainly, both stones could physically be just as advertised and the "intense" purple of the larger stone might be a real beauty. Nonetheless, rough stones can be very difficult if not impossible to trace back to the originating mine. As another check of the stone, a prospective purchaser may wish to inquire about paperwork of origin, which may include one or more intermediaries.

One last note to consider is cutting, clarity, and color. Especially in the case of the 0.65-carat stone, realize that depending on the shape diamond desired you're likely to lose much of the carat weight to the cutting process. Further, the "SI" rating wouldn't even be guaranteed by a gemological institute. A such, you could end up with an "I" stone weighing around 0.35 carats. The color issue is similar in nature. No guarantee, but likely close to what the stone really is.

Due diligence may be rough, but it is your responsibility.[16]

Very large rough stones that stay intact during formation deep within the Earth are rare finds indeed.

Not only that, these stones must survive extraction and pounding by "crushers" used to separate these crystals from the ore dug from the mine. Many roughs are unintentionally broken into smaller specimens during the mining process. More often than not a broken stone can be salvaged as its remaining part(s) can be cut separately depending on where the stone splintered. Obviously a single rough stone surviving as a whole piece provides many more cutting options, which in turn enhances overall value.

Reportedly the second-largest rough diamond of all time examined by GIA was a 1,138 carat stone. This single-crystal natural diamond is larger than the 995 carat Excelsior, yet smaller than the epic Cullinan, weighing in at 3,106 carats.

The 1,138 carat crystal comes from the DR Congo region as a natural Type Ia diamond high in nitrogen. An infrared microscope had to be used in identifying this stone as a diamond since its size prohibited fitting other examination tools.

Its grayish color was likely influenced by inclusions contributing to irregular crystal growth and the stone had a very weak blue fluorescence. The stone must have had a relatively rapid ascension given the evidence of dissolution on the stone's surface.[17]

Determining Value:
One Part Science, Three Parts Art

Receiving the correct answer to the wrong question really turns out to be the "wrong" answer.

When it comes to valuing diamonds, "50 shades of grey" barely scratches the surface of the variety and complexity involved in attempting to nail down a definitive diamond value.

You've heard the line "it depends" many times before, yet if there ever was a case in which "it depends" hits the nail on the head, diamond valuing is it. Unfortunately too many diamond buyers think they're getting a carved-in-stone valuation, when in reality their white knuckles are just clinging to a piece of opinionated paper.

"Knowledge is power."
Francis Bacon

In essence, value is what one perceives it to be.

One only needs to review De Beers' historic global role in the diamond industry to get an idea of how diamond value ebbs and flows. It should be no surprise that the price you pay for your dream diamond is influenced by many factors well beyond your control.

Popularity has provided a wave on which colored diamonds are surfing quite well, to say the least. Auction houses such as Christie's and Sotheby's hold years of record sales proof. The "invisible" market hand of supply and demand certainly has its say in diamond value based on macro and micro economic factors. Of course a particular diamond's unique characteristics have their own influences upon value. Even specific mines from which the diamond originates adds or subtracts to the value equation.

Getting back to the wrong question/right answer dilemma, make sure the valuing technique applied to your situation is a true fit for your intentions. Are you looking to insure your diamond or are you interested in resale value? Are you looking to buy or do you want an idea of market value? What about obtaining a value estimate for another purpose such as asset and wealth determination?

An appraiser needs to know what your goal is in order to estimate value to any close degree. "Market value" is often misunderstood, being that it is a legal concept that varies per jurisdiction. This is where laymen get confused. Assuming "Fair Market Value" (FMV) is "fair" may be where the trouble starts. Remember that what you paid for a diamond was transactional. That deal did not solidify anything. You may be able to turn around and trade it in for much less or sell it to a private party for a profit. The possibilities are as varied as the opportunity at hand.

There's a reason gemologists don't really issue "certificates." Issued diamond reports are just that, reports. They are similar to balance sheets for companies, a snapshot in time. Just as a balance sheet does not indicate true value, a report is not a "certification" per se, much less a guarantee, of diamond value. Estimates may be close to a figure one might actually be able to obtain on the open market. Then again, value can change as quickly as the ink dries on that estimate.

"Down and dirty" diamond valuing can be had from pricing charts.

A quick search on your favorite browser will return a plethora of links with which to search diamond value. Be aware that the discussion of "value" in this section may be better interpreted as "price," which is what these charts really provide. Nonetheless, we'll stick with the word "value" at this point.

A good rule of thumb is to assume that price chart "values" can become obsolete in a short span of time. This built-in obsolescence can occur due to many factors ranging anywhere from lack of updates, erroneous calculating formulas, biased data points, location, etc. The list of variables goes on and on.

Also keep in mind that some price calculators can be accurate for some period of time due to luck or the accuracy employed by the vendor. Take note of any fine print as you would with any other financial decision. Be highly suspicious of any price calculator, chart, or printout that even hints at guaranteeing anything.

Clearly, price calculators, value charts, or what have you, are not created equally and most of all garbage-in-garbage-out is common sense application.

Ultimately, no matter what source of information you refer to, you're the judge at the end of the day. Getting a great diamond deal is a combination of knowledge applied to the opportunity offered by the right stone at the right time. It is understandable that timing is not always a priority for certain diamond purchases. Nonetheless, a patient and informed buyer is more likely to come out ahead of the game.

Rapaport Group provides many independent pricing tools to assist professionals in their quest to remain tuned into industry news and pricing trends. The Group was established in 1976 and by 1978 had published its first Price List. Trusted by both

> *"Knowledge isn't power until it is applied."*
> Dale Carnegie

buyers and sellers, this independent benchmark can be subscribed to for electronic delivery. Historical Lists can also be had.

As a primary source of price information in the diamond industry, the average person can learn much just by picking up on a few trends and a detail here and there that will pay dividends in awareness.

In "Market Corrections," a PDF by Martin Rapaport provided in preparation for the Rapaport Groups "Expand Your Horizons" conference in Las Vegas, NV, it was stated, "We believe in fair markets and reject the notion that the interests of suppliers are more important than those of buyers." Truly free markets are free flowing as far as price is concerned. Since Rapaport's Price Lists gauge the markets accurately on a weekly basis, they have become the global standard to evaluate diamond prices. This List and other premium value aggregators act as monitors over industry sentiment, which boils down to value and price. As mentioned earlier, the Rapaport List is quite accurate, but it's no guarantee of spot-like prices, which may have something to do with the word "Report" reflected in labeling.

The List is an easy-to-read grid with a simple formula to calculate diamond prices. Much information is provided on the Rapaport site (www.diamonds.net/Prices). There is even a short video clearly explaining a few basic elements of how diamond prices are calculated. The List shows prices in US dollars and reflects New York asking prices at high cash values.

RapNet Trade Screen™ provides real-time prices based on 1 million-plus diamonds for sale on RapNet. This B-to-B platform is an online marketplace for reputable diamond professionals, but believers in the trickledown theory who are not in the industry are likely to make out what the market is up to in due time without this instant access.

The "Market Correction" PDF also outlined RapNet as pricing by the market, "not based on Rapaport opinion." Prices are independent asking prices provided by trade quotes. Further, the publication stated, "A fundamental value, purpose and function of the Rapaport Group is to create, promote, and support fair, transparent, competitive, and efficient markets." In addition, "Rapaport remains firmly committed to maintaining transparent competitive markets and honest pricing at all times, including during periods of declining prices."

Rapaport Auctions is another tool of extensive global reach for maximum exposure to market prices. A few Rapaport offices are based in the USA, India, China, Hong Kong, Israel, Dubai and Belgium.

Even "experts" disagree at what value represents. Prices change and value can be perceived as conditional at times. Diamond pricing guides range from rudimentary data fields to market-driven subscriptions that dealers live by.

Although appearing on the surface as a science, diamond valuing, with its sometimes unexpected ebbs and flows, is an art one must learn to exercise.

Diamonds are a work of nature's art. Never forget that physically examining one is still the best way to ensure you're getting what the paperwork indicates. Diamond Trading Centers (DTC's) exist for a reason, the hands-on approach remains an integral valuing metric. There is no mystery in this conclusion, for the layman can test this principle themselves by strolling down to the nearest jewelry shop and exploring the world of dazzling diamonds and their sparkling mystery.

No matter the type of party to a diamond negotiation, there are many flavors. Jewelry stores, estate sales, private deals, auctions, pawn shops, and broker-driven deals are all part of the excitement, all due to a hardy little spectacular stone.

For the uninitiated, remember that a price tag is a starting point of opinion. Profit is an acceptable part of business dealings and, depending on the side of the table you're on, an honest, unbiased opinion of value is in the eye of the beholder. Each party has a bottom line best figure in mind and their own means to justify it.

So, pleasant diamond hunting! In this industry, seeing is still a part of believing.

Mazal u'Bracha! ("May the deal be with luck & blessings!")[18]

Typecast Crystals

With a twinkle here and a twinkle there, did you ever wonder what type of diamond you have?

Part of a diamond's value is now attributed to their crystal structure and particular elements therein. At the most basic level, diamonds have been classified as either Type I or Type II. Let's stick with the facts and explore a thing or two about diamond "Type."

> *"Twinkle, twinkle, little star, How I wonder what you are. Up above the world so high, Like a diamond in the sky."*
>
> Jane Taylor

India was well-known as the only source of diamonds for hundreds of years, beginning as far back as 400 B.C. Admiring terms such as "limpid" and "ice white" have been used to describe the beauty of diamonds from India's historic Golconda region.

Being clear and transparent defines "limpid," which is a term still used in exclusive diamond industry circles. "First water" was, and is, used to unofficially declare a stone to be of the finest quality. This lingo was most common prior to the proliferation of GIA certificates and also included the phrase "whiter than white" to exemplify the purity of these early Indian diamonds.

To the casual observer, the "4C's" sums it up nicely. For Diamantaires, additional diamond traits such as proportion and specific cut add value. In the auction and investment world a "Type" designation on a certificate (report) makes all the difference.

With technological advancements and buyer preferences that prefer a deeper connection to diamond history as well as favoring perceived value of a diamond, "Type" classification is gaining popularity, and driving prices.

This is where the gemology of diamonds weighs in heavily using FTIR. With detection sensitivity, marking nitrogen at just a few parts per million spectrophotometers, specifically Fourier Transform Infrared (FTIR), can readily determine diamond type.

Nitrogen makes the difference. Only 2% of diamonds have virtually no nitrogen, making them "Type II" diamonds, while "Type I" stones contain some nitrogen and are the overwhelming majority of diamonds.

Although the diamond quality of the Golconda region was highly regarded, the diamonds were not perfect. Yes, it is theoretically possible for a "perfect" diamond to exist, but most diamonds have some sort of issue that nixes a "perfect" grade. Even some synthetic stones have been known to include man-induced imperfections in an attempt to fool the unwary.

As beautiful crystals that diamonds are, it is only possible due to carbon. During the formation of diamonds in the Earth under high pressures and temperatures, nitrogen is usually incorporated, as is the case with 98% of all natural diamonds.

Type I diamonds can have pairs of nitrogen atoms classifying them as Type Ia or isolated nitrogen atoms making these stones Type Ib.

Rare as they are, you can now see how blue diamonds have been attracting high values. Boron creates the blue color which can be found in Type IIb stones, yet not all Type II's are blue. No nitrogen is found in Type IIb stones, whereas boron and nitrogen are absent in Type IIa stones.

As with any other asset, value is usually found in scarcity as well as perception of some desired trait. The historical Golconda region of India produced many Type IIa diamonds.

Combining technology, historical significance, and scarcity, you have a grand recipe for escalating value. The diamond industry has made "Type" a branding function, which has created a flurry of activity and interest in these stones that once upon a time graded like all others.

Possessing a Type IIa stone is a level of purity ("first water") that can command up to about 15% pricing premium. Remember, presence of nitrogen is essentially considered an impurity in a stone, so the lesser the better. Even better if that level of nitrogen is as few parts-per-million as possible. The fewer the parts of the whole, the more "invisible" that nitrogen essentially becomes and, surprise, perceived value increases.

Structurally and chemically speaking, there is only a trace difference in the amount of nitrogen between a Type Ia and IIa stone. Today, markets value this small distinction on a grading certificate. Your eye can't make out the difference, but since an infrared inspection can, that is all that counts.

Very simply, a Type IIa is the market standard. A IIa designation has even pushed aside the venerable "triple EX" cutting grade that dominated the market just years ago. Time will tell how long these measures of quality on the high end of the market will take to trickle down. That might be awhile since only the major labs have spectrometers capable of splitting hairs over how many extra atoms of nitrogen actually exist in the crystal structure, never to be seen by the naked eye.

Senior VP of lab and research at GIA, Tom Moses, was reported as saying most of the Golconda region diamonds were not Type IIa. Despite this and the fact that centuries have gone by with no diamonds coming from Golconda, this region's name is tossed around as if recently mined IIa stones from another country are entitled value by mere association.

Since there is no scientific test to establish where a stone definitively came from geographically speaking, Type IIa and

Golconda spoken in the same breath is puffing at best and possible fraud at worst.

One must be careful interpreting labs issuing letters simply referring to the Golconda region without certifying the stone originating from that area. Brazil, Central Africa, and South Africa currently produce Type IIa stones that may or may not be as revered as any existing Golconda-era diamond.

There is a distinct difference between a Type IIa stone and Golconda. Not all IIa diamonds came from that region and certainly none are mined there today. It's best to treat a IIa certified grading as the "cherry on the cake" for auction hype, popular perception, and ultimate value-add purposes.

Christie's catalogs began discerning and labeling stones by type around 2007. Although many diamond sizes can be "typed," the ten-carat level and above is very common for investors "buying certs," not the diamonds themselves.

"Super D"...

...that is the contemporary term used to describe a "whiter than white" or "first water" colorless diamond. Many retailers now want the Type IIa designation on certificates. Not only is this practice now accepted as setting the stone apart from others, it adds to the bottom line.

A $150,000 per carat stone gets attention. So does one raking in $220k per carat.

Sotheby's Spring New York auction handled a 100.2-carat Type IIa D IF (internally flawless) diamond that brought in $22 million. Graded by GIA, the cut-corner rectangle shaped stone split the pre-sale estimate figure. A much smaller 22.3-carat marquise made up the 150k per carat take with a $3.3 million sale. Not bad considering price pressures on luxury items recently. It was another Type IIa D If stone.[19]

Ever popular, deep yellow "Canary" diamonds are very rare and considered "Type Ib," given their darker color. The presence of nitrogen atoms, which absorb blue light and are uniquely concentrated and dispersed throughout the diamond, are a factor in color. Orange, brown, and greenish diamonds are members of the Type Ib family.

Pale yellow diamonds contain clustered nitrogen atoms in the carbon lattice and are classified as "Type Ia" diamonds. Type I diamonds can also be colorless and, together with yellow tones, make up about 98% of all diamonds.

While each type has its benefits, the purest of the pure are "Type II's," with their rare clarity and virtual absence of nitrogen.

Is "Type" missing from your diamond's gemological report?

Large carat investors may squawk about it, but for the typical consumer there is really nothing to worry about. Simply chalk up "Type" reference as a strict selling point because when it gets down to it, neither Ia nor IIa are superior to each other, at least as far as the naked eye can tell.

Diamond Detectives Find Crystal Fingerprints

Some siblings do nothing but complain about their parents while others cherish the special connection and wouldn't trade it for the world.

> "'Are these real diamonds?' I once asked, and she said, 'Why have them if they're not?'"
>
> Elizabeth Berg

Well, diamonds don't complain and neither do some of their proud owners. In fact, when presented with evidence that polished diamonds came from the same rough stone, these same owners are elated. Similar to a simplistic genealogical search, top notch gemologists can prove "family ties" between specific diamonds. It's an amazing feat of behind-the-scenes detective sleuthing that confirms these connections.

Science that establishes the "sister stone" link involves X-rays and tomography. Although originating from the same basic building block of carbon and forming under minimum pressure and temperature extremes, the growth history of crystals and their resulting imperfections are distinctive nonetheless. Technically speaking, lattice defects are structural and imaged by X-rays while tomography detects chemical aspects unique to each rough stone.

Diamond "fingerprints" can be developed by combining these scientific physical and chemical elements. It doesn't matter what shape or quality the diamonds are after being cut from the originating rough stone since they retain a core lattice structure and chemical tags.[20]

"Sister Stones" is an unofficial term for diamonds cut from the same rough. Valuation of a pair of diamonds certified to have originated from the same rough is subjective and can be marketed in any number of ways. If the popularity of auction prices based upon diamond "Type" is any indication, there is room for diamond "fingerprinting" to have a shot at further differentiating and adding value to diamonds with this distinction. It is further respected that, with all the clamor over a diamond's "Type" these days, it is no stretch to expect a certificate to call out the fact that the inspected diamond is the "sister stone," for lack of a better term, of one or more other diamonds. Certainly, there is some value-add proposition to be had in these situations. Take the "Past/Present/Future" setting layout for example. Three diamonds from separate rough stones are not likely to be worth as much as all diamonds birthed from a single rough "mother" stone mounted on the same ring.

It's not hard to imagine a buyer paying a slight premium to acquire side stones from the same rough that the center stone was cut from. After all, diamonds mounted with other diamonds usually must be "matched" closely in color and clarity in order to avoid an odd visual effect. This is no secret, it's simply common sense that the average consumer can catch on to if not observe with his or her own eye.

Going a step further, the same concept can apply to small stones mounted in a cluster or channel style with the main diamond as focal point, all cut from the same rough stone. Although not necessarily practical to cut a rough in this fashion, a special order from a customer that is willing to foot the bill can usually get their way.

The value options are numerous. Necklaces, earrings, bracelets, and combinations such as ring/earrings can all tow the "sister stone" marketing angle quite well.

A Vision of Value

Diamonds are a work of art, natural art.

Having been formed without the intervention of man, natural diamonds are unlike any other mineral on Earth.

There are no other luxury treasures comparable to diamonds and their inherent value.

A piece of paper alone does not define substance or value. No matter how many changes occur in the diamond industry, the universal law of true value reminds us all that when you've got something great, there is no need to try to "fix" it.

Let us not forget or attempt to rewrite history. During Biblical times, civilization realized the value of true wealth. Value was so elementary that people understood that to survive one must watch over that wealth with an eagle eye. One-third was kept in the form of jewelry for the sole purpose of preparation in case of uncertain economic times. That wisdom still rings true today.

Part of a diamond's value is in its portability. Another is as a dependable storage of wealth and yet another value factor is sealed in its inherent value that it was born with.

Yes indeed, diamonds are spectacular due to their diversity. Every stone has its own make-up, a personality of sorts, that can't help but shine through. Although synthetic gems are in fact man-made, they lack the true inherent value of natural diamonds. Gem-quality imitators have their place in the market, but they also stand as a reminder of the true and enduring value of natural diamonds.

Of course the process of grading diamonds is merely a presentation of opinion. The free market itself will attribute value to each unique stone. As we've seen, not even professional jewelry auctioneers can nail down a value equation. There is a reason

> *"Angels are like diamonds. They can't be made, you have to find them. Each one is unique."*
> Jaclyn Smith

pre-sale price ranges are broadly set. With record-breaking sales occurring year in and year out, some of these price estimates underestimated reality.

Value begins at the source. Some mines, such as the Ekati and Diavik in Canada, house some of the highest grade diamond ore in the world.

The valuation of diamonds is an art with objective science principles used as tools to verify what we already appreciate, inherent and natural radiance stands the test of time.

CHAPTER 11

FAKING IT

T HE DIAMOND INDUSTRY can be a mixed bag of challenges and opportunities.

Over the years, technological advances have made the diamond trade quite interesting for consumers, investors, and diamantaires alike.

World diamond supply levels are dropping. This fact is a boon for investors, puts the squeeze on prices for consumers, and further opens up opportunities for diamonds that aren't...well..."real" natural diamonds.

Diamond industry participants have been adjusting and shifting strategy in order to remain competitive to challenges both inside and outside the industry. Of particular interest is the inroads made by "fake" diamonds and how they have and will change the way the industry does business.

Under Pressure...Again

"Pressure, pushing down on me, pressing down on you..."

That is the opening line of the song "Under Pressure," co-written by David Bowie and the super group Queen. The song speaks of the type of pressure that can affect lives.

Pressure is also known to build character. Another type of pressure persists in building up and creating the most beautiful natural creation on Earth, diamonds.

With the searing heat of over 2,000 degrees C and a force beyond about 60,000 atmospheres, nature turns carbon into a strong and stunning sought-after mineral.

In the 1950s, Lazare Kaplan and General Electric Company furthered Sweden's first demonstration of synthesis, diamonds under man-made high pressure and high temperature.

Arrival of the late 1990s opened the technology door to public awareness of how a High Pressure High Temperature (HPHT) process could alter natural diamonds. Transformations were amazing. A once ignored dim diamond became a sought after color grade D after treatment. Best results came from Type IIa diamonds and the FTC-suggested discloser. Gemological Institute of America (GIA) cooperated by inscribing "HPHT PROCESSED" and/or "IRRADIATED" on the girdle of processed diamonds.

The process essentially duplicates the heat and pressure the stone was subjected to during its creation. That original molecular stress that brought about a certain degree of yellow or brown shading is not popular in a colorless (white) diamond. The original colorless state, through the HPHT process, can be restored at the molecular level in the crystal.

Critics insist that one must assess the long term value of any treatment of diamonds. HPHT obliterates any value for investment purposes even after being sold at a steep 20–30% discount from natural diamond prices. Further, you'll have to search high and low to find a jeweler willing to negotiate at trade-in time, and good luck on the secondary market.

There have also been reports of treated diamonds clouding up years later, which makes one wonder how "permanent" diamond alterations are.

Keep in mind that a treated diamond may have had its origins in a mine, but that doesn't automatically classify it as a natural diamond in its entirety.

Dyeing and irradiation treatments have been used to darken areas of black diamonds. Many "black" diamonds are found with gray, white and clear areas. HPHT is a common treatment used to nudge these lighter sections of the stone closer to the hue of the more dark areas of the stone.

"Bringing Good Things to Life"

Permanency is serious business.

In New York and Belgium, Bellataire Diamonds embraces change to the fullest. Their business is taking "ultra-pure" natural diamonds and applying a process called HPHT to refine the characteristics of the original stone.

Although the "permanent" nature of this process is debated by experts, Bellataire emphatically answers the question, "Is the Bellataire process permanent?" with a resounding, "Yes, the process is permanent." Essentially, Bellataire fosters change for the sake of a permanency.

Ultimately, Bellataire's value proposition is permanent change. Change, through the application of a proprietary process, is applied to fairly rare nitrogen-free Type IIa diamonds. This HPHT technology has roots dating back to the 1950s.

Bellataire calls this process a restoration. The unique process restores diamonds that were destined to become "extraordinary gems." Bellataire self-describes their diamonds as "The Diamond Nature Intended."

Bellataire raves about the beauty of their diamonds and brings attention to the fact that the Bellataire logo and unique number is laser-inscribed on the girdles of their diamonds. It is also true that due to the difficulty of distinguishing from other diamonds, Bellataire's altered diamonds are identified only by gem lab equipment or said inscription.

With all the consumer concern over other less favorable diamond enhancements, Bellataire claims their diamonds are "never laser-enhanced, irradiated, fracture-filled, or altered in any way that would compromise their all-natural content."[1]

Fakes Alive? Get Real!

Remember the Memorex commercial from the 1980s? That company made audio and video cassettes advertised with the famous tag line, "Is it real or is it Memorex?"

Although Memorex never made its duplicating debut in the diamond business, there are plenty of "diamonds" that aren't authentic, natural diamonds, in the market that are much harder to distinguish from the natural masterpiece that we've loved and cherished for hundreds of years.

Despite modern lab-grown diamonds, imitations have been with us much longer, yet still leave some wondering if these impressive "fakes" can be called "diamonds."

Synthetics are sly, to say the least. They have the same crystal structure, optical, and physical properties and chemical composition as a natural diamond. Synthetic diamonds are also called "cultivated," "cultured" and man-made.

So what is classified as a diamond these days?

Simulants have subtle differences. Most notably they are look-alikes of natural gems. Simulants are known as "imitations," "simulated diamonds" or "substitutes" and can also be natural or man-made.

Confused yet?

Know this: there are only two types of diamonds: natural diamonds and synthetic diamonds. Anything else is just that, something else…but not a diamond.

On the "anything else" (simulated diamonds) side of the coin are nature-created elements (white sapphire, quartz) or man-made (cubic zirconia or CZ, moissanite, glass, yttrium aluminum garnet) substances.

Essentially, then, what we end up with can be categorized as mined diamonds, lab-created diamonds, and diamond-like materials. That being said, it is easy to see how consumers confuse the term "synthetic" with "fake" when "simulant/diamond-like materials" are the real imposters.

> *"'Are these real diamonds?' I once asked, and she said, 'Why have them if they're not?'"*
> Elizabeth Berg

In a past finding, the FTC agreed that "laboratory-created," "laboratory-grown," and "[manufacturer-name]-created" more clearly communicates the real intent behind the term "synthetic." Also, "Laboratory Grown" is inscribed on every synthetic diamond of which GIA writes a report.

Big Bank Signals Synthetic Sins

In their "Disruptive Technology in Mining" report, Citi Research declared "lab-grown diamonds" to be a "growing threat to the diamond industry."

Citi Research is a division of Citigroup, which has its head office just blocks from Tiffany & Co. main store in New York.

The 80-page report identified man-made diamonds as a "disruptive technology" that will have ripple effects upon the mining industry. Martin Rapaport, a diamond industry insider, also addressed this issue in a report titled "Sinthetics," which calls on the diamond industry to police their own and do a better job of making it easier for consumers to differentiate between natural and synthetic diamonds.

Long term, Citi's suspicions are that consumers will slowly warm up to man-made diamonds and will no longer outright reject them in favor of the real thing. The fact that these imposter diamonds have been around for many decades and most are still used in industrial applications suggests that any substantial "threat" needs more time to mature.[2]

Supply Chain Shenanigans

The subtitle of Martin Rapaport's "Sinthetics" report asks, "what should we do about it?"

Rapaport is referring to synthetic diamonds as a challenge to the integrity of our diamond industry.

The report goes on to discuss the good and bad of technology and the fraud and misrepresentation that can ultimately hurt the pricing power of authentic, natural diamonds.

In fact, it has been reported that unscrupulous companies have actually bought diamond grading reports for the purpose of creating a diamond to match the report details elements. Some synthetic diamonds have even had the GIA logo laser-inscribed with a grading report number to assist the deception.

Rest assured, most diamonds and their certified grading reveal the true nature of the stone, but we can't ignore the reality of imposters slipping through the cracks every now and then.

As with many things in life, disclosure equals transparency, a key ingredient of trust.

In this day and age, average citizens are aware that "fake"

diamonds are part and parcel of the marketplace, due to ethical marketing and disclosure. Also, consumers are quite familiar with laminate floors and countertops, look-alike brick and other similar alterations of products across multiple other industries.

In the last model year, Ford boldly pushed the limits of tradition in favor of massive change. At a distance, as well as up close and personal, a gleaming pick-up truck on the showroom floor or in your driveway looks the same whether it sports a steel or aluminum body. You don't have to be an engineer to realize that aluminum used in place of steel for a "rough-and-tough" pick-up truck has turned heads, quite a few in the industry for sure. Of course, the point is that Ford never attempted to hide the fact of "going aluminum." Although pick-up truck purists make no bones about their skepticism concerning this major change, there are significant advantages for the much lighter weight yet "tough" new aluminum body construction.

Congratulations to Ford for handling this major change effectively. Those along the diamond supply chain could learn a few business lessons from the auto industry giant, particularly when it comes to standing by your product to ensure that your customers get the facts.

For argument's sake, let's say there was absolutely no way to determine if the diamond on your finger is natural or not. If this situation were the new reality, what value would you place on this stone, since no one would know if it is natural or synthetic? With this new reality, one outcome would be prices of a "natural" diamond falling to that of the imposter (fake) diamonds. Or, worse yet, the going market price of the fake stone might shoot up toward that of natural diamonds. Either way, this would flood the diamond industry with waves of doubt and instability. Long-term diamond value would suffer.

Fortunately, this is not the case. A key point is that the diamond industry is in the best position to verify distinct differences between synthetic and natural diamonds, has the equipment to detect these differences, and even document them. However, without ultimate disclosure to the consumer, "integrity" and "trust" are hollow hopes.

Thanks to the infamous De Beers' "diamonds are forever" marketing slogan, symbolic value has been attached to diamonds, specifically, to naturally occurring stones. Natural diamonds are truly unique in that they mark special occasions and are the ultimate physical representation of true, pure love.

Nonetheless it has been argued that synthetic diamonds can actually benefit, not threaten, the existence of natural diamonds.

Industry insiders along the diamond supply chain can no longer point the finger at "fake diamonds" while labeling them a scapegoat for the industry's woes. Synthetics have proven to be worthy competition, they are here to stay.

Rapaport keenly hints that the "buck stops" with retailers. They are the last line of defense to ensure that if natural and synthetic stones are mixed, procedures are in place to reveal and disclose the truth. Loading up jewelry display cases with undisclosed synthetic diamonds clearly isn't the solution, much less ethical. B2B players, unlike consumers, have the inside knowledge to identify and control infiltration of synthetic diamonds. Common sense dictates that consumers have a right to know what they are buying, real or fake.

Opposition from downstream (distributors and the like) on the diamond supply chain complain that it is too expensive to test each and every stone. Sources known for mixing stones are China and India. They also take the position that infiltration of synthetic stones is an unintended consequence of "batch" testing, which has been industry standard for some time now. This random selection of diamonds from a shipment pool for testing obviously has flaws. Many times there is no written authentication of the testing itself or details of the testing method. Retailers are justified in their concern of what is seen as "forced" misrepresentation of stones and the erosion of integrity that results across the entire diamond industry.

Overall, the one-of-a-kind aura of natural stones is a powerful marketing tool. Rapaport speaks of being and remaining "Supplier of Choice." Natural, authentic diamond retailers don't have to "defend" the value of natural stones. That is a reactive stance. Instead, they need only to clearly position the facts to make synthetics "climb the marketing hill." Since the beauty of natural diamonds is undeniable, this is a point of leveraged differentiation. Value inherent in being "the real thing" is the ultimate basis for a higher price point for natural diamonds.

Technological investment in the diamond field has been occurring for some time now. At first glance, tech advancements are welcome. On the other side of the coin, credibility must be upheld to safeguard "consumers against the risk of undisclosed treatments and synthetics," says Rapaport.

In addition to setting natural diamonds apart, synthetics have already been accepted as an avenue to expand profits. Diamond retailers can also take a cue from the music industry, where the opening entertainment is simply a prelude to the main act. The same spotlight may shine on both, but the sparkle from the star of the show (natural diamonds) is a step above, spectacular![3]

Persuasive Pledge

One takes notice upon running across a business that says what it means and means what it says.

Here are a few excerpts from a mineral vendor's "Pledge to My Customers" declaration:

"All minerals offered will be naturally crystallized specimens, no fakes, no dyes, no irradiation, no crystals glued on matrix."

"Only the exact item pictured on the site will be shipped, no substitutes."

"Photographs will accurately represent each item, no exaggeration, enhancement, or retouching flaws."

"Mineral species and localities will be accurately listed on labels with each specimen."

"All historic labeling, if available, will be included with each mineral."

"Returns are gladly accepted. No questions asked, no explanation necessary."

"All mineral specimens have a lifetime guarantee: if the mineral specimen is ever tested, and I incorrectly identified the mineral species, I will refund the cost of the original purchase and shipping, the cost return shipping, and the cost of the test."

"I will continue to freely share my knowledge with others and contribute to the study and appreciation of minerals."

The above are just a sampling of the owner's commitment to customer satisfaction that can be applied to not only the diamond industry, but many other businesses in order to establish the kind of integrity and trust that fosters repeat business.[4]

The 4 D's

That is why the ubiquitous "4 C's" depend on the "4 D's" for their very existence.

Without safeguards allowing natural diamonds to be authenticated and proven as such to consumers with integrity, the outlook would be grim for the jewelry industry.

A top-notch security system has built-in layers of protection to ensure your property, wellbeing, and other assets remain safe.

Such is the case with the "4 D's" in the quest to separate natural stones from synthetics.

The end game is documentation. This gives consumers and investors the peace of mind that the diamond they now own is authentic. For the customer, trust is earned, which prompts repeat business. On the investment front, a certificate of authenticity makes resale of any asset a smooth transaction as well as enabling liquidity.

Documentation, disclosure, and detection allow one to differentiate between natural and synthetic stones. All four of these "D's" work in synergy supporting each other.

A manufacturer is the affirmative source of any paperwork necessary to document the chain-of-custody of a diamond, which becomes critical in detecting any "leaks" in the supply chain. Declarations on invoices, direct delivery (with a tamper-proof seal) and grading reports are tools to help ensure integrity remains an integral part of calling out synthetic stones posing as natural diamonds. Grading reports aren't a sure thing, but they do enhance the paper trail.

Detecting synthetics is a deterrent to illicit activity and guards against accidental mixing. Machines such as the Automated Melee Screening (AMS) from De Beers detect synthetic diamonds and can be costly. Originally only available to De Beers sightholders, a three year lease for an AMS ran about $25,000 per year.

Parcel (batch) became popular due to the expense of testing every diamond to a 100% confidence level, especially small melee stones.

"Peppering" a parcel of natural diamonds with fake stones is a more difficult trick to get away with now that GIA offers World Federation of Diamond Bourses (WFDB) members diamond testing instruments.

Once detection is completed, full disclosure becomes a center stage, necessary and legal requirement.

With as much as 90% of the world's diamonds being cut in India every year, the task of disclosure can seem at first glance to be insurmountable. India has over 2,000 cutting factories and over 300,000 cutters. Adding to these numbers are polishers, suppliers, and distributors. Open market diamond trading involves many twists and turns in the path of a diamond on its way to the consumer. There are many handlers of a single diamond when a broker receives an order and searches any number of suppliers for fulfillment.[5]

To Test or Not to Test

Unlike the Kimberley Process (KP), synthetic diamonds can be tested and identified in an objective manner even after they're sold. One cannot simply look at, much less "test," a diamond and legitimately declare it a "blood" diamond, or not. Although clearly effective at deterring conflict diamonds worldwide, the KP is not an airtight, proof-positive system. To a limited degree, the same can be said of synthetic diamond testing, at least concerning large mixed parcels of stones.

How? In the case of mixed parcels, the WFDB borrowed portions of KP conflict diamond language that introduces instances of second-guessing. Despite the requirement of an "affirmative" statement on invoices declaring the shipment contains natural diamonds, there may be multiple statements depending on how many suppliers held the stone at any given time along the chain-of-custody. What we end up with is a supplier statement based on their supplier's statement, which came about from possibly any number of previous supply statements. As you see, the term "cloud-on-title," used in real estate to question the validity of ownership of claim is relevant here.

The problem is compounded with small melee stones in large quantities. It is extremely difficult and expensive to track the source of all these stones. Open markets, with their characteristic "chain reaction of transactions," make it easy for all along the transaction chain to rubber-stamp invoices with assurances of product identity that may not really be the case.

In order to ensure that retailers' and consumers' protection is at the highest level, disclosure must relate to the circumstance at hand. Have an order of synthetic diamonds? The invoice or memo should clearly state such. Can't be definitively sure what type of diamond a parcel contains? Boldly reveal that fact as "Sold AS IS" or "Sold AS IS. Not tested." Has the sample been tested? Indicate "Sample Tested" with a tolerance level denoted as a percentage.

At the retail level, proactive testing of diamonds is critical to maintain a high bar when it comes to customer trust in a jeweler. Along the supply chain, testing can occur at any point. Nonetheless, retailers represent the last stand when it comes to releasing a diamond to the public and the first to hear complaints if a stone advertised as natural comes back from grading as a synthetic.

Think of testing as adding value. As mentioned above, the "threat" of synthetics is only as real as one will allow. Natural diamonds are truly unique. Nothing comes close to the pride in a customer's voice confidently declaring, "I own a natural, one-of-a-kind diamond."[6]

Synthetic? Yes, it is…No, it isn't…Yes, it is…

Erring on the side of caution is usually the best practice. Verified scientific evidence is vital in debunking any unsubstantiated claims concerning diamonds and other jewelry. Without a definitive answer from industry authority figures, confusion would reign.

Antwerp became involved in a controversy over natural versus synthetic stone detection between De Beers (backed by GIA) and the European EGL and EGL Hong Kong.

At the heart of the issue was a specific type of diamond, an "IaAB." De Beers claims a synthetic of this pure type cannot be replicated while EGL Hong Kong states both DiamondSure™ and DiamondView™ systems (both by De Beers) failed to detect the alleged synthetic stone that their associated company's DiamaTest™ system identified correctly.

Over the last several years, much controversy has risen over synthetic diamonds making their way into parcels of natural diamonds. Many safeguards have been implemented to curb this practice. Industry insiders such as De Beers, EGL, and GIA have successfully remained ahead of the curve of detecting the ever-improving "diamond-like" quality synthetics.

When a stone is suspected of being synthetic, systems like those offered by De Beers provide three options to determine if such is the case. DiamondPlus™ actually examines natural diamonds to detect high pressure, high temperature (HPHT) treatments. Diamond View™ determines whether the stone in question is in fact natural or synthetic, while DiamondSure™ is the initial screening system designed to pick out Type II diamonds that may be synthetic.

Unless a cutting edge development in the era of synthetic diamond creation is being hidden from the industry, De Beers is scientifically correct in its position that a lab cannot replicate the natural nitrogen aggregation sequence in Earth born diamonds. Any stones not matching this complex natural structure are set aside for "further testing" by De Beers' machines based on their algorithm that reveals heat treatments on synthetic stones.

In the case where a stone was subjected to a secondary treatment in an attempt to hide the primary treatment, a classification of "undetermined" is a likely outcome.

Prior to persistent reports of lab stones being mixed with natural melees (under one-carat), back in 2013 chemical vapor deposition (CVD) synthetics were uncovered at the labs of International Gemological Institute (IGI) in Antwerp and Mumbai.

With this continuing infiltration of synthetics, bourses in Dubai, Hong Kong, New York, Tel Aviv, Tokyo, and other centers around the world have received detection instruments from De Beers.

GIA assured that the DiamondCheck device gives no false positives. All diamond samples are labeled "natural," "non-diamond" or "further lab testing for treatment or synthetics."[7]

"Treating" Carats to a Color Correction

A substitution is just that, an imposter, a pretender.

A substitution, commonly known as a "fake," can look the part at a distance. Upon closer examination, most will agree there is nothing like the real thing.

This isn't to say that treated diamonds don't have their own character and attraction. Both synthetic and treated stones have price and uniformity of color advantages that are very appealing to the uninitiated. "To each their own," as they say.

What you must consider, however, is stability, in every sense of the word.

Naturally colored diamonds have stood the test of time. Significant price appreciation has extended for well over a decade-and-a-half.

Treated or synthetic stones have long-term weaknesses that may not be obvious up-front. Resale value is going to be less than stellar. Color coming from treatment can change over time. That colored hue may hang on for years, but long-term staying power is not guaranteed. You'll need to prove the origin of a stone and have a certificate from a reputable lab in order for a serious auction house to give it the time of day on the block. All in all, serious buyers demand natural diamonds since nothing else is as exceptional, rare, or unique. Similar to their colorless sister stones, no two colored natural diamonds are the same. True intrinsic value is difficult to justify when it comes to synthetic or treated stones.

Irradiation is used to darken the hue of colored stones to produce a richer look.

Creating colored diamonds in a lab utilizes man-made methods to duplicate the "tricks" nature plays when forming natural stones of color. A lab performs "magic" when treating a colorless diamond that has a tinge of yellow. A thin coat of blue coloring is applied, neutralizing the yellow and thus enabling a higher color grade.

In the case of purple stones, a basic guideline followed by professionals is the premise that the natural purple's deformation lamellae has concentrations of color while the treated stone are saturated throughout. This color distribution scheme is a common way to delineate enhancement from naturally occurring color.

Natural fancy colored stones are born similar to pearls in that introduction of a foreign element into the carbon is one method of birth. Pressure and natural radiation are two separate ways in which colored diamonds originate. No matter what origin, natural colored stones are very rare, which reflects upper tier pricing. That is to be expected at a typical 10,000:1 ratio of natural fancy colored stone to colorless.

Lab stones simply simulate natural beauties. What took our beloved Earth eons to birth can be accomplished by a lab in a matter of weeks. Carbon is common to both the natural stone and its purely synthetic substitute. Today's technology is very impressive in that a man-made stone has only subtle crystal structural differences from a natural stone.[8]

Chameleon Colored Carats

For some time now, a variety of products have been flying off retailer shelves, allowing people to whiten their teeth. Dentists are still able to charge higher fees for their special whitening systems, since the cheaper versions publically available either couldn't live up to expectations or don't maintain that bright Hollywood smile long enough.

It's really no stretch of the imagination to hear that in May of 2015 GIA labs in Israel issued a "laboratory alert" warning that previously graded diamonds changed color, all on their own!

You don't have to be a gemologist to suspect that eventually this was bound to happen. GIA suspects the submitted diamonds were subjected to some kind of temporary color altering treatment. As GIA investigated, the clients identified with this issue had their diamond submissions suspended. GIA also alerted industry trade bodies. Submitting stones to any lab for grading without disclosing a known treatment or alteration can be considered fraud.

The alleged treatment of these diamonds masked their inherent color for a short period of time. This was no small feat since the color change, discovered after grading certificates were issued, was up to three color grades. That variance is large enough to warrant up to a 60% price premium in diamond price in many cases.

Grading reports of these diamonds were recalled and RapNet delisted all the offending diamonds.[9]

What's the difference between a "Classic" and "Reverse" chameleon?

First we must distinguish olive green from light yellow chameleons. Then we must determine which type of chameleon reacts to changes in heat and light.

"Classic" chameleons are olive green and react to both heat

> *"Beauty is in the eye of the beholder."*
> Oliver Platt

(thermochromic) and light (photochromic), while "Reverse" (light yellow) type only favor heat for their color changing habits.

Have you figured out this odd puzzle of color?

The "Classics" like to go from olive green in hue to yellow or brownish yellow while the "Reverse" transition into intense greenish yellow from light yellow. The chameleons were first documented in the early 1940s but have unknown geographic origins. Thirty-nine such chameleons were studied. Having been purchased between 1987 and 2004, they came from Tel Aviv, Antwerp, and India.

Did you realize that chameleons were world travelers?

As rare gems, Chameleon diamonds are very unique minerals. In 2005, a study (A Gemological Study of a Collection of Chameleon Diamonds) examined these GIA or EGL graded diamonds concerning color change surrounding particular circumstances that included heating to approximately 150 degrees Celsius and prolonged storage in the dark. Testing must be strictly controlled since prolonged heat may permanently cause color change.

"A Green Diamond: A Study of Chameleonism," a report from 1995 delved further into "Classic" chameleon characteristics related to thermos-chromic properties.

To return to the subject of a temporary color changing treatment that threw GIA for a loop early in 2015 illuminates something more complex than already known chameleon diamonds.

As answers become clear, we are likely to see game changing elements, as seen from Yehuda Treatment (1980s) and Bellataire diamonds (GE & Lazare Kaplan; 1990s). These technological events forced the gemological world to develop protocols based on extensive studies (thousands of stones studied) pursued to identify, detect, and understand the underlying new treatment.

With Yehuda and HPHT, the color change was quite stable

and permanent. This latest "now-you-see-it-now-you-don't" spontaneous color-changing witnessed by the gem industry is, shall we say, revolutionary. Remember, several hundred diamonds received the GIA stamp of approval, which lasted a very short time indeed.

Only time will tell what "trigger" may have been part of the reversal of color after the grading process was officially completed.

How extensive might this color reversing magic be?

Thus far, the overwhelming stone size was greater than 1 carat. Some of these color-shifting stones were up to 5 carats. Those were graded in New York or California. Despite the flurry of activity and police presence at the Israel lab, graded stones at that lab were capped at the 3 carat weight and below.

Ultimately, what we have here, is a reversible treatment process that leaves no traces, was meant to defraud, and demands unequivocal answers to restore market tranquility. The good news is that turmoil in any industry almost always elevates that market to new levels of stability and prosperity.[10]

Mother Stones Stand for Stability

Diamond grading labs and diamond trading centers around the world have systems for detecting synthetic and treated diamonds. These methods and machines are technologically necessary tools that assist in drawing the line between what is classified as a natural diamond and the rest.

A much older and similar comparison technique is a set of Mother Stones used as a base line for judging diamond color when grading diamonds.

Replicas of the Mother Stones are acceptable as an objective basis for grading. The average consumer may not know that all colorless diamonds are not the same color. In the same way a synthetic or treated diamond suffers a price discount on the open market, so does the "whiteness" of a colorless diamond or the hue and saturation of a colored stone. A "dim" (yellowish to brownish) colorless diamond loses value, as does a weak hued and/or less spectacular saturated colored stone.

Reference stones (Mother Stones) used to grade diamond color are part of a thorough grading process that includes ever-advancing lab systems to detect man-made diamonds.

No Cover-Up Here

Worn out phase? Cliché statement? Hardly.

Despite the true advantages and inherent beauty of natural diamonds, there will always be room for healthy competition.

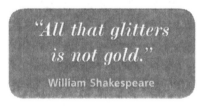

"All that glitters is not gold."

William Shakespeare

Imitators have their place, but it's the consumer that ultimately calls the shots by voting with their feet and dollars at the register.

A copied work of art can be admired, but no matter how you slice it an original is priceless. All else pales in comparison. Real diamonds equal real value.

Natural diamonds, colored or colorless, are like authentic artwork, one of a kind.

CHAPTER 12

DIAMONDS IN DANGER

"WHAT IS THE *status of the alarm?*"

"*Fully functional,*" the operator said, checking the signals coming in from the Diamond Center. "*The vault is secure.*"

"*Then how is it that the door is wide open and I'm standing inside the vault?*" That is what a surprised Mr. De Bruycker declared while moving about within the breached vault in the subterranean chamber area of the Diamond Center in the Antwerp Diamond District.[1]

Mr. De Bruycker and Mr. Peys, both members of the Diamond Squad, arrived at the Diamond Center that morning in response to a frantic call alerting them that the vault had been compromised.

The above conversation occurred between De Bruycker and the vault alarm company after he requested a nationwide alert be issued by headquarters.

Their worst fears had been realized.

The Antwerp Diamond Center had been robbed. Over 100 of the 189 safe-deposit boxes had been broken into and their contents (cases, satchels, backpacks, etc.) had been strewn into a heap in the middle of the vault floor.

How could this have happened?

The Diamond Squad

In 2003, the year of the heist, about $3 billion in gem sales were reported in the Diamond District, a true perpetrator's paradise.

Oddly enough, three years earlier the Belgian government hired Peys and De Bruycker to head up the newly formed Diamond Squad. As specialized "diamond police," the squad was to keep watch over the Antwerp Diamond District.

It was determined that a small, tight-knit crew were the likely perpetrators and the robbery was initially a success for several reasons.

First, the venerable Diamond Center had been penetrated undetected…no alarms and no police. As the cliché goes, "Like a thief in the night," the robbers slipped in and slipped out of the Diamond Center vault, a colossal challenge on its own.

Second, an estimated $100 million in jewelry, loose diamonds, gold, and other valuables were stolen. In fact, the thieves made off with more than they could carry. Many security boxes remained unopened and strewn upon the vault floor were beautiful treasures, left behind in the thieves' hasty departure.

Heist of the Century

Authorities had difficulty figuring out just how the robbers pulled off such a grand theft and escape given the heightened security in the Antwerp Diamond District.

Over 60 video cameras saturate the three-square-block Diamond District and the area is also under 24-hour police surveillance. There was even a private security force.

Doppler radar, a seismic sensor, and a lock with 100 million possible combinations were just a few of the many layers of security protecting the vault area. Infrared heat detectors, a magnetic field, a locked steel grate, and a light detector were also part of the security layers. The vault door itself was about one foot thick and weighed in at three tons.

The vault was thought to be impregnable.

Enter Leonardo Notarbartolo, born Palermo, Sicily, and leader of the heist clan. He claims he found himself in a replicated vault room hidden under black tarp inside a warehouse outside the limits of Antwerp.

It was clear to Notarbartolo that the diamond dealer, a true *diamantaire*, used pictures from a small pen camera to construct the replicated surroundings they both stood within. Notarbartolo, who showed up to the warehouse by request of the dealer, hadn't heard from the dealer for about five months. Notarbartolo claims the dealer made clear his intent to provide necessary resources to break into the Diamond Center vault and the replicated vault certainly was proof that he was serious.

They had both briefly met at a café overlooking the Diamond District about five months prior where, upon leaving the café and taking a stroll outside the District area Notarbartolo, claimed the diamond dealer asked him if the vault could be broken into without alarm. He said the dealer paid him a substantial "fee," even though Notarbartolo's answer was that a vault break-in and successful escape was not feasible. That fateful meeting at the warehouse changed his mind since the *diamantaire had also upped the ante with a niched crew of top-notch thieves.*

Notarbartolo fell in love with being a thief at the very early age of six after rifling through a sleeping milk man's pockets. As he grew older he assembled small teams of specialized thieves to pull off detailed jobs. All along he honed his tracking and observation skills by following jewelry salesmen around Italy in order to observe their habits.

By his own admission, Notarbartolo pulled off many major jobs by 2000 and found himself making frequent trips to his new office at the Diamond District, making deals while infiltrating the diamond industry's insider secrets. In fact, it got to the point where his visits to the vault were frequent enough that the guards became complacent.

Snarling Security Systems with Hairspray, Tape and Wire

The three-ton vault door with six separate layers of security didn't make a difference.

That same door's combination wheel with 100 million possible combinations wasn't even a factor.

The dual motion/heat sensor and light sensor inside the vault did not deter the heist crew either.

You see, Notarbartolo's countless visits to the vault revealed a major security lapse. The original vault key, of which the heist crew had previously fabricated a foot-long duplicate, was hanging freely in the utility room. Prior to opening the vault, a guard would return from this room. The heist crew's hunch was correct. At the time of the break-in they made a bee-line to the utility room and grabbed the original key to gain entry.

The sensors were effectively bypassed with everyday hair spray and tape.

The day before the heist in February, 2003, Notarbartolo took advantage of a brief moment alone in the vault to disable the motion/heat sensor by applying hair spray on its outer lens. He did this while under video surveillance yet no one caught him in the act.

The crew disabled the light sensor after gaining access to the vault with common tape. Keeping the lights off while opening the vault door and approaching the sensor in the dark was all it took to defeat this vault defense. Notarbartolo's crew had practiced this action time and time again in the diamond dealer's mock vault built in the old warehouse.

Once inside the vault, one crew member systematically made his way to the main system's electrical feed in the ceiling, then bridged the inbound and outbound wires. This cut electricity to the vault's technological defenses and provided the thieves with a large safety margin.

A simple bridge of wire, tape, and hair spray were strategically used to defeat one of the world's most "secure" subterranean vaults. As you can see, these "hacks" that the thieves used were very successful.

Of course, it didn't help the reputation of the Diamond Center that the vault key was left openly available in a common utility closet.

Diamond Games and Back Door Break-Ins

Before reaching the vault, Notarbartolo's crew had to gain access to the Diamond Center itself.

A crew member called "The King of Keys" cunningly selected a neighboring run-down office building whose lock he picked at around the midnight hour. The back of this building had a private garden adjoining the Diamond Center. Better yet, this area lacked video surveillance. A ladder, hidden earlier, was used to reach the Diamond Center's second floor terrace.

The crew avoided setting off an infrared detector by utilizing a low thermal conductive polyester shield made specifically for this purpose.

During this early maneuver to penetrate Diamond Center defenses, Notarbartolo was in his Peugeot, on a nearby street, monitoring a police scanner. His cell phone was at the ready, waiting to hear from his crew soon after they breached the vault.

It is interesting to note that the "Diamond Games" semifinals were in Antwerp at the time of the heist and a big reason the Diamond District was deserted. These games championed Antwerp as king of the gem world and many diamantaires were in attendance. The winner would receive a stone-encrusted tennis racket worth nearly $1 million.

Notarbartolo saw Antwerp as a thief's paradise. He posed as a Italian gem importer and his charm soon christened him as the "Jolly Jeweler," even though his French language was not up to par. Diamond jewelry stolen in Italy could easily be sold for cash in Antwerp after being taken apart, the perfect locale to fence hot diamonds.

An Antwerp espresso café that Notarbartolo frequented was in the middle of the world's diamond trade. In the summer of 2001, he peered out of the café window and watched hundreds of millions, if not billions of dollars in diamonds pass by the café in the satchels, cases, and other protective carrying devices of the diamond traders. At the end of the day the diamonds were stored in the Center's vault.

In 2003 De Beers controlled about 55% of the global diamond supply as the world's largest diamond-mining operation. Many De Beers distributors were Antwerp-based and a monthly shipment of rough diamonds in about 120 boxes arrived at the Diamond Center from London. These deliveries, worth millions, were known as "payday" and left the Diamond District flush with wealth. Within two days Notarbartolo's crew made their move against one of the hardest targets (the vault) they'd ever seen.

Conspiracy Theory or Insurance Fraud?

The Italian mafia's reputation is known worldwide and for some time Notarbartolo, and his family, had long been suspected of being members. Their ties to the Sicilian mob were suspected by the Italian "anti-mafia" police and even Notarbartolo's extended family was beleaguered by accusations.

With that history in mind, and a good dose of common sense, Notarbartolo planned to return to the Diamond Center after the heist, hoping not to arouse suspicions of the police. Had Notarbartolo been absent immediately after the heist, or worse yet disappeared altogether, he most certainly would be listed as the number one suspect.

The crew's intentions were to split the loot in Milan. In a prison interview from 2009, Notarbartolo stated that his crew took only $20 million in jewels from the vault since that was all they found. Police estimated, due to diamond dealer claims, about $100 million worth of jewels were stolen from their security boxes during the vault heist.

Why the apparent $80 million difference?

Notarbartolo claims he was set up, used as a pawn for insurance fraud committed by the diamond dealers themselves.

Assuming Notarbartolo's claims to be correct, the diamantaires stood to gain by a windfall with limited, if any, fallout.

The theory unfolds like this:

A diamond dealer, or dealers, as the case may be, plans an elaborate insurance fraud scheme.

They carefully approach an expert thief (Notarbartolo) with alleged mob connections to rob the Diamond Center vault.

The dealers, already primed with inside knowledge, assist in basic heist plans, being vigilant to avoid getting their hands dirty by staying far away from the planning efforts.

Once their unsuspecting thief commits to the heist, the dealers follow through with the second phase of their clandestine plan by secretly removing from their own security boxes the bulk of their assets, diamonds.

With an ironic twist representing true mob motive, the diamantaires ensure staying "clean" by carefully calling orders from the top, minimizing communications, and covering their tracks every step of the way.

At the time of the heist, the dealers' alibi is their attendance at the Diamond Games.

Predicting building pressure and questions from authorities after the heist, the dealers either shrug their shoulders while displaying shock at being "robbed" and remain silent, or deflect focus from themselves by pointing the finger at someone else, such as an Italian "outsider" like Notarbartolo.

With virtually no proof of diamond dealer involvement, much less any accusations from their "own kind" in the Diamond District community, they move forward with insurance claims by declaring themselves victims of property theft.

Notarbartolo seems to believe he was set up and used like pawn.

You decide, dazzling diamantaire genius or delusional diamond thief?

It is no surprise that part of the diamond trading business is done "under the table" in the Diamond District. Citing the close knit family and culture element, many go as far as to say a percentage of diamond trading in Antwerp is "off table." If that is the case, then it is no stretch of the imagination to suppose that the Diamond Center may have involved a "now-you-see-it-now-you-don't" diamond disappearing act prior to heist, courtesy of local diamond dealers.

Further, it makes one wonder why a crew like Notarbartolo's would risk such a complicated heist upon one of the world's greatest concentrations of wealth, with all the security obstacles to overcome, only to divide up $20 million.

Does it not seem more plausible that Notarbartolo, his crew, as well as the diamond dealers themselves would risk an illegal venture of this magnitude only if the payoff was substantial?

What do you believe?

Getting Caught Holding the "Trash"

The hardest part was over. Notarbartolo and his crew made it out of the breached vault and the Diamond District without alarms, police radio chatter, or private security being aware of their presence.

But one of the crew, a long-time friend of Notarbartolo's, was about to sink the whole deal just as they were in the midst of making their getaway.

"Speedy," as he was called, was not wanted by the others on this job in the first place. He was considered a liability. Notarbartolo, despite his better judgment, stuck up for his friend and made Speedy part of the team anyway. Friends since childhood, Notarbartolo stayed loyal to Speedy despite knowing he routinely "came apart" after a job.

They were about to destroy incriminating evidence when Speedy started showing signs of a panic attack. Speedy was a willing participant in the "perfect" heist with millions of dollars' worth of jewelry and diamonds to show for it, yet he couldn't control his growing anxiety leading up to his inevitable panic attack.

In an effort to calm Speedy down, Notarbartolo detoured from their route and onto a path that led into brush cover and a forested area. The garbage bag full of evidence in the car's backseat had to be disposed of now, to appease Speedy. Before Notarbartolo could find an area and the means to rid them of the evidence, Speedy lost it.

Stories differ on what happened next. Some say they tried to burn the evidence. Others say Speedy spread the bag of evidence around and that several diamonds were found. Yet another report stated that Diamond Center security videotape was amongst the rubbish.

No matter the condition of it, the evidence was abandoned on land on which the owner had repeated problems with dumping and littering. Having come across yet another pile of garbage, Van Camp, the land owner, made his usual call to police, who were at first reluctant to investigate. Van Camp's passing of information that the "trash" contents were unusual got a response. After piecing together a surveillance invoice with Notarbartolo's address from the refuse and finding a few loose diamonds, Belgian diamond detectives alerted Italian police who were now primed to search Notarbartolo's house.

Although Notarbartolo attempted to stall police at the Diamond District while being questioned, they eventually made their way to his home where, loaded down with bags and a rolled-up carpet, family and friends appeared to be in a hurry taking out the "trash."

Everyone present was taken into custody. The "trash" contained prepaid SIM cards whose stored data logged being in the Diamond District locale during the heist. "Monster," "Speedy," and "Genius" were three Italians linked to cell phones the SIM cards showed were called repeatedly.

Overcoming significant odds of bypassing a high security diamond vault wasn't good enough for a clean getaway. It all came tumbling down due to a paper invoice and a few SIM cards that helped piece together the puzzle of who had done it.

Had police arrived at Notarbartolo's house minutes later, the evidence would have been gone.

Out of Prison and Back in Hot Water

In 2014, several months after being released from prison, Milan police found Notarbartolo with over two pounds of rough diamonds in his BMW.

He had already served six years in prison and now was being detained due to the Diamond Center diamonds never being recovered and the discovery of stashed diamonds in a "convicts" car.

Basilio Foti, Notarbartolo's lawyer, is advocating the return of the diamonds based on the fact that they are industrial grade, rather than precious, diamonds.

Aren't rough diamonds "rough diamonds"?

No. Notarbartolo was found with virtually untraceable industrial grade diamonds. Although it looks suspicious, common sense would dictate that prosecutors would have to prove that these are the same diamonds from the Diamond Center heist.

The confiscated diamonds are likely to be back in Notarbartolo's hands unless it's proven that they are linked to the Antwerp heist or that he stole them from someone or someplace else. He claims that he paid 10,000 euros for the bunch of them, a cheap price, since they were less valuable industrial grade.

Rough diamonds are not certified by the diamond industry as they are soon to be cut and polished for their intended purpose based on their inherent quality or lack thereof, gem quality or industrial.

Via laser-etching logos and certification numbers that are invisible to the naked eye, gem quality polished diamonds are blessed with a unique identity.

Proving, with no uncertainty, the diamonds found in

Notarbartolo's BMW are the same from the diamond heist of six years ago will be almost impossible.

Could they be the same diamonds?

Yes, it's possible. There just isn't sufficient evidence to prove it.[2]

Antwerp's Diamond Center Vault, Tough, but no Fort Knox

The Antwerp Diamond Center is listed as number five in a *Top 6 Guarded Vaults in The World* comparison.[3]

What vaults beat out Antwerp, and why?

You may be surprised to learn that even with all the technology and electronics in our modern society, a plain key, yes, the kind most of us use to lock the front door to our homes, remains a critical layer of defense guarding the Bank of England Gold Vault. Second only to the NY Federal Reserve in the amount of stored gold, this UK vault has multiple three-foot long keys in addition to a voice recognition and bombproof door.

Antwerp's door had one such key for its three-ton door. Although this foot-thick door could withstand nonstop drilling for twelve hours and included a seismic alarm alerting of the first turn of a drill bit, it was bypassed.

Voice recognition programing and multiple physical keys of the UK vault make things more challenging for even the most cunning thieves.

And yes, it's true, the Bank of England Gold Vault was used to protect bank staff during WWII.

Even though standing at number six on the list, the UK vault has a few security features that have kept is secure from prying thieves.

As you'd expect, Fort Knox security makes it virtually impossible to get through their blast proof 22-ton door. There is no "hacking" into the Knox vault, they don't "make an app for that," all joking aside. In fact, the secret code to gain entry is divided amongst ten people and is stored "off-the-grid," no server or network vulnerability to be compromised. Sorry techno geeks, tried-and-true "old school" security measures keep Fort Knox safe 24/7.

Thus the genius behind the simplicity of the Antwerp break-in and getaway. Antwerp's security setup was overly dependent upon technological defenses.

Many times, physical "old-school" security wins the day. Unlike the Diamond Center Vault where the thieves casually crept in through a "back door" leading to the subterranean vault area, back at Fort Knox you'd have to get past the electrified fences, armed sentinels, and four-foot-thick granite.

Sure, the steel and copper safe-deposit boxes in the Diamond Center had 17,576 combination possibilities and also required a key to open, but as we see, the thieves literally drilled away that defense. Fort Knox obliterated that weakness by designing vaults tucked inside of vaults. Even the most beefy drill is useless in this situation. Remember, only the main vault door in the Diamond Center had a seismic alarm to warn of any drilling upon it, a feature missing from the safe-deposit boxes.

Oh, and don't forget the 30,000 soldiers from Fort Knox's military camp ready to jump into action at the first sign of trouble.

Notarbartolo's gang sat in waiting for a night break-in when no guards patrolled the building. Recall that long before the Antwerp heist, Notarbartolo became a trusted and charming insider, known as the "Jolly Jeweler," who was frequently invited into Antwerp vault rooms for merchandise inspection.

Antwerp's underground vaults are known as one of the densest concentrations of wealth worldwide. However, unlike Fort Knox and other "open space" security zones, the Diamond Center is cramped for space, which worked to Notarbartolo and gang's advantage.

Ranked the number one "guarded vault in the world" for the basic reason of simplicity and physical security presence, Fort Knox remains the toughest "nut" to crack.

Gold Under Wall Street?

Would you believe the United States would guard foreigners' gold behind a 90-ton steel door about 80 feet below ground, surrounded by rock on all sides and watched over by company of expert marksmen?

Fort Knox isn't the only secure location with patrolling marksmanship trained officers. The Federal Reserve Bank of New York has its own stationed guards too, earning the number two spot on the *Top 6 Guarded Vaults in The World* list.

An estimated $270 billion in gold bullion is estimated to be in this bunker, or vault, if you wish to call it that. Trusting in the security of America, foreigners own about 98% of the gold secured here. This bunker holds about 25% of the world's gold, minus a few percentage points if China and other nations keep buying up gold supplies.

The bunker is only blocks away from Wall Street and is listed as number five of nine on the *World's Most Ridiculously Secure Safes and Vaults*.

Sure, a 90-ton door wouldn't even fit in the subterranean Antwerp Diamond Center, but Notarbartolo would most likely have passed on any monetary offer to attempt breaking into the NY Federal Reserve with its tight security.

Seeds Guarded Better than Antwerp Diamonds

Believe it or not, there is a plan for our survival after a dreaded doomsday scenario.

On the rock island of Spitsbergen in the desolate Arctic Circle is the Svalbard Global Seed Vault. Otherwise known as The Doomsday Seed Vault, this post-apocalyptic protector of seeds took over an old copper mine site.

Ranking as number three on the *Top 6 Guarded Vaults in The World* list this vault has meter-thick steel reinforced concrete walls, motion sensors, and airlocks. Beyond the exterior blast-proof door are four heavy steel doors blocking the corridor leading to the chamber that secures the seeds.

Nicknamed the "Seed Vault," it ranks number two of nine on the *World's Most Ridiculously Secure Safes and Vaults.*

The goal of the vault is to "preserve crop diversity," and nothing says "keep away" more than its Arctic location of about 620 miles South of the North Pole. Very remote indeed.

Oddly enough, Antwerp's Diamond Center vault does not even appear on this *"ridiculously secure"* world list of nine vaults.

Vault Versus Nuclear Fallout

Coming in at number 7 of 9 on the *World's Most Ridiculously Secure Safes and Vaults* list is the Teikoku Bank of Hiroshima.

Unlike the surrounding security features found at the Bank of England Gold vault, Fort Knox, New York's Federal Reserve, or Svalbard Global Seed Vault, the Teikoku Bank's claim to fame earning its keep on the list was strictly due to the Mosler vault itself, not the bank.

The Bank building, and miles around it, had little hope of survival upon the dropping of Little Boy on Hiroshima during WWII. The bank's surrounding neighborhood was obliterated, but the Mosler vault sat undamaged. The interior was just as intact as the minute before the bomb blast. The exterior of the vault was scorched.

There was no arguing with the integrity of the Mosler vault since ground zero was confirmed to be about a football field away from the bank.

If you've ever wondered why the word Mosler may have sounded familiar, it is most likely due to the heavy advertising this company embraced after the war touting the security of their vaults.[4]

Sure, Notarbartolo got nabbed by carelessly disposing of heist evidence, but at least he and his crew didn't try to blow up the three-ton Diamond Center vault door to gain entry.

GIA, Grading Gems and Catching Crooks

What does Jack Nicklaus, a lost or stolen diamond, and a GIA data base have in common?

In an effort to assist law enforcement, the GIA (Gemological Institute of America) began setting up a database in the 1980s to complement their diamond grading reports in the hopes of stemming criminal activity.

Stones in the database labeled lost or stolen are compared to stones submitted for grading, whether from a private party or by law enforcement request.

Multi-million dollar diamond heists have involved world agencies such as the Scotland Yard, FBI, and international law enforcement. Many times these cases ultimately call upon GIA for expert assistance in solving the crime.

In the case of pro-golfers Jack Nicklaus and Greg Norman, GIA quickly alerted the FBI after identifying stones they submitted for grading. Sentenced with 40 years in prison, a Florida man defrauded the pro-golfers by selling them stolen diamonds. The diamonds were previously evaluated by GIA and as such the case moved along quickly, since the suspected crook was already under FBI investigation. GIA's system allowed the FBI to confirm the stones and trace them back to the Florida man.

Many of the world's diamonds are graded by GIA which certainly helped Scotland Yard solve a $15-20 million dollar diamond robbery. In this case, gemological identification was used by GIA's highly trained gemologists to confirm a match with submitted stolen diamonds.

GIA's database uses many factors such as fluorescence, symmetry, clarity, proportions, measurements, and polish to identify stones. Even a recut stone's identity can be determined in many cases as a potential match. Laser inscription of a stone makes it more difficult for lower level technologically challenged thieves to cash in on stolen stones.

Crime syndicates with international enterprises are much more adept at not only stealing diamonds, but at profiting from their trade or outright sale. Their sophisticated operations fund other criminal activities. This risky conduct forces them to find ways to counter GIA technology and related theft detection practices.

FBI special agents often remark that common crooks that make their way into large criminal enterprises start off in jewelry theft, a "gateway crime."[5]

Jewelry Thefts Around the World

The alluring nature of dazzling diamonds has always captured the attention of those not only with good intentions but misguided motives as well.

From the typical jewelry store robbery to global underworld masterminds, criminals and diamonds can't seem to resist each other…an addictive love affair that never seems to cease.

Just when law enforcement believes they've created a better "mouse trap," it seems those with less than admirable goals are frequently a few steps ahead of getting caught.

Let's take a look at some of the events in which the law and the lawless have crossed paths.

$50 Million in 5 Minutes

With the surprise of military precision and lightning-quick timing, a band of eight robbers burst through Brussels airport's security perimeter, stole an estimated $50 million in diamonds, and disappeared without firing a shot.

A Brinks "diamond and jewelry services" truck was in the process of delivering the diamonds directly to an aircraft at the moment of the heist. For "security" purposes, the transfer of the diamonds, from armored truck to aircraft cargo hold, had to be completed within a 15-minute time frame.

Passengers who were already seated in the target airplane said they "saw nothing," even though the robbers pulled up and surrounded the airplane brandishing military-like assault rifles. In fact, passengers only became aware of the attack after their flight was cancelled minutes later.

Similar to other historical heists, including the Milan Damiani showroom raid in 2008, the Brussels airport heist robbers were dressed in police uniforms with airport security arm bands.

The five-minute raid (February 18, 2013) was so fast that authorities are convinced that it was an inside job and that the robbers were clearly professional criminals and most likely had some degree of military training.

The robbers raced up to the aircraft in two police type vehicles, a Mercedes van and an Audi car, with blue lights flashing for effect.

A manhunt in Belgium and the Netherlands was initiated immediately given the brazenness of the heist and value of the stolen gems, which had come from Antwerp, the world capital of the diamond trade.

Afterwards, the airport hit-and-run authorities found an empty burned-out car that may have been used in the heist.

A "Hollywood Heist"... Foiled.

From *To Catch A Thief* in 1955 and *The Pink Panther* in 1963 to modern day heist films, such as *After The Sunset* and *The Score,* gems have fascinated and lured criminals since the first gem glittered in their greedy little eyes.

Many times dramatic crime films mimic real life, but sometimes the opposite is true. Movie magic has a way of bringing criminal conduct to life by exposing the intricate planning and execution of high-stakes heists right before our eyes on the silver screen.

The attempted Millennium Dome heist in London had all the elements that Hollywood could hope for in a successful blockbuster.

A real world plot twist caught the heist hoodlums by surprise.

Fakes were swapped for the actual gems the night before by authorities who were previously tipped off. As expected, a heavily armed crew of thugs ran into the Millennium with gas masks and sledgehammers, which they promptly used to smash display cases filled with "gems." What was to be the heist to end all heists came to an abrupt end when police officers, dressed as cleaning crew, pounced upon the perpetrators and saved the day. Law enforcement even pre-planned and nabbed the getaway speed boat.

This attempted and failed heist valued at about $700 million occurred in 2000. By 2003, *The Italian Job* (remake of the 1969 version) hit the screens featuring a spectacular speed boat get-away scene wherein the robbers, in cinematic style, got away.

Had the real life Millennium Dome heist succeeded, the world-famous Millennium Star diamond (203.04 carats) and 12 blue diamonds (118 carats total) would have slipped away by waterway getaway, leaving owner De Beers empty handed and going down in history as the undisputed heist of all heists.

Lights, Camera...Makeup?

Despite crafty disguises, these robbers left a cell phone in a getaway car, which became the loose end that led to the arrest of 10 men. Charges ranged from conspiracy to commit robbery to attempted murder.

In this heist, looks can be deceiving.

Men walking into Graff Diamonds (London, August 2009) wearing expensive suits does not qualify as a "disguise." However, having altered skin color and professionally applied prosthetics certainly did raise the bar of deception in the robbers' favor.

They exited the store with about $65 million divided among more than 40 pieces of stolen jewelry and sped away from the scene, but not before firing shots into the air.

Although several arrests were made, the stolen merchandise was never recovered.

Queen Elizabeth II Meets Harry Winston!

Speaking of disguises, recall that in 1999 Whoopi Goldberg appeared at the Oscars as Queen Elizabeth II of England adorned in diamonds on loan from the House of Harry Winston in Beverly Hills.

Yes, the same store in the chain of Harry Winston fame, one of which was the target of a Paris heist in 2008.

Although toting guns, not a shot was fired and these rogue robbers were disguised with female clothing and wigs and are still at large. The fact that a police station was right down the street was of no consequence. They had a plan, great disguises, and made a clean and quiet getaway.

In about 20 minutes the heist was over. This crew knew employees by first name and the location of a "secret" safe, which allowed for an estimated $107 million to be taken from this Paris Harry Winston store.

Sticking with the Hollywood scene, it's Oscar time....

Empty for the Oscars

Under the distraction of nearby construction noise, this crafty crew of criminals dug through a four foot wall to claim their booty of gems.

The front door armed guards and high tech security system were both bypassed with ease. The location was the Damiani showroom in Milan, Italy (2008).

In fact, this heist was pulled off with no weapons and fake police uniforms. Oddly enough, a woman had been complaining to police about early-morning noise in the neighborhood, but the complaint was dismissed due to construction in the area. The fact that she lived next door to the showroom did not raise any red flags.

Surprise and disguise were key to stunning showroom staff. After penetrating the wall, the robbers lay waiting in the lower level until late morning when they entered via an interior unarmed and unmanned door.

These robbers took the additional step of tying and gagging the staff before rounding up approximately $20 million in goodies (diamonds, rubies, and gold) and disappearing.

Authorities, once again, suspected assistance from someone on the inside.

The timing of this heist was almost perfect...almost.

Although the showroom had reduced staff due to preparations for a private showing and the perpetrators are still on the run, the total haul most likely would have been significant if not for most of the valuable pieces being on loan to Hollywood stars attending the Oscars as the heist took place. One such piece was the "Sahara Bracelet," boasting 1,865 diamonds at 47 carats.

Crème de la Crème

The undisputed global underworld currency remains diamonds.

In what other way can wealth be stored at highly concentrated value, concealed, and readily transported? When underworld players and crooks alike think "currency, par excellence," they think diamonds.

The economic term "elasticity" cuts to the chase concerning the inherent value of diamonds given their superior characteristics just mentioned. Diamonds are a unique blessing to criminals wishing to store wealth "off-the-grid"...the true pièce de résistance in their world.

Being "elastic" in nature, diamonds fit neatly into the illegal strategy and structure of the criminal world. No doubt, diamonds are flexibly compatible with the need and desire to store wealth in many ways.

Money launderers and terrorist funding operations buy drugs and pay for illegal arms via diamonds.

Diamonds form a "bridge of trade" in the underworld by retaining their value and having limited inflationary or exchange rate weaknesses. They are also easily exchanged for other currency and commodities.

Conflict (blood) diamonds still circulate at some level despite the Kimberley certification process putting a fine dent in illicit diamond trading.

Smuggler's Blues

By far the preferred method of criminals to convert diamonds to cash is to stay "under the radar" as best as possible. Elaborate, on-the-spot, attention-getting burglaries do occur, but are not as common compared to other crimes involving diamonds.

Avoiding guns, disguises, and possible physical assault charges due to participating in a robbery does not guarantee getting away with a crime, however, as a diamond company employee discovered.

Attempting to transfer large sums of cash out of South Africa with no satisfactory explanation is a great way to grant yourself attention you don't need. The employee's net worth was put under investigation after authorities confiscated a large stash of cash in said employee's possession while attempting to leave the country. It didn't help that the cash was hidden to begin with.

This attempted "money flow" led to charges under the Prevention of Organized Crime Act of 2004. A history of cash transactions by this employee further cast suspicion.

Detection and prevention of diamond-related crimes have made great strides, but then again so have evasion and savvy of criminals.

It's a "cat and mouse" game that never seems to let up.

CHAPTER 13

CARATS FULL OF CHARACTER

How DOES A stone, randomly found by a shepherd boy, end up mounted in a head ornament worn by the Earl of Dudley?

Initially thought of as only a pretty pebble, what was to become the "Star of South Africa," an 83-carat diamond, was discovered in 1869 by the 15-year-old boy near a field on the banks of the Orange River in Africa.

Also known as the "Dudley Diamond," the colorless diamond was cut to 47 carats. Oddly enough, the Earl of Dudley was a member of the Ward family, a son of which was jeweler to King Charles I. The family's great wealth was directly tied to a foundation of mineral resources.

The "Star of South Africa" is not to be confused with another famous diamond, the "Star of Africa."

In 1888, De Beers Consolidated Mines was the entrepreneurial pursuit of Cecil Rhodes. By the turn of the century, De Beers was well on its way to dominating the world rough diamond market for the next 100 years. The fields the shepherd boy strolled through were in Kimberley, a name associated with the beginnings of the modern diamond market.

Great wealth and rivalries sweep the Kimberley region (formerly known as "New Rush") after the discovery of diamonds. Just prior to the rush, the diamond, briefly mistaken for a pebble, was sold to a neighboring farmer for about 500 sheep, 10 oxen, and a horse. That farmer had previously sold a 21-carat stone (found in 1866) to a Hopetown business who in turn sent the new diamond off to England where it ended up with the Countess of Dudley.

It wasn't until 1974 that the diamond was sold at auction in Geneva.[1]

India's Diamond Indulgence

Historians estimate that from as early as 400 B.C. diamond trading was occurring in India. That's an amazing 2,400 years ago, and close to 2,250 years before the "Star of South Africa" was found in Africa, setting off an epic diamond rush.

Not only did diamond trading begin in India, but the first recorded history of the diamond has Indian roots. The fabulous qualities of diamonds were recognized by early astrologers and Hindu priests. At that time divinity was thought to have multiple pure qualities and a particular Hindu God was represented by a diamond's colors. Divine quality was equated with the unique characteristics of diamonds.

India's rivers and streams were the alluvial gathering grounds for diamonds and the Indian wealthy class enjoyed their share of these spectacular stones. Soon Western Europe benefited from "diamond caravans" that made their way to medieval markets in Venice. Elite Europeans loved the fashionable adornment provided by diamonds.

India's diamond dynasty began to wind down in the early 1700s, soon after which Brazil took center stage as major diamond supplier for the next 150 years.

Before India was relegated to the history books, many famous gem-quality diamonds came out of the infamous Deccan Highlands region, such as the Hope Diamond.

Before ending up in the Smithsonian Museum, the Hope family owned the 45-carat diamond, but not before royalty had its hands on it. It is believed that George IV was once an owner as well as Louis XVI. "French Blue Diamond" was the Hope's name prior to the French Revolution, when it disappeared for about twenty years. Though this rumor is unverified, the diamond was likely recut to disguise its sordid past.

Having been stolen from the crown jewels, it seems that the Hope diamond curse fulfilled what was assumed to be superstition, by bringing bad luck to a few owners. Taking the good with the bad, lore tells us that even as a symbol of love, diamonds supposedly bring ill will to those with greedy intentions. Misfortune, according to legend, is the price to pay for anyone possessing a stolen stone.

Another controversial Indian diamond, the 109-carat Kohinoor, is related to royalty outside of its founding country. Queen Victoria snapped up the Kohinoor after the Anglo-Sikh Wars. Now that the Queen Mother has passed and colonial rule is no more, India wants this treasure returned. Bloodshed surrounds Kohinoor history. Persian and Indian rulers have had possession of this famous stone at various times.[2]

Ancient Times... Trillions of Carats

A diamond's alluring beauty was so strong that thousands of years ago many believed these stones to possess supernatural powers.

At one point it was believed that a diamond could only be

broken if smeared with fresh goat's blood. Many civilizations prized this stone that was well known for its hardness, power, and natural beauty. In fact, diamonds were thought to be able to not only detect but detoxify various poisons.

Dreaming of diamonds was said to be a precursor to happiness, wealth, and overall success. Pharaohs associated diamonds with the Sun, symbolizing truth, courage, and power. In addition, ancient writings tell of illness being cured from those who gazed upon a diamond around Abraham's neck.

Roman and Greek history had a long history and admiration for diamonds. Even Venus, the goddess of love, was said to be influenced by the diamond. Speaking of love, it was also thought that diamonds tipped Cupid's arrows. Taking a look on the other side of this gem it was said that if a person lied, a diamond they owned would grow dim.

> "Diamond polishing is the constant search for greater brilliancy, more life, a more vivid fire in the diamond."
>
> Tolkowsky (from *Diamond Design*, 1919)

To these ancient peoples, diamonds came for the tears of gods and even as fragments of the outer rings of stars as well as falling stars themselves, spreading these stones across the land. Julius Caesar wore diamonds as magic objects that was considered to be a stone of champions.

'Dia-mon-d' was otherwise known in ancient Greek as "Adamas," which translates to unbreakable and unconquerable. Believing their muscles would be strengthened and that they would be invincible, Greek warriors wore diamonds. Courage was also thought to be a benefit of diamonds. Wearing them in battle was "sure" to bring victory.

Wearing a diamond on the left hand is a carry-over from ancient times when bravery was believed to bestow upon the wearer who wore diamonds close to the skin on the left side of the body.

Accounts vary as to whether meat or mirrors were used, but Alexander the Great's luck paid off upon running across the "Valley of Diamonds."

Diamonds and jewels filled a rocky valley. Amongst these treasures were living "terrible creatures" which were depicted in a sixteenth-century Turkish manuscript as snakes.

Alexander the Great (Iskandar) suggested using meat to procure the diamonds. Throwing meat into the deep valley would tempt the birds to snatch up the diamonds with their talons where they stuck to the meat. As habitual animals of nature, the birds would fly up and out of the valley and drop the meat in preparation for feeding. Alexander's soldiers would then pick the diamonds out of the meat after shooing the birds away.

In another account, mirrors were used to scare the guarding snakes out of the valley.[3]

Looking to the skies, thousands of years before powerful telescopes, could it be early astrologers were on to something? During ancient times, astrologers had linked diamonds to the heavens. Today, some white dwarf stars are thought to have diamond cores. The mass is estimated to weigh in at over two-and-a-quarter trillion metric tons at about 10 billion trillion carats. Truly amazing![4]

A Bigger, Bolder Beauty

Who could be humble if a stunning diamond was named in their honor.

Such was reality for Sir Thomas Cullinan, whose South African mine sourced a 3106-carat beauty in 1905. Dubbed the "Cullinan Diamond," it is the largest gem-quality diamond in the world and was discovered during a routine inspection 18 feet below the surface, when a superintendent took notice of a flash in the wall above him.

King Edward VII of Britain was presented with the stone by the Transvaal provincial government as a birthday gift. The best part of this story is how Edward planned to receive the diamond.

During these times, any word of riches, such as the Cullinan diamond, would bring attention. So, as a diversionary tactic, King Edward devised a plan to ease any worry of losing the diamond to thieves.

Being deceptively simple, the Cullinan diamond was to be sent in a plain box, no markings, no security, nothing to alert anyone to its contents. A phony decoy diamond would be sent via steamer ship from Africa to London, accompanied by many detectives to complete the illusion of a grand transportation.

Now the complication of how to best cut this rock arose. Today computer software is used to scan a stone and present return-on-investment (ROI) analysis of various cutting scenarios. Obviously no such help was available in the nineteenth century.

Asscher Diamond Company was assigned this formidable cutting task. Leader Joseph Asscher of Amsterdam, who had cut a stone one-third the size of the Cullinan (the famous Excelsior Diamond), was put up to the task. In preparation, Asscher studied the Cullinan for six months before attempting any cuts. Drama struck right out of the gate as the steel blade broke without any effect on the diamond. Cut number two did the trick, the rest is history.

This gigantic stone was cut into 105 separate diamonds. The two largest (530-carats and 317-carats) are set in the British Crown.

Setting quality aside, a Brazilian stone found in 1893 set a record at 3167-carats. Called the "Sergio Diamond," it is a non-carbonado black diamond. The theory is that, thanks to the Big Bang, this stone fell out of space from a meteor.[5,6]

Diamonds as Birthstones

Early fascination of gems mixed with supernatural beliefs led to diamonds and other gemstones being inextricably linked to astrology.

It wasn't until the mid-1500s that gemstones were widely used as birthstones and the signs of the Zodiac.

It is interesting to note that several rows of stones on a breastplate of "judgment" were part of the instructions given to Moses in chapter 28 of Exodus. Stones of the like are also found in the book of Revelations in the New Testament.

Foundation Stones were said to set the month/stone order. This traditional order has changed over the years, however. What has remained constant is the diamond being the birthstone of April, aligned with the Zodiac sign of Taurus. Coincidentally, one trait of those born under the Taurus sign is the appreciation of the finer things in life, of which diamonds certainly qualify. In addition, Tauri prefer predictability, which the diamond delivers with its strong, stable crystal core structure.[7]

The diamond is said to benefit the moon sign of Taurus more than any other stone.

Beneficial attributes of diamonds include improved health, enabling the resolution of marital issues, as well as promoting progress in financial endeavors. "Getting the love of your life" also ranks high when it comes to the many benefits of diamonds.

Since the sign of Taurus "rules the throat," accessories such as scarves, pendants, and necklaces, incorporating diamonds, are sure to be compatible.[8]

King of Crystals

What could be more impressive in diamond history than the marriage of Mary of Burgundy to Maximillian of Austria in 1477?

This union occurred during the Renaissance period and was the first instance of a diamond being used as an engagement ring. Maximillian took heed and followed the wise words of the ancients by choosing the third finger on Mary's left hand to place the diamond. Excellent choice, as it was believed this finger was directly connected to the heart by the Vein of Love.

> *"Diamond is the most valuable, not only of precious stones, but of all things in this world."*
>
> Pliny, Roman Naturalist

Artisans have their own love affair with diamonds, too. A diamond's natural shine and beauty only comes about after cleaving, cutting, and polishing.

No doubt, diamonds are objects of desire...always in demand.

That grand, mesmerizing sparkle dancing across a diamond's crown is just one characteristic that lets us know we're in the presence of a very special gemstone.

The magic of mosaic patterns of light diamonds create is amazing to behold.

This panorama of light is artistic in its vibrancy and vitality. It must be witnessed, in person, to fully appreciate its beauty. The purity and permanence of diamonds are undeniable, making them the King of crystals, reigning over all gemstones.

Diamonds personify value and true emotions, the very best.

No doubt, excellence, purity, and a symbol of love have been the hallmarks of the diamond for centuries.

Yes, indeed, the lore, beauty, and attraction of diamonds extend well beyond the mineral itself. We are in awe of a diamond's intense brilliance and life revealed by its stunning scintillation.

Diamonds truly are forever, the crème de la crème of gems.

CHAPTER 14

TRAVELLING
FOR PLEASURE
AND PROFIT

T RAVELING OVERSEAS IS exhilarating!

Securing a fabulous diamond deal for a client at the same time is even more thrilling. Having close to three decades of tenure in the gem industry allows me the joy of guiding clients on the path of freedom, both geographically and financially.

A Match Made in Heaven

My love for travel and diamonds began at an early age.

As a young girl, my parents worked for airlines and I was in awe and starry-eyed seeing and hearing about all of the exotic destinations they visited. Naturally, my time with the Air Force was unforgettable and allowed me to spread my wings. Gems were also an early favorite of mine. While my sister collected dolls, my fascination was focused on collecting gems and jewelry. After serving in the Air Force I followed up on another goal and became a certified gemologist through the highly respected Gemologists Institute of America (GIA). The amazing education and hands-on experience I earned at GIA enabled me to fulfill another dream by launching a jewelry business that I own to this day.

Your sincere interest in gems combined with my extensive yet refined background will prove worthy for any diamond search and gem related investment goal you may have. Knowing the industry "ropes" is key in any business.

> "An investment in knowledge pays the best interest."
>
> Ben Franklin

Having a solid foundation of knowledge is like possessing a flawless diamond. I continually draw upon and update my GIA training in order to best serve my clients. It is no surprise that GIA issued the first diamond grading reports in 1955 that have become universally standard. Additionally, they graded the infamous Hope Diamond in the late 1980s and revealed synthetic diamond identification processes in a groundbreaking article published in "Gems & Gemology" in 1996.

That legacy makes me proud and keeps me on my toes, given all the changes the gem industry has seen over the years. After all, Richard T. Liddicoat's contributions to gems and jewelry at GIA earned him the title, "Father of Modern Gemology." As a gemologist myself, it is a pleasure and a privilege to provide you with accurate information in the realm of the diamond world.

Mazal U'Bracha!

Pick your destination…invest in your dream diamond and let it shine!

Diamonds are found the world over. Whether it be from mines, alluvial fields, or ocean-based vessels sucking these sparkling stones up from the deep, diamonds are just part of the adventure.

On the surface, such a declaration relating to the venerable diamond may be a bit off-putting, but the details are intriguing. Operating under the "all-under-one-roof" concept, the Israel Diamond Exchange (IDE) ranks as one of the most sophisticated diamond centers in the world, boasting approximately 3,000 members. Directly employing 20,000, the Israeli Diamond Industry contributes to tourism and banking as well.

Utilizing a trading hall and private offices, visitors and members can conduct business in safety within the business framework. Outside of the walls of the diamond trade offices, an energetic business center surrounds the diamond complex of which the diamond industry has been largely responsible for creating. This urban development, Ramat-Gan, is economically vibrant and is a benefactor of a world diamond center that was established in 1937.

Yes, it is a "supermarket" of diamonds. It is said that at the IDE, virtually any diamond type can be purchased. Large to small, round to heart-shaped, white to colored stones, and even innovative Israeli special cuts are to be had. The jewelry trade loves Israel for its almost never-ending availability of sparkling stone. It is truly a diamond buyer's dream.

And, of course, Israel is well known as a most inviting tourist destination in its own right. The history is rich in flavor going back over two-thousand years to Biblical times.

Israeli diamond polishers are expert craftsmen specializing in medium and large stones while offshoring smaller stones only to import them back for grading and sorting, then exporting to the world's market including North America, Europe, Asia and beyond.

With key roles in the World Federation of Diamond Bourses, International Diamond Manufacturer's Association, World

Diamond Council, and the Kimberley Process, Israel is a prominent player in the world diamond arena.

As a leading hub of trading and manufacturing of polished diamonds, great deals can be had. Arabs, Chinese, Americans, Indians and others know that "mazal u'bracha" is the accepted code among diamond dealers, meaning "may the deal be with luck and blessings."[1]

Whirlpools, Kangaroos, and Diamonds

Many time zones away from the Israel Diamond Exchange is Australia, with its wealth of natural wonders.

Not widely known for diamond mining by the average person, this shining facet of Australia surprises many folks. As a very popular tourist attraction, the Argyle mine resides in East Kimberley of Western Australia.

Flying tours offer spectacular birds-eye views of both the mine and ancient Bungle Bungles formations within the wondrous Purnululu National Park.

Dare to compare sandstone and diamonds?

Bungle Bungles are naturally sculptured formations that display diversity above ground for all to admire. They are unrivaled in scale anywhere in the world. Once you witness the beauty of the special beehive domes and other sandstone formations, you'll understand why this special place is protected by buffer zones and beloved by the Aboriginal peoples.

Like the above-ground unique Bungle Bungles, the nearby Argyle mine releases another one-of-a-kind natural wonder, diamonds. Due to its singular qualities, the Purnululu (Bungle Bungles) National Park was inscribed on the World Heritage List in 2003. Once above ground, diamonds share their natural innate beauty and are a testament to the evolutionary history of our great planet Earth.

The sheer scale of Purnululu can also be appreciated by heli-copter as well as hiking on designated paths. Cathedral Gorge is an astounding must-see. With almost an entire 360 degrees worth of vertical sandstone cliffs, the Gorge was formed by wet-season waters that also create cascading waterfalls. A massive pattern of each season's whirlpool is a sight to behold.

Like pure natural diamonds, one can't compare the special features of Bungles to anything else you've ever seen. Hiking Piccaninny Creek makes you wonder if you've stumbled into a different world.

Having become one of the world's largest suppliers of natural colored diamonds, Argyle opened in the mid-1980s. Argyle is also at the top of the list of largest diamond mines in the world, colored or colorless.[2]

One can feel the impressive scope of the Argyle mine opera-tions in person. The Kimberley operation produces approximately 20 million carats a year and is a great boost to local tourism.

Exquisite Argyle stones range from pale pinks to intense purple-reds and are sought by world-wide investors and collec-tors. Pink diamonds are the popular and prized signature stone from this area. Top-grade colored investment diamonds, no matter the source, benefit from the popularity of common stones being pulled from the Argyle mines. Many are commanding prices close to 20 times their colorless diamond cousins.

Pink Jubilee Is Pure Glee

Australia's largest rough pink diamond, dubbed the "Argyle Pink Jubilee," weighed in at 12.76 carats and was unearthed from the Argyle mine. It found a permanent home at the Melbourne Museum.

"It's taken 26 years of Argyle production to unearth this stone and we may never see one like this again," stated Argyle Pink

Diamonds manager Josephine Johnson. In 2012 another pink beauty, "Martian Pink," sold at Christie's auction house for over $17 million.

Now part of Australia's mining history, the Jubilee shares exhibit space with more than 3,000 minerals and gems after being donated to the museum by Rio Tinto, Argyle's owner.[3]

More good news comes out of Northern Australia regarding the "Merlin" project.

The pilot project operated by North Australian Diamonds, Ltd. since 2013 is known for "super white" high clarity diamonds. A 104.73 carat stone, one of Australia's largest, came from Merlin. Marketing will be under the "Merlin" brand as Australian stones to further emphasize the recognized quality.

Promising international diamond market strength combined with Merlin diamond premium quality has led to a run-on-mind (ROM) parcel assessment increase to over $330 (US) per carat.

Resource support such as these further buttresses the overall market for gem-quality diamonds and in turn provides a "floor" for investment-grade stones.[4]

Cognac and champagne natural diamonds is another claim to fame for Argyle. The US market has embraced these colored stones.

Similar to agreements in Canada, respect and concern for the ecology and environment includes land use agreements with the Aboriginal community.

Outback Odyssey

Australia's Opal Capital embraces a one-of-a-kind lifestyle that has attracted attention from the jewelry and tourism worlds.

Almost everyone and everything is underground in Coober Pedy, Australia. They even have underground camping in this

Southern Australian Outback between Adelaide and Alice Springs.

As a gemologist who respects stones of all kinds, Coober Pedy stands by its status as the largest opal producer in the world. "Whiteman's hole in the ground" comes from the Aboriginal "kupa piti," and is how the town name Coober Pedy came to be.

The rose-colored sandstone walls make underground living and working more pleasant. No cramped, damp, or dark caves here. You'll find motels and hotels, shops, backpackers, churches, and even a swimming pool.

Sure, there are other Opal mining towns, but you'll never forget a visit to Coober Pedy.

Diamond Beginnings to Start Again

World class diamond exploration meets a historic diamond era in India.

Back as far as 400 B.C., India was the diamond capital of the world. For hundreds of years India retained this title until stone discoveries in Brazil led to the changing of the guard. Brazil relinquished the crown to Africa and today we see diamonds being mined in countries around the world.

Rio Tinto's record of successful world diamond mining has turned its attention to the Indian state of Madhya Pradesh where they plan to invest $500 million in a Bunder mining project as soon as environmental clearances are secured.

If history is any guide, this venture could be a massive hit for Rio. They found gargantuan deposits that haven't been seen in the last 40 year in India. Best of all, a light bulb will instantly go off in any diamond connoisseur and serious investor's head. Long ago it was the Golconda region in India that brought the first "investment" grade diamonds to the world. Famous, rare, and rich in nature, the European aristocracy and well-to-do loved these Indian stones. So famous were these diamonds' clarity that today auction houses and high-end jewelers refer to rare "Type II" diamonds as "Golconda-like" and other cozy terms to assume association with the "best of the best."

Sold for $21.5 million in 2012 at Christie's Geneva Magnificent Jewels auction, the "Archduke Joseph" diamond is world famous. Dating back to the ancient Golconda mines, it retains more than the stone's inherent value.

Overall, history confirms the quality of India diamonds and Rio's find of eight diamondiferous pipes in cluster is very good news for the industry.

Any online search will return a plethora of travel options in and around India that are sure to thrill. Many a deal have been made by distant brokers, but nothing beats witnessing diamond history at the source and collecting memories as well as dazzling diamonds.[5]

Go Wild in Africa

No zoo or reserve can capture the majesty of a being out in the wild in Africa.

Seeing the king of the jungle roaming the plains in its home-land is a priceless wildlife experience. South Africa is the ultimate destination for many safari goers. Variety and numbers of other amazing animals such as elephants, rhinos, cheetahs, and others are sure to please.

South Africa has plenty of plenty of remote escapes from urban life." Kruger National Park provides brave visitors the chance to get close to untamed beauty, safari style.

Just because you're exploring the wildlife out in the open doesn't mean that you can't experience luxury. "JoBurg" (Johannesburg) offers many boutique hotels at the five-star level as well as tourist attractions.

Diamond history runs deep in Africa.

Not many are aware of the off-shore diamond ships. Many miles out to sea, these diamond-finders have hundreds of feet of pipe that search the ocean floor for rough diamonds. Although fishermen work hard in Alaska, my vote is for diamonds being the "greatest catch," hands down.

In 1905, one of the largest diamonds was discovered in South Africa. This monster weighed in at 3,106 carats and was found only 18 feet below the surface in the oldest diamond "pipe" in the world. The fact that King Edward VII was given this great diamond dubbed the "Cullinan" is not the most interesting fact.

Safely transporting this spectacular stone was the real challenge. A diversion had to be devised to protect against any possible robbery. The solution was simple, send it under normal package post! It's true, the 3,106-carat colossus Cullinan was sent in nothing more than a brown paper covered package. The diversion was another package sent via steam ship surrounded by a posse of guards and fanfare.

Diamond City

Almost equidistant as the crow flies between Johannesburg and Cape Town is capital Kimberley of the Northern Cape Province.

Rich in colonial history and the home of the birth place of Harry Oppenheimer during the diamond rush era, Kimberley is an art lover's retreat. Amongst the numerous jewelry stores is the William Humphreys Art Gallery holding a collection of fine art by Dutch, English, and French masters of the sixteenth and seventeenth centuries. Rock art and contemporary pieces can also be found in the area. Talented artisans in Kimberley offer crafted jewelry as custom mementos of your visit.

Ghost tours, mine museums, and battlefields of the past South African War coexist in this diamond capital of the world.

Thanks to the diamond rush of the 1870s, you can look back at the glittering past by touring a once-operational mine. At one time there were five large holes used to access dormant volcanic pipes in which diamonds waited to be released. One hole, dubbed the "Big Hole," remains uncovered. About the size of eight football fields, this hand-dug crater-like hole sinks almost 2,700 feet below surface grade.

Adjacent to the "Big Hole" are original buildings and the Kimberley Mine Museum, which recreates the excitement of the diamond rush days.

Belgravia, just a few miles from the diamond capital, boasts many homes built during the diamond mine's peak of activity. At one time this region was said to contain more millionaires than anywhere else in the world. As one of Kimberley's oldest residential suburbs, it is easy to understand why wealth congregated here along with the mining dynasty family that turned South African into a top producer of diamonds.

The Cape is Great

A slice of luxury awaits you in Cape Town.

At the extreme tip of Africa is Cape Point, a "promontory." This scenic mountainous landform juts out into the ocean majestically. You can observe waves roll in and crash against the Cape of Good Hope for hours and still want to stay for more. Words and pictures can't do this wondrous scenery the justice is deserves.

Campos Bay is like a pastoral retreat. Known as the posh area of Cape Town, amazing views of the ocean and the surrounding landscape are at your doorstep.

On Cape Town's famous waterfront is the Clock Tower Precinct, against which the Table Mountains make a perfect backdrop. As a massive landmark, the flat topped mountains are a sight to behold. A special treat awaits those that ride the Aerial cableway for a view of a lifetime. Occasional low cloud cover during sunrise and sunsets make the view from high above on the mountain look like a colored puffy cotton dream. From the Table vantage point scenic points are Lion's Head, Signal Hill, Kloof Corner, and Devil's Peak.

Down in town learn about the Great Kimberley Diamond Rush where you get to dress up as a miner while exploring a replica mine shaft. Feel what it was like to free diamonds from their resting place with realistic sound and lighting on the tour.

Paying tribute to a stone most precious is the Cape Town Diamond Museum. Continue your quest for knowledge and exploration by checking out the Shimansky Diamond Experience where diamonds are "transformed into amazing creations of fire and light" at the Shimansky workshop.[6]

Cape Town is a retreat to luxury and just another reminder of how diamonds are an integral part of the world economy and an incredible opportunity for diversifying your wealth.

Canada

Known to some as the "Top of the World," Canada has continued sprinting forward in the diamond industry since arriving on the scene with a giant splash in the 1990s.

Fraser Institute's 2014 survey rated the world's second-best mining investment jurisdiction in the world to be Saskatchewan.

Canada, that others affectionately call "The Great White North" has several diamond projects underway which are likely to boost its share of world production to about 15%.

There is much to see and do in many of Canada's cosmopolitan cites. Vancouver, Toronto, Montreal, Calgary, and others each have a style of their own.

It is in Edmonton where I am the proprietor of a jewelry store called The Gem Gallerie. Over the decades of ownership I've come across sophisticated clients who see much more value behind diamonds than the sparkle. Having grown up in an airline family, I recall a time when only the well-to-do flew. That changed after the late 1970s with the deregulation of airlines in the United States. Soon enough middle class families were able to fly the friendly skies. This scenario is not that different than De Beers' loss of its large monopolistic-like control of the diamond industry. Today investing in diamonds is within reach of those that never thought it possible just years ago. With an expert in the industry that knows the ropes, investing in diamonds has become a reality for those willing to take action after thorough counsel.

Stornoway Diamonds and Mountain Province Diamonds are expecting mining projects to begin producing in 2016. Mountain's joint venture with De Beers is to be operational in the third quarter. Estimated at 1.6 million carats per year, the first diamond mine (Renard) ever in Quebec is under construction with a mine life of about 11 years.

Pikoo is a new Canadian diamond district with North Arrow Minerals being part of this project as the most advanced exploration company in the district.

Along with Russia, Canada helped put an end to the virtual strangle hold of De Beers' industry domination. As such, there are opportunities for those in-the-know to make investment decisions in the Canadian diamond arena.

Large colorless gem-quality diamonds still come from the Diavik mine (Rio Tinto) in the Northwest Territories. The 6-7 million carat annual output stands testament to the grand scale involved in this mine's epic success.

Track record is important in the competitive world of diamonds and investing. As a member of the Canadian Diamond Bourse and the World Federation of Diamond Bourses, I'm committed as a business owner and gem lover to the best interests of my clients.

Certainly cold calculations and nerves of steel are traits necessary to keep one grounded for pure financial concerns. On the "warmer" side of the equation, intuition and love of these precious stones sustains your "preferred dealer" status in the trade and allows amicable negotiations that leave all parties coming out as winners.

Amazing Alberta

The Great White North beckons again with the prospect of a diamond rush on the horizon.

Consisting of over 142,000 acres, the Alberta Diamonds Project is part of Grizzly Discoveries Inc.'s, new permits, enabling further searching for diamonds. Three diamond "pipes" (kimberlite) have revealed microdiamonds and there are 28 pipes in the field of a diamondiferous nature.

The Buffalo Head Hills area is in diamond exploration mode on these highly prospective lands. Given that the Northern Alberta region has about 48 kimberlitic pipes over three separate areas, with 26 of those identified as diamondiferous, who would blame them?[7]

Persistence and patience has been the key to the Canadian diamond story.

It was back in 1991 that two dogged geologists put Canada on the world diamond map. Before hitting pay dirt, Chuck Fipke and Stew Blusson simply would not give up on a hunch. They did whatever it took, from renting helicopters to establishing a "camp," in which some relatives and hired help lived under less than ideal conditions. What seemed to the world as an overnight success took years and years of planning, restarts, frugal living, and pure dedication to the cause, even when all seemed dim.

Alberta has already been blessed with oil and gas reserves, amazing geography, and international gateway cities, so an economical diamond find would be a wonderful compliment to the Alberta province. Bolder Investments (B.C.) mining specialist stated:

> "Diamond exploration is for believers, for people who have a long-term perspective and who make high-risk investments."
>
> Dorothy Atkinson

Yes indeed, great things in small packages come to those who wait.

Investors from the "Old World" of Europe and the Middle East have already put down funds for Alberta diamond exploration. Unlike Ekati, Canada's first diamond mine, the Buffalo Head Hills (BHH) area already is prepped with skilled labor, roads, utilities, and infrastructure to accommodate the initial influx of activity resulting from any green-lighted primary mine opening.

While waiting for the diamond hunt to shine, Alberta is already known for its jaw-dropping and eye-popping scenery.

Part of the United Nations Educational, Scientific and Cultural Organization (UNESCO), the Alberta Rocky Mountain parks are a geological gem in and of themselves. There are working ranches in the West and dinosaur bone digs in the Southern Badlands. Canada also boasts 17 total UNESCO significant areas to explore.

Plenty of activities are sure to keep you busy, such as hiking, cycling, fishing, camping, golfing, horse riding, wildlife viewing, and star gazing. Many specifically seek out Canada's cold thrills such as snowboarding, dog sledding, ice fishing, and skiing. And who could forget the Northern Lights viewed from your own cabin or lodge during a weekend getaway?

Gateway cities of capital Edmonton and Calgary are vibrant cultural centers with fine dining, spectacular shopping, and amazing arts. Alberta's South is bordered by Montana with the West dominated by the majestic Rocky Mountains and pleasant prairies to the East. As everyone knows, the Arctic tundra is knocking on the Northern hinterland of the Northwest Territories.

The "Bar U Ranch" is a ranching outfit with roots back to the 1800s where you can relive the cowboys and cattlemen adventures of the olden days. By the 1870s, Mounties did what they could to tame the wild frontier. Canada's fur trade reaches back even further in time to the 1600s and kids will love the fact that Alberta has a dinosaur fossil concentration that is the largest in the world.

On the Western front is a natural jewel in the form of a National Park. Banff offers unparalleled access to the Canadian Rocky Mountain experience. Several alpine towns offer the call of the wild while providing amenities to accent your experience. Culinary delights are sure to be had and your choice of a private chalet or alpine castle awaits your arrival. Banff has been described as a cultural oasis with year-round festivals, museums, and even a vibrant night life.

When was the last time you breathed in the crisp mountain air or enjoyed the view of mighty mountains, fabulous foliage, and a wonderful waterfront?

There are two national parks to the West of Calgary and, if you choose, a quick flight over the border to the "Big Sky Country" of Montana offers the treat of a few more national parks, one aptly named "Lewis & Clark."

Long before the Ekati mine came to be, a member of Grizzly Discoveries, Inc., found diamond indicator garnets in MacLeod River (West of Edmonton and North of Banff) near what some call God's country. Grizzly hunts for silver and gold in B.C. and Buffalo Head Hills are part of Grizzly's mineral permits, which encompass almost four million acres of land.

With headquarters in Edmonton, Grizzly hopes to find a KIM "pipe" (Kimberlite-Indicator Mineral) targets that will finally back up Alberta's long reputation for tremendous potential for diamonds deposits.[8]

Armed with magnometers, ATV's, a small team of geologists and the enthusiasm of those that went before them, the Grizzly crew maintains the adventure and exploration spirit of the diamond hunt.

Dive in and get a Canadian vacation guide. Plan an adventure. You never know when the headlines will again read, "Diamonds Found!"

The diamond dream is still alive in Canada.

Believe!

A Diamond Port of Call

Arrive in style at the Port of Antwerp!

Antwerp's cruise terminal can make your decisions to combine business and pleasure all the more profitable and fun at the same time.

Antwerp's Diamond District is where all of the cutting and polishing businesses have an office. First trades occur here for "fresh" diamonds, as they have for decades. "Choice" is an understatement and bargaining is expected, as this is the center of diamantaires and "sights" (set sales to client buyers). Thousands of loose diamonds are handpicked by those with an eye and intuition for value. Brokers and buying groups are the name of the game at the renowned Diamond Exchange. Planning ahead of time is crucial for dates, times, and contacts.

Antwerp's old world origins and contemporary flare is something to behold. Be sure to check out the diamond museum, diamond factories, and the fashion museum along with the local culture and arts.

Investors need to know that Antwerp handles about 8 in 10 of all rough diamonds while about one in two of all cut diamonds find their way through Antwerp. Naturally, then, it pays big dividends for top tier sophisticated gemstone investors to broaden their horizons. Keeping overseas options open is the hallmark of a great deal and profit making for any major diamond investment.

"State Side" Gems

Not much attention is on the United States when it comes to diamonds, or even other gemstones for that matter.

Best known around the world as a consumer nation, the US keeps the gemstone world humming along very nicely by importing well over $20 billion in gemstones per year. Diamond producing countries of the world have good reason to thank "Uncle Sam" for being almost 99.9% dependent on foreign gemstones.

A diversity of gemstones are produced in the US, but only in nominal quantities.

Seasonal workers man some very small mines in the US. As of 2011 just about 1,000 workers were reported, in the entire country, as part of the gemstone mining industry.[9]

There are a few bright spots that have gotten attention that may pique your interest, however.

In the Spring of 2015, a visitor to the US's only operating

diamond mine found an eight-carat diamond in under 20 minutes and legally left the premises with said diamond in hand.

That fairly large stone was identified as a diamond for free by site staff and the patron only paid an eight dollar admission fee for the privilege of searching the mine for any gemstone they could find.

Crater of Diamonds State Park is the only mine in the world where you can be the miner as a layperson, no experience required. Since the 1970s, tens of thousands of diamonds have been found by visitors who got to keep their carats for free. All diamonds found have been colorless, brown, or yellow, and each year around 100,000 visitors rush to Arkansas to take a stab at striking diamond "pay dirt."[10]

Two attempts were made by private ventures to mine diamonds, thanks to volcanic kimberlite "pipes," until about the 1970s when the national park took over the land. The volcanic neck simply was not economically feasible for commercial purposes. Although many regions of the US have been proven to hold diamonds, the quality and quantity are only suitable for very small operators that are but a speck in the scheme of world production.[11]

Many would be very happy to run across a few hundred dollars that no one else laid claim too.

How ecstatic might you be stumbling across $10,000 dollars?

In North Carolina, about a dozen locations allow you to keep any gemstones you find. More than one emerald estimated at over $10,000 in-the-rough were found by visitors, as reported by the Huffington Post and ABC News websites. Pay-to-dig mines are quite popular and populous in North Carolina, yet many are unaware that rubies, sapphires, and emeralds are a staple in this area of the country.

A good hint at the quantity of gemstones found can be gleaned by local businesses whose skilled cutters and bench jewelers can readily turn your gleaming gem into jewelry.[12]

Sapphire, opal, quartz, emerald and even diamond are several of the minerals that the "Gem Stones of the United States" Geological Survey Bulletin 1041-G tells us can be found in the Palmetto State.[13]

Don't let the state bird fool you, wild turkeys aren't found on the beach in sister-state South Carolina. Vacation towns, such as Myrtle Beach, are famous for golfing and just as fabulous as the subtropical beaches. The oldest city, coastal Charleston, is home to Fort Sumter, where the opening shots to the Civil War were fired.

Back to North Carolina and right up the coast is the Outer Banks, famous for the first emeralds for commercial sourcing in the US. Tiffany & Co., were the former owners of the Crabtree Emerald Mine in the western area of the state, which mined until 1990. Also inland is the spectacular Blue Ridge Mountains. Enjoy horseback riding, whitewater rafting, hiking and other activities.

It would be hard to miss the Grand Strand, a 60-plus-mile magnificent stretch of uninterrupted beach land. There's plenty of surfing, scuba diving, fishing, boating, and golfing to be had. On the Western edge of the state is the Great Smokey Mountains and a national park.

All is not lost in the US for gemstones of higher value. February is the month that most of the relevant US miners of gemstones sell their special stones directly. Both rough and cut stones abound at the Tucson Gem and Mineral Show in Arizona. This is your chance to speak directly to miners and the person who likely mined and/or cut the stone you can't keep your eye off of. Many of the vendors are more than happy to speak with you, not only about the stones but the operations they love so much from which the stones originated.

Be sure to take an expert in the industry with you when venturing to New York, one of the world diamond trading centers. Don't be fooled by the fact that volume here is not a direct match for the hub-like activity in main trading centers overseas.

They don't call it the "Big Apple" for nothing. Be prepared and stay on your toes when trying to close that big diamond deal.

Globetrotting for Gems

Major world centers of diamond cutting and trading are in New York, Tel Aviv, London, Amsterdam, and Antwerp. Primary processing centers, where diamonds are evaluated, cut, and sold reside in Tel Aviv, Antwerp, and New York.

I must admit that some of my gemstone investing clients have found spectacular success State-side, on occasion, since about 80% of diamonds are sold in the US. Of particular interest to value seekers are large and unusual rough diamonds, which tend to make their way through New York.

No doubt, finding and securing a gem-quality diamond takes perseverance and expertise…as well as someone that "knows the ropes." Leveling the playing field is essential to securing a great diamond deal. Too many amateurs have discovered that "going it alone" has consequences in the competitive diamond investing environment.

Having been to many gemstone hot spots over the years, it would take a great portion of this book to reveal all I've experienced as a gem lover and investor.

In appreciation for all the beauty and splendor the world has to offer surrounding the great gems this Earth has gifted us with, I would be remiss to not bring to your attention a few other gem destinations.

Be an explorer both in travel and as an information-seeker in order to "keep your ear to the ground" when moving forward with any financial decision.

Thailand, Burma, Sri Lanka, and Brazil all have ties to either the diamond and/or gem industry. Many locations left me not only with a great gem deal, but with awe inspiring wonder and amazement with the culture, place, and times.

It's a time-tested investment principle you've heard again and again, location, location, location.

Similar to real estate deals, the location of your diamond investment can make a difference. Many times, travelling afar to a Diamond District is required to secure the best deal. At other times, especially when least expected, an auction house may be nearby or a private sale of some sort pops up. When opportunity knocks, at least take a peek through the peep hole.

Remember, if you structure the deal correctly, there are ways to defer, or even reduce, costs. Also, you can combine business and pleasure by vacationing during a portion of your investment trip and still write-off costs within tax guidelines, legally.

With respect earned worldwide, diamonds have virtually no boundaries. Best of all, with an expert negotiator or agent by your side as a guide, you'll be the proud owner of your dream diamond in no time!

Selecting "The One"

There may be plenty of "gem quality" diamonds available, but only a select few that qualify as "investment grade." Being "In the hunt" for such a rare diamond can seem like searching for the proverbial needle in a haystack. Nonetheless, my clients love the payoff of perseverance. Patience pays off.

Knowing the ubiquitous "4 C's" means you know most key details about buying a diamond. True or false?

False! Informed diamond investors follow the "2 B's" and "2 D's" as I call them.

"Buyer Beware" (2 B's) is a great rule to live and invest by. Due diligence is any prudent investor's redeemer that ultimately leads to profit. Many savvy investors I've been an agent for appreciated my tips and tricks to avoid diamond investing "landmines." As you'd expect, red ink is not welcome within investment portfolios.

As a long time GIA (Gemological Institute of America) certified gemologist, jewelry store proprietor, and gem investor I significantly shorten my clients' gemstone learning curve, thus mitigating their risk.

Being an industry insider also benefits my clients when it comes to the 2 D's Diamond Districts. Israel and Amsterdam are quite obviously diamond "strongholds," more specifically, Mumbai, Tel Aviv, Antwerp and New York. Of which the ins and outs must be understood in order to successfully navigate diamond deals. Also, don't underestimate the value of the secondary districts, especially through the sale of estate jewelry in markets like Los Angeles."

Well before venturing into the diamond investing world, it would behoove serious investors to:

- Choose and trust your gemstone agent wisely
- Develop a budget (diamond shape, size, etc.)
- Target the source (Diamond District, wholesaler, etc.)
- Have a plan for contingencies
- Leave emotions out of the deal

Although online resources can aid in gemstone investing, it is usually better to examine a stone in person. Let's just say gemstone statistics that look good on paper may lose their luster in person. Not many people make major purchases (car or home) without a test drive or walk through respectively, so why risk committing your hard earned money on a "virtual" (unseen) diamond?

From Bench Warmer to Starting Lineup

The more things change, the more they stay the same, until now.

Diamonds have become accomplished "alternative" investments, so much so that colored diamonds are not so "alternative" anymore. In the rhinestone world of traditional investing, what was once considered avant-garde has slowly become a new standard in and of itself. Diamonds have slipped onto center stage and skeptical investors are taking notice.

> *"It's hard to be a diamond in a rhinestone world."*
>
> Dolly Parton

How are investing and diamonds similar?

Just like the world itself, there will always be many facets to each. One must be open to new ideas and possibilities while remaining disciplined in approach. Clinging onto only one method or outdated theory can prove detrimental to an investment portfolio's overall return. Old habits are hard to break.

Bain & Co.'s infamous 2014 "Global Diamond Report" was prepared with the assistance of the Antwerp World Diamond Centre (AWDC). It factually illustrated how diamonds recently survived a major world "crisis" event, which became known in the United States as the "Great Recession." As a safe harbor asset, any gemstone loss was temporary with early relief of recovery while traditional asset mainstays such as securities and real estate remained "underwater" and at best stagnant years to come. Investment grade diamonds were one of the few bright spots in the wealth arena.

Barclays, a wealth and investment management firm, released "Wealth Insights, Profit or Pleasure?" which explored motivations behind "treasure" investment trends. In cooperation with

Ledbury Research, this 15th volume of Wealth Insights surveyed more than 2000 high-net-worth individuals in 17 countries around the world.

This report is a wealth of key points tracking precious gems and jewelry's rise in the wealth of top net-worth individuals around the globe.

Matching the reality of world market instability, many respondents surveyed in communist, socialist, and monarchy-based governments had precious jewelry as a high percentage of their wealth. Out of the 17 countries, the top 5 belonged to the type of government just listed with ownership rates of precious jewelry at over 85%.

Why?

Uncertainty of government intentions concerning citizen possessions led many to hold wealth in portable form, free from the threat of instant lien, levy, or seizure. Even some republic-based governments ranked high on the list of well-to-do citizens with high jewelry wealth content too.

Let this be an objective lesson for us all.

Even in Biblical times people had to be vigilant and wise with their limited "wealth" if they were to survive not just natural disaster but intruding "government" as well. Having been around the world to witness how other cultures value gemstones, there is a clear correlation with the rule of thirds. Many peoples throughout different cultures kept one third of their wealth portable, in precious jewels. As Greece recently proved, many paper assets, whether it be currency or securities, are not necessarily backed by good faith or good credit, no matter what the contract preaches.

With no intent to pitch any specific security, I must say that it is telling that the Lundin family have taken up a 20% stake in a junior diamond company that has exploration projects in Canada. The Lundins have a successful investment record in resource markets and are bullish on diamonds in particular. Prior to that junior company stake, the Lundins first diamond investing venture was a home run. Lucara Diamonds was the company and has been the best resource stock for a few years.

Diamonds have been warming up for years, albeit quietly. Those in the know have been investing in and racking up profits for many, many years. Look no further than Warren Buffet's lengthy track record investing in the diamond sector.

Investors around the world have been able to keep a big secret, until now.

Diamonds have been blowing the doors off assets once assumed to be the bread and butter of the investment world. The returns cannot be denied. Once a backup alternative, diamonds as investments have earned a spot on the "starting lineup" of portfolio management.

Once again, another quarter rolls into another year of record-breaking sales of diamonds and other gems at Sotheby's and Christie's auction houses. This public proof can't be denied any longer, diamonds are top dog in investing.

Move over "rhinestones," the new world is aglow with diamond sparkle!

An International Investment

Around the world my traveling observations have also confirmed that much of the "good" money is snapping up investment grade gems at increasing rates, becoming mainstream assets.

It is no coincidence, then, that GIA founder Robert M. Shipley's tremendous impact on the world of gems included his worldly view of gems as needing a "comprehensive, international approach for...evaluating gemstones."

It's been a long time coming. Gemstones, especially diamonds, are being accepted for the value they bring to the table.

Has the perfect storm arrived or is it still on the horizon?

No matter the timing, one thing remains undeniable: gemstones have gained more than a foothold in strategically planned investment portfolios around the globe. Are you going to board on time for this trip of a lifetime?

Invest in the dream, it's time to shine!

FOOTNOTES

Chapter 1

1   http://www.smithsonianmag.com/science-nature/diamonds-unearthed-1-144200432/?no-ist
2   http://guide.diamondpriceguru.com/diamond-and-ring-basics/4cs/how-are-colored-diamonds-formed/
3   http://www.guinnessworldrecords.com/2015/preview/index.html#4/z
4   http://queenofcolordiamonds.com/2013/03/
5   http://www.williamgoldberg.com/famous-diamonds/
6   http://thejewelryloupe.com/pink-diamond-sets-auction-record/
7   http://thejewelryloupe.com/in-the-pink-rare-diamoands-bring-record-prices/
8   http://www.smithsonianmag.com/science-nature/diamonds-unearthed-1-144200432/?no-ist
9   http://www.jewelsdujour.com/2015/04/the-perfect-100-02-carat-diamond-sells-for-22-million-at-sothebys/
10 http://observer.com/2015/04/sothebys-perfect-diamond-fetched-22m-but-these-rocks-sold-for-even-more/
11 http://www.guinnessworldrecords.com/2015/preview/index.html#4/z
12 http://www.diamonds.net/Magazine/Article.aspx?ArticleID=46283&RDRIssueID=121
13 http://www.gia.edu/gia-faq-analysis-grading-pearl-classification-report-nacre-thickness
14 http://www.gia.edu/analysis-grading-sample-report-colored-diamond?reporttype=colored-diamond-grading-report
15 http://www.leibish.com/diamonds-continue-to-beat-warren-buffet-and-his-thirst-for-coke-article-864
16 https://invest.usgoldbureau.com/fancy-colored-diamonds
17 http://www.langerman-diamonds.com/encyclopedia/6-53/angola.html
18 http://www.langerman-diamonds.com/encyclopedia/1-3/colored-diamonds-vs_-colored-gems.html
19 http://www.gia.edu/gia-faq-analysis-gradinggrading-report-colored-stone

Chapter 2

1   http://robertpmiles.com/buffetgems.html
2   http://www.gurufocus.com/news/254632/a-diamond-in-the-rough—warren-buffett-talks-jewellery
3   http://www.helzberg.com/category/about+us/our+history.do
4   http://robertpmiles.com/buffetgems.html
5   http://www.leibish.com/

colored-diamonds-compared-to-other-investment-opportunities-article-594

6   http://diamondcolors.com/Fancy-color-diamonds-investment-guide

7   http://diamondcolors.com/Fancy-color-diamonds-investment-guide

8   Wealth Insights Profit or Pleasure? Exploring the Motivations Behind Treasure Trends (Barclays Report; 2012

9   Wealth Insights Profit or Pleasure? Exploring the Motivations Behind Treasure Trends (Barclays Report; 2012

10 http://www.newyorker.com/magazine/2006/10/23/the-40-million-elbow

11 http://articles.latimes.com/1999/oct/17/news/mn-23281

12 http://www.cracked.com/article_19650_5-priceless-works-art-destroyed-by-unintentional-hilarity.html

13 http://www.diamonds.net/News/NewsItem.aspx?ArticleID=51637&ArticleTitle=Market+Comments+3%2f12%2f2015

14 http://abcnews.go.com/Business/celebrity-homes-sold-loss-california-york/story?id=16303634

15 http://www.leibish.com/colored-diamonds-compared-to-other-investment-opportunities-article-594

16 The Diamond Insight Report (De Beers; 2014)

17 http://www.rarecoloreddiamonds.com/investing.html

18 http://www.leibish.com/colored-diamonds-compared-to-other-investment-opportunities-article-594

19 http://www.diamondsinafrica.com/investment-diamonds.php

20 http://www.melee.pro/whatismelee.htm

21 https://diamondlighthouse.wordpress.com/2014/05/23/history-of-the-diamond-engagement-ring/

22 http://www.melee.pro/whatismelee.htm

23 http://www.diamonds.net/News/NewsItem.aspx?ArticleID=51637&ArticleTitle=Market+Comments+3%2f12%2f2015

24 www.SoulCurrency.org

Chapter 3

1   http://diamondintherough.com/spotlight

2   http://diamondintherough.com/buying-guide/about-us

3   http://www.johnbetts-fineminerals.com/jhbnyc/gifs/59582.htm

4   http://www.guinnessworldrecords.com/2015/preview/index.html#4/z

5   Diamondintherough.com

6   http://www.johnbetts-fineminerals.com/jhbnyc/diamondtest.htm

7   http://www.craterofdiamondsstatepark.com/newsletter/view.aspx?mid=22639

8   http://money.cnn.com/2015/11/19/investing/second-biggest-diamond-lucara/

9   http://www.bloomberg.com/news/articles/2015-11-26/ceo-wants-more-than-60-million-for-biggest-diamond-in-a-century

10 http://fortune.com/2015/11/19/lucara-diamond-biggest/

11 http://www.bloomberg.com/news/articles/2015-11-19/biggest-diamond-in-more-than-a-century-discovered-in-botswana

12 http://www.bloomberg.com/news/articles/2015-11-26/ceo-wants-more-than-60-million-for-biggest-diamond-in-a-century

Chapter 4

1   http://www.bloomberg.com/apps/news?pid=newsarchive&refer=&sid=a8gfjAeq
bw3I
2   https://kimberleyprocessstatistics.org/public_statistics
3   http://www.bloomberg.com/apps/news?pid=newsarchive&refer=&sid=a8gfjAeq
bw3I
4   http://www.craterofdiamondsstatepark.com/
5   http://www.npr.org/templates/story/story.php?storyId=96564952
6   http://www.smithsonianchannel.com/videos/how-a-140000000-ship-earns-her-keep/30832

Chapter 5

1   http://www.bloomberg.com/apps/news?pid=newsarchive&refer=&sid=a8gfjAeq
bw3I
2   http://www.npr.org/templates/story/story.php?storyId=96564952
3   http://www.npr.org/templates/story/story.php?storyId=96564952
4   https://weatherspark.com/averages/28312/Ekati-Diamond-Mine-Northwest-Territories-Canada
5   http://www.npr.org/templates/story/story.php?storyId=96564952
6   http://www.bloomberg.com/apps/news?pid=newsarchive&refer=&sid=a8gfjAeq
bw3I
7   http://www.diamonds.net/News/NewsItem.aspx?ArticleID=47376&ArticleTitle
=Fipke+Holdings+to+Sell+Ekati+Share+to+Dominion+Diamond
8   http://www.biv.com/article/2015/2/whos-getting-sued-feb-17-2015/
9   http://www.forbes.com/sites/anthonydemarco/2014/04/28/warren-buffett-to-sell-signature-diamonds-at-berkshire-hathaways-shareholders-weekend/
10 http://www.cnbc.com/id/101548522
11 http://www.thecanadiandiamond.com/cdc.html
12 http://www.ddcorp.ca/operations/canadamark
13 http://lunaticg.blogspot.com/2011/10/2012-queen-diamond-jubilee-gold-coin.html
14 http://www.harrywinston.com/our-story/hope-diamond
15 http://phx.corporate-ir.net/phoenix.zhtml?c=65233&p=irol-newsArticle&ID=1775627&highlight=
16 http://www.nnsl.com/frames/newspapers/2013-02/feb11_13bh.html
17 http://www.mountainprovince.com/project/project-overview/
18 http://www.cbc.ca/news/canada/north/deninu-kue-first-nation-gets-rights-to-diamond-benefits-1.2886207
19 http://www.mountainprovince.com/files/5314/2842/5225/MPV_NR_Closing_of_Debt_Facility_April_7_2015_FINAL.pdf
20 http://www.firestonediamonds.com/operations/mining-operations/liqhobong
21 http://www.mountainprovince.com/industry/industry-overview/
22 http://stellar-diamonds.com/operations/sierra-leone/tongo-project

Chapter 6

1   http://engagementrings.about.com/od/Eco-Friendly/tp/The-Best-Eco-Friendly-Bridal-Ring-Brands-Part-1.htm
2   https://web.duke.edu/soc142/team7/Social,%20Political,%20and%20Environmental%20Issues.htm
3   http://www.abazias.com/video/education_politics_in_diamonds.asp
4   http://www.pacweb.org/en/pac-and-the-Kimberley-process
5   http://www.un.org/press/en/2012/ga11205.doc.htm
6   http://www.pacweb.org/en/diamond-watchlist
7   http://www.pacweb.org/en/united-arab-emirates

Chapter 7

1   http://abcnews.go.com/Entertainment/photos/celebs-engagement-rings-5780615/image-21543604
2   http://boards.weddingbee.com/topic/what-is-the-average-center-stone-size-for-engagement-rings-in-your-area/
3   http://www.nytimes.com/2014/02/01/your-money/with-engagement-rings-love-meets-budget.html?_r=0
4   http://stylenews.peoplestylewatch.com/2012/01/05/drew-barrymore-engagement-ring-picture/?xid=rss-topheadlines
5   http://www.huffingtonpost.com/2014/09/18/jenny-mccarthy-loses-wedding-ring-honeymoon_n_5842044.html
6   http://www.brides.com/wedding-dresses-style/2012/06/celebrity-engagement-ring-photos#slide=2
7   http://www.mtv.com/news/2135312/nicki-minaj-kim-kardashian-beyonce-engagement-rings/
8   http://iconicrock.blogspot.com/2013/11/holly-madisons-engagement-ring.html
9   http://stylenews.peoplestylewatch.com/2014/05/21/amber-heard-engagement-ring-photos-johnny-depp/
10   http://design.jared-diamonds.com/engagement-rings/neil-lane-bridal-settings/
11   http://www.boomsbeat.com/articles/5456/20140620/50-interesting-facts-about-david-beckham-is-ocd-one-of-the-wealthiest-soccer-players-in-the-world.htm
12   http://www.prnewswire.com/news-releases/carrie-underwood-2014-48th-annual-cma-awards-wearing-over-53-million-us-dollars-of-johnathon-arndt-jewels-on-the-red-carpet-281728551.html
13   http://engagementrings.lovetoknow.com/designer-engagement-rings/carrie-underwood-engagement-ring

Chapter 8

1   Diamonds: Timeless Gems in a Changing World
     Global Diamond Report (2014)
     Prepared by: Antwerp World Diamond Centre (AWDC) and Bain & Company
2   http://www.euromonitor.com/the-rise-of-luxury-spending-and-high-income-earners-in-emerging-markets/report
3   http://www.ft.com/cms/s/0/d686b8dc-d489-11e4-8be8-00144feab7de.html#axzz3ZU2fQMyU
4   "Market Correction" by Rapaport USA (2015)

5   http://www.pricescope.com/blog/retail-diamond-prices-slightly-april
6   http://www.pricescope.com/blog/us-jewelry-spending-millennials-buying-more-any-other-age-group
7   Diamonds: Timeless Gems in a Changing World
     Global Diamond Report (2014) Prepared by: Antwerp World Diamond Centre (AWDC) and Bain & Company
8   Diamonds: Timeless Gems in a Changing World
     Global Diamond Report (2014)
     Prepared by: Antwerp World Diamond Centre (AWDC) and Bain & Company
9   http://www.bloomberg.com/news/articles/2015-07-31/when-chinese-stocks-crash-this-top-ranked-fund-steps-in-to-buy
10   http://www.wsj.com/news/articles/SB10001424127887323826804578468980022101580
11   http://www.forbes.com/sites/myuan/2015/02/05/colored-diamonds-asias-new-fancy-best-friend/
12   http://www.wsj.com/news/articles/SB100014241278873238268045784689800221015 80
13   http://www.businessinsider.com/chinas-slowing-economy-is-a-big-problem-2015-6
14   http://www.economist.com/blogs/economist-explains/2015/03/economist-explains-8
15   Diamonds: Timeless Gems in a Changing World
     Global Diamond Report (2014)
     Prepared by: Antwerp World Diamond Centre (AWDC) and Bain & Company

Chapter 9

1   http://4csblog.gia.edu/2012/how-diamonds-shape-up
2   http://famousdiamonds.tripod.com/koh-i-noordiamond.html
3   http://www.gia.edu/gia-about/4Cs-Cut
4   https://www.diamondlighthouse.com/blog/2015/04/get-in-shape-the-history-of-diamond-shapes/
5   https://www.diamondlighthouse.com/blog/2015/04/get-in-shape-the-history-of-diamond-shapes/
6   https://www.diamondlighthouse.com/blog/2015/04/get-in-shape-the-history-of-diamond-shapes/
7   https://www.diamondlighthouse.com/blog/2015/04/get-in-shape-the-history-of-diamond-shapes/
8   http://4csblog.gia.edu/2012/how-diamonds-shape-up
9   http://4csblog.gia.edu/2012/how-diamonds-shape-up
10   https://www.diamondlighthouse.com/blog/2015/04/get-in-shape-the-history-of-diamond-shapes/
11   https://www.diamondlighthouse.com/blog/2015/04/get-in-shape-the-history-of-diamond-shapes/
12   https://www.diamondlighthouse.com/blog/2015/04/get-in-shape-the-history-of-diamond-shapes/
13   http://www.williamgoldberg.com/famous-diamonds/
14   http://www.williamgoldberg.com/famous-diamonds/
15   http://www.internetstones.com/guinea-star-diamond-famous-jewelry.html
16   http://www.history.com/this-day-in-history/burton-buys-liz-a-diamond

17   https://www.diamondlighthouse.com/blog/2015/04/get-in-shape-the-history-of-diamond-shapes/
18   https://www.diamondlighthouse.com/blog/2015/04/get-in-shape-the-history-of-diamond-shapes/

Chapter 10

1   http://yourdiamondteacher.com/diamond-polish
2   http://sarinelight.com/En/AboutUs.aspx
3   http://www.gemologyonline.com/diamond_dictionary.html
4   http://www.diamondregistry.com/news/ideal.htm
5   http://www.diamondregistry.com/news/giaideal.htm
6   http://sarine.com/diamonds/choosing-your-diamonds/the-4cs/
7   Gemguide.com
8   http://www.gia.edu/gia-faq-GIA-grade-diamond-cut
9   http://www.gia.edu/gia-news-research-GIA-innovators-liddicoat
10   http://www.gia.edu/gia-news-research/de-beers-reduces-rough-prices-too-little
11   http://www.polygon.net/jwl/public/trade-resources/jewelry-insights/two-160-carat-diamonds-discovered-at-letseng-mine-in-lesotho-en.jsp
12   http://www.ddcorp.ca/operations/sorting-and-selling
13   http://www.ehudlaniado.com/home/index.php/diamond-pricing/pricing-diamonds-from-the-rough
14   http://www.pbs.org/wgbh/pages/frontline/programs/transcripts/1209.html
15   http://sarine.com/products/advisortm/
16   http://www.gemrockauctions.com/auctions/diamonds/rough-diamonds/
17   http://www.gia.edu/gems-gemology/lab-notes-very-large-rough-diamond
18   http://www.diamonds.net/Prices/
19   http://www.gia.edu/gia-news-research/de-beers-reduces-rough-prices-too-little
20   http://www.gia.edu/gems-gemology/winter-1998-diamonds-cut-same-rough-sunagawa

Chapter 11

1   http://www.bellatairediamonds.com/WhyBellataire/FAQs.aspx
2   http://www.forbes.com/sites/timtreadgold/2015/03/11/dont-laugh-citi-says-man-made-diamonds-are-a-growing-threat-to-the-real-thing/2/
3   http://www.diamonds.net/Docs/Synthetics/Sinthetics.pdf
4   http://www.johnbetts-fineminerals.com/
5   http://www.diamonds.net/Docs/Synthetics/Sinthetics.pdf
6   http://www.diamonds.net/Docs/Synthetics/Sinthetics.pdf
7   http://www.diamonds.net/News/NewsItem.aspx?ArticleID=46436&ArticleTitle=Synthetics%2bAre%2b100%2525%2bDetectable
8   http://www.allcountries.org/articles/diamonds/fancy_colored_diamonds_information_on_natural_versus_synthetic_colored_diamonds.html
9   http://www.gia.edu/gem-lab/laboratory-alert-may-2015
10   http://www.idexonline.com/Memo?id=40755

Chapter 12

1   http://archive.wired.com/politics/law/magazine/17-04/ff_
    diamonds?currentPage=all
2   http://www.wired.com/2009/07/organizer-of-worlds-biggest-diamond-heist-
    found-with-rough-diamonds/
3   http://www.uncoverdiscover.com/facts/top-6-guarded-vaults-in-the-world/
    bank-of-england/
4   http://mentalfloss.com/article/31219/9-worlds-most-ridiculously-secure-safes-
    and-vault
5   http://www.gia.edu/cs/Satellite?pagename=GST%2FDispatcher&childpagenam
    e=GIA%2FPage%2FSearchResults&c=Page&cid=1355954564260&q=robbery

Chapter 13

1   http://www.capetowndiamondmuseum.org/about-diamonds/south-african-
    diamond-history/
2   http://www.gia.edu/diamond-history-lore
3   http://www.themorgan.org/collection/treasures-of-islamic-manuscript-
    painting/26
4   http://www.capetowndiamondmuseum.org/blog/2015/06/15-fascinating-
    diamond-facts/
5   http://www.capetowndiamondmuseum.org/blog/2015/04/the-biggest-diamond-
    in-the-world/
6   http://www.history.com/this-day-in-history/worlds-largest-diamond-found
7   https://www.gemsociety.org/article/foundation-stones-new-testament/
8   http://www.gempundit.com/blog/gemstone-for-taurus/

Chapter 14

1   http://www.israelidiamond.co.il/english/news.aspx?boneid=3024
2   http://www.riotinto.com/diamonds-and-minerals-162.aspx
3   http://www.jewellermagazine.com/Article.aspx?id=2675
4   http://www.merlindiamonds.com.au and "Corporate Overview" (2012; PDF)
5   http://www.mining.com/rio-tinto-to-spend-at-least-500-million-to-advance-
    diamond-project-in-india-44089/
6   http://www.shimansky.com/shimansky-difference/
7   http://www.ags.gov.ab.ca/minerals/diamonds/
8   http://albertaventure.com/2005/12/diamonds-in-the-backyard/2/
9   http://geology.com/gemstones/states/
10 http://geology.com/gemstones/states/arkansas.shtml
11 http://pubs.usgs.gov/bul/1042g/report.pdf
12 http://geology.com/gemstones/states/north-carolina.shtml
13 http://pubs.usgs.gov/bul/1042g/report.pdf

Visit us at www.perfectlyclear.diamonds

You should visit this page to learn how you can win over customers for a lifetime and create a new generation of younger, enthusiastic diamond and gem lovers.

Jewelry stores, organizations and associations related to the gem and jewelry industry worldwide.

Visit us at: www.perfectlyclear.diamonds/reseller

CPSIA information can be obtained at www.ICGtesting.com
Printed in the USA
LVOW10*1912230616

493875LV00004B/79/P

9 780983 130888